# Praise for *Thinking Allowed on Schooling*

Mick Waters

future

policy,

perspe

Unlike

insightf

we can

With hi

on the

tional l

experie

invested

and dis

tion fro

critique

teachin

outcom

Mick Waters has produced the right book for the right time. He penetrates to the heart of the many open discussions we are having about education today. We may not agree with all he says, but we cannot help but be stimulated to think at a deeper level by reading this book.

Dr Anthony Seldon, Master, Wellington College

*Thinking Allowed on Schooling* is a truly seminal work, which should become required reading, not just for head teachers and those charged with delivering education, but for all those with an interest in how our children become educated rather than simply schooled, how they become engaged members of our society rather than tabloid stereotypes. Mick Waters goes beyond analysing the triumphs and failings of our system. He suggests practical solutions to the miasma of challenges facing us today, with a clarity and sharpness of thinking, liberally interspersed with humour and humility – things that political masters only achieve unwittingly. This is a brilliant contribution to a discussion that is yet to be had.

This is a 'must read' for anyone involved in education, including the politicians! Mick's common sense approach to education – that is so evident in his inspiring, motivational talks that have endeared him to teachers across the country – is exemplified and expanded on in this book, which is full of words of wisdom. In this era of radical educational change, this book should be our educational bible as we strive to find a better educational system that, in Mick's words, 'moves away from undue, short-term political influence,' towards a system and curriculum that truly serves the needs of children. I shall be buying multiple copies of this book, to ensure that all of the staff at our school have the opportunity to read it!

**Iain M Erskine, Head of The Fulbridge Academy in Peterborough**

Listening to Mick is always a pleasure – his down-to-earth, common sense beliefs are forged from exhaustive research, vast experience and a commitment to providing high-quality learning experiences for our young people, regardless of their backgrounds. His book is no different – it is as thought provoking and challenging as I had hoped it would be. I am looking forward to some very interesting and productive staff development sessions, using his questions and suggestions as the basis for discussion and change.

**Siobhan Collingwood, Head Teacher,
Morecambe Bay Community Primary School**

Professor Mick Waters is not afraid to challenge our beliefs and our practices in this new book.

His holistic approach takes the reader beyond questioning and evaluation with a passion that demands action. He offers so many suggestions for new ways forward that it will have your head spinning.

Whilst I do not necessarily share all the views expressed, this book is stimulating and thought provoking at all times and I would recommend it as a 'good read'.

**Mrs Brenda Bigland CBE, Education Consultant, Trainer and Coach**

*Thinking Allowed on Schooling* is, of course, an inspiration!

Unlike most educational books, this one will not be read and then shelved. Mick's absolute commitment to the best education for our children is apparent throughout, as he shares his wealth of knowledge and experience. The book, whilst being accessible and colourful, provides enough hard-hitting research and challenging quotes and examples to make it a very interesting read for people at all levels of education and a credible point of reference for years to come. I hope that *Thinking Allowed on Schooling* will become both a valuable source of guidance for educators and an essential read for future Secretaries of State!

I am a head teacher and therefore not in the business of critically evaluating and editing material for publication, so I can't be of help in reviewing the language, organisation and structure of the text itself. But I can comment on how the book could, and has already, helped me as a practicing head teacher. *Thinking Allowed on Schooling* justifies my exhaustion; it also revels, with me, in the joy of schools and education, making me laugh out loud and nod my head at shared experiences! *Thinking Allowed on Schooling* sets out, with real clarity, the very complex context for education and the huge agenda faced by schools. It gives enough history for us educators to understand how we got into this educational situation, and enough inspiration and guidance to help us prioritise, refocus and manage things better for our children and our communities. I liked the book being crammed with page after page of things I'd wanted to have explained, and reminders of why we are all trying so hard to get 'it' right. I felt reassured that I could have this book on my desk as a constant source to tap into – for clarity, reflection and deeper thinking. It is helpful to have chapters focussed on crucial things like pedagogy and curriculum, aspiration and assessment. It worked well for me that each section concluded with What could we do/What might be done? – clear next steps which we can all consider and/or act upon. I have pulled out key messages to help clarify our strategic thinking as a school (when I'm given the go ahead to share the content) and have clung onto 'innovate with integrity' and 'learning which is irresistible'. The book has highlighted some key questions I need to ask of myself as a leader, of our team within the school and of the parents and children. I think that this book will become invaluable to senior leaders within education and could go a lot further towards raising standards than Ofsted Inspections, testing systems or political grand speeches ever will!

I feel very privileged to have been asked to read this book and even more privileged (though not surprised) that Mick is willing to share so much with us all.

To conclude – what could Mick do next? Find a structure to update schools leaders and teachers with filtered information to help us prioritise; a way to help us feel informed but not overloaded with information and political claptrap. Press for a National Council for Schooling. Pat himself on the back (for once) and know that he has provided us with something practical and tangible that WILL make a difference to education in our schools.

Caroline Vernon, Professional Colleague

Mick Waters has done it again. Sometimes you read something so blindingly obvious that you wonder, 'Why didn't I think of that?' But whereas most of us only manage to glimpse parts of the problem and fragments of possible solutions, he pulls all those elements together, succinctly and coherently. He presents educators and policy-makers alike with a challenge that is huge and daunting, to be sure, but which, in his masterly analysis, is eminently capable of being addressed – if only we have the will to do so.

That analysis is dispassionate, but there's no mistaking Mick's passion for education and for its purpose that we owe to our children, but in which we so often fail them. Notwithstanding his clear love for teaching and for teachers, he doesn't flinch from criticising the uninspiring and formulaic; nor does his flinch from laying the blame firmly at the doors of the qualification-obsessed policy-makers and the data-dominated inspection system for creating and perpetuating the focus on what is narrow, tedious and purely utilitarian.

Mick is a positive thinker – hence the book's title. So, although he paints a bleak picture of the current state of affairs, he also offers solutions: they are challenging but realistic, if only policy-makers would find the courage. If we don't pick up the gauntlet Mick throws down, we risk (as he writes graphically) continuing to 'beat the drum of progress and march to the drum of tedious accountability'.

Dr Bernard Trafford, Headmaster, Newcastle upon Tyne Royal<br>Grammar School and former Chairman, HMC

In this highly readable book, Mick gives a brilliant review of the Good, the Bad, and the Plain Old Ugly of the current educational landscape. He is right to conclude that we need 'an Education Spring - a rising of intolerance about the way schooling is being manipulated in a piecemeal and uncoordinated way to serve too many purposes with unclear measures'. His call for the establishment of an elected National Council for Schooling as a way forward is also spot-on. It is, indeed, time for politicians to hand over the direction of the Profession to the Profession itself.

Andrew Chubb, Principal, Archbishop Sentamu Academy

# THINKING
# ALLOWED
# ON SCHOOLING

## MICK WATERS

Independent Thinking Press

First published by

Independent Thinking Press
Crown Buildings, Bancyfelin, Carmarthen, Wales, SA33 5ND, UK
www.independentthinkingpress.com

Independent Thinking Press is an imprint of Crown House Publishing Ltd.

British Library Cataloguing-in-Publication Data
A catalogue entry for this book is available
from the British Library.

Print ISBN 978-1-78135-056-0
Mobi ISBN 978-1-78135-075-1
ePub ISBN 978-1-78135-076-8

Edited by Ian Gilbert

Printed and bound in the UK by
TJ International, Padstow, Cornwall

Dedicated to three lads:
Philip, Thomas and Matthew

# Author's note

Dr Ishmail ran the end of his reflex stick up the sole of my foot and his expression changed. Apparently my toes curled the wrong way. Within no time he was organising MRI scans. A few weeks later and a couple of days before I was due to chair the annual three-day North of England Education Conference in Leeds, I found out that I would need tricky surgery on the spinal cord in my neck and it would take a few months before I was up and running. Not that I often run.

Here was the chance to write the book I had been asked for before and so often put off because of pressure of work. When, coincidentally, Ian Gilbert offered to edit it the project was underway.

How long does it take to write a book? It depends when we start counting. It could be said that this book has taken a career to write. It is a collection of thoughts that have built up as I have reached the twilight of my career. The shadows are long behind me as I head towards a setting sun. At the same time, it has taken just a few months of actual writing during my convalescence and the Olympics and then onwards through the autumn and winter of shifting educational activity. Some will expect a book on children, teaching approaches and classroom practice, a book full of ideas to try, for that is how I have always worked. There is relatively little of that here. Instead, it is a book about the state of schooling in England and it reflects the many conversations I have had with those I have met who are trying to make the system work for all our children and young people. It is a book to pick up, dip into and hopefully debate, wherever it is that we work in the schooling system.

While we might write a book alone we also need help and support. The team at Independent Thinking Press has helped me enormously and Ian has been a great source of wisdom. In my career's worth of thinking, I have been sustained by a family that has tolerated and supported my unending appetite for getting involved in schools and their work. Across the country and beyond, I am proud to know professional friends who have provided me with so much inspiration as I have worked alongside them, glimpsed their incredible practice, shared their enthusiasm for teaching and wondered with them how it could all be better. In the book there are references to schools but I do not name them; the people involved will recognise themselves and for each of those I mention, there are many similar examples.

I hope you enjoy the book and that, whatever your involvement with schooling, there is something in it to make you think. I have always believed that improving schooling is about shedding light, offering challenge and building confidence and reassurance. I hope the book does that in fair proportion.

It is a book about schools so it will hardly be a blockbuster. My operation was a complete success and my follow-up tests came to a climax with the repeat reflex test on my feet. This time the toes went the right way. This book is for you, Dr Ishmail, and all the colleagues who helped me to recover. It is my educational toe-curler.

Mick Waters

# Contents

# Some background, explanations and disclaimers

It was relatively early in my teaching career when I realised the point of the old joke about someone asking directions and being told, 'If you were trying to get there, I wouldn't start from here.' It dawned on me that there was a world of difference between education and schooling and if we were truly trying to offer education to young people, we really would not organise schooling in the way we do.

As a novice head teacher I found myself restrained by resources, staffing structures, tradition, habit and parental expectation. Maybe I couldn't change the world but I could change a bit of it; I could make it as good as possible for the people we are meant to serve, the children in our care. I remember thinking that my task was to make the most of a bad job or to make a silk purse from a sow's ear. This is not to be negative but realistic. I have taken the same attitude to every job ever since: keep the highest ideals and at the same time be pragmatic. Do the best for the young people in whatever way you are allowed and give them the best experience and prospects possible.

I reflect that it must have been the same for the bosses of the train companies in the mid-1980s. If we were really to run the rail system properly we would want to start again. Wider tracks, bigger, longer trains, more lines in the right places, better tunnels and modern stations would all be top of the list. However, the infrastructure was already there so it was a case of making the most of it and giving the passenger the best travel experience possible. It may not be perfect, and there are plenty of moaners, but the reality is that the railways are generally better than they were.

The history of the school system in England places a similar burden on those trying to make it work for the future. This is one of the reasons why sections of this book dwell on the background to our current situation. History can create insight, although it may not stop it repeating itself.

I have tried, though, to make the book readable without too many references to academic texts and official papers (although these are listed in the bibliography). The risk in this is that points may appear to be unsubstantiated or conjecture. There is personal opinion and much of what I have written is a commentary on what I see in the hundreds of schools in which I spend time in the course of a year as they go about their daily business. I am with them because I might be teaching a class or two with the teachers watching. I still think this is one of the best forms of teacher development; watching your own class with someone else. I don't do it a lot, but enough to still be that teacher I was when I started out. I might be in schools at the invitation of a head or governors to discuss ways forward. I might be speaking at a conference or seminar with teachers, heads, governors, parents or employers. All of these exchanges over many years have fuelled the writing in this book.

One real problem I encountered in writing the book is the use of the collective noun. We all do it to describe teachers, schools, children, parents, inspectors and politicians as though all of their category was the same – yet we know they are not. We generalise and in every generalisation we recognise there are subtle differences and polar opposites. Maybe not all children in Africa walk ten miles each way to school and there are many children in Africa who wouldn't wish to go to school if the opportunity were freely available. We realise that not everyone who left school with few qualifications, like Lord Sugar and Sir Richard Branson, ended up as successful multimillionaire business leaders. Not everyone who goes to private school ends up as a success and some people who can't read do very well for themselves as adults. Please forgive the use of the collective noun where it needs forgiveness and be charitable as you read the text in the way I might have intended.

I hope the book is one that can be opened at any section and enjoyed as a 'think piece' for its own sake. Because of this, there is the occasional repetition as the same issues can affect a range of agendas. Some sections are longer than others and some much more focused on the practice of schooling that might be discussed at a staff or departmental meeting. I have integrated some previously written articles into the text where they fit and I have tried to respond to changes of policy late in the process of publication. Here and there are some musings and passing thoughts that might make the reader think again about the routine of their world. Sometimes these are humorous, a wry reflection on the odd world of schooling.

Schools are fascinating and busy places and there is much that happens in them that is very funny and sometimes absurd. One of the sadder aspects of recent years is that teachers and others who work in schools seem to have less time to laugh with the children and each other at some of the amusing things that happen. Childhood should be joyous and schools should feel part of that happy outlook.

# ... on the confused purpose of schooling

During the month that you are reading this around 50,000 babies will be born in England. Most will be greeted with joy and be referred to as wonderful and a miracle. Some will be unwanted but most will be loved. What might we hope for these children as they begin their life's journey that many predict will see most of them living into the next century? Most parents would say that they want their child to grow up to be contented, happy and fulfilled.

During their lives our young people will have more opportunity than ever before and will face more complex challenges. The chance to travel is greater than ever with the prospect of journeys into space becoming fact rather than fiction. Most will need to work to sustain themselves and their families; some will move beyond routine work and achieve significance, celebrity or greatness. At today's rate, one in every three month's batch will become a star for a while on television or film and one every month will make a music recording. Some will take on representative roles; ten of our babies every year will become a Member of Parliament. One baby in every six month's batch will become an Olympian.

In our batch of babies, society needs some who are pioneers, exploring new frontiers in science, technology or engineering. We will need people who can make things and sell them. We will need people to grow things. There will need to be some who seek a just and fair society on behalf of all of us and there will be those who seek to help us to avoid conflict and uphold rights. We will need people to entertain us. We will need people to do the dirty jobs and the unthinkable tasks that most of us would turn away from. We will need people who are happy to work behind the scenes to make things happen. We will need people to whom we can turn to for organised solace and comfort. We will need people who are brave. We will need those who will care for others and nurture talent. On top of all this we will need leaders to organise the very society in which we live.

Our hopes for our young are a compromise between their personal fulfilment and our needs as a prosperous and secure society. Can we describe our hopes for all our children so that they might enjoy fulfilment in their adult lives?

## Our hopes for our young people

Most would agree that we would want our young people to be *competent and confident in themselves*. What that means might provoke debate but surely we need individuals who are able to cope in familiar and novel circumstances. They will require the basics of reading, writing and numeracy plus those even more essential skills of concern for their own health and well-being.

Next we might want our youngsters to grow up and *act with integrity*. This is a challenging aim – easier to say than do and with lots of implications in many contexts. It is about more than behaving in the way demanded by elders; it relates to self-control, being critical and developing and retaining a sense of honour and respect. How can we encourage our young people to act in a decent way towards themselves, towards others, their community and towards their planet? From an early age children are aware of many examples where adults do not act with integrity and there are harsh lessons to learn about the ways we might not trust each other.

We would expect our young people to be ready to *take responsibility, to support and nurture others*. This would involve working hard, sometimes in teams, sometimes leading, showing determination and commitment and developing character. It would demand willpower, self-control and respect. It would encompass many of the qualities that business leaders constantly emphasise as vital.

Most would hope their children will grow up being *fascinated by the natural world* and *intrigued by our attempts to manipulate that world,* including *a growing recognition of human achievements and failings.* These are the elements that have been part of the English school curriculum over time; the aspects that are organised into subject disciplines and over which there is so much debate about what should be included.

The importance of enjoying and taking part in *the creative, cultural, sporting and innovative* aspects of society and recognising the valuable contribution they make to our lives is also something that would be included in our hopes for young people.

Growing up in a modern society means we would need our youngsters to *appreciate the cultures, orientations and sensitivities of other people.* Again, this is easily said but makes high demands in terms of our own society where we see communities both at one and at odds with themselves and others.

It is vital that young people are *ready and qualified to take on the next stage of their learning* as they pass through the gateways in their adult lives. This does not necessarily mean having exams or certificates but it does mean that they have sufficient resources to convince others that they can take the next steps – the tickets to pass through doorways.

Within all this, we would want our young to develop *the capacity to reflect on and recognise their contribution to their world, its value and their developing spirit.* Essentially, though, we would want our young people to be *fuelled with a desire to learn* that will be with them for the rest of their lives.

Most would agree with the hopes described above; there is a broad general consensus about our ambitions for our young people. The various elements of this list are interdependent on each other for success. It is easier to appreciate the differences in society if there is some knowledge of history and geography. Innovation comes more easily when basic principles of science, engineering, art, design and mathematics are clearly grasped. Enjoying and working hard at sport or culture helps to develop responsibility and in turn is much more easily developed if conscientiousness is already there.

The difficulty comes when we decide which aspects of the list are in the province of our schools. Schooling sets out to support society in nurturing its young people. All schooling is part of education, but not all education takes place in school. School is but a small part of a very big whole. Should that small part be a segment of the education experience – the subject disciplines? Or should the small part of education that is schooling be an inner or outer concentric circle giving a rounded experience that complements life's wider education? Schooling happens for about 1,200 hours per year between the ages of four and eighteen. Matthew Syed, in his excellent book *Bounce*, quotes research that reckons that high-level performance comes with 10,000 hours of practice. On that basis, each child will be excellent at one-and-a-half things by the time they leave school. Perhaps we need them to practise the specific art of learning so that they leave school as excellent and committed learners ready to take on all they meet.

As our children leave the schooling system they will be less than a quarter of the way through their lives and they will have spent less than 20% of their time in school. We are surely not expecting finished human beings at school leaving age? Is it not more realistic to expect that when they leave they are primed for the future – ready to move forward with confidence, curiosity and commitment? That is not to say they should be without knowledge or working skill sets in literacy, numeracy and oracy, but to have the presence of mind to know that their educational journey has only just begun. They need to be aware of the markers and signposts that lie ahead.

We have recognised standards in schools which are easily definable: test and examination results. Through tests of literacy and numeracy in primary schools and a few GCSEs in particular subjects at the secondary stage we seem to assume that we have a shorthand method for evaluating the quality of schooling. We apply this evaluation on a national level and, through various subsets, to the individual school.

Those who find their school standards high or rising find it difficult to disagree that their school is good. Yet are results in exams and tests all we seek? What about the list of hopes above?

Society seems to want more from its schools than the basics established during the Victorian era that heralded state education, yet it finds it difficult to express exactly what it does want. The infant school that decides to abandon the nativity play because of the need to teach the basics would probably be castigated for denying the children one of life's formative and memorable experiences. But is seeing our child on stage really about their education or simply one of those rites of passage that as parents we have come to expect? Is teaching them to recite a line, sit here, move there and not pick their noses really educational? Is it formative? There is a big difference between being directed and being creative. Do we think enough about not only the purpose of having all children appear in a nativity play each year but also about the purpose of school itself?

Is the annual round of treats, visits and parties that follow the tests and exams really a good use of time if children are meant to be acquiring standards? Is the post-SATs residential for Year 6 a break from the slog of the previous months or is it a more meaningful educational experience (building independence, teamwork, sharing success, learning new knowledge and skills, seeing subject disciplines in context and forging lasting memories) than the SATs preparation could ever be? Are schools meant to be less of a factory producing 'scores' and more of a chance for our children to be supported in meeting our hopes for them collectively? Do we really think our schools can take responsibility for the behaviour of all of our children? If so, the claim that educational standards in London are better than ever rings hollow in the face of the riots of 2011.

Schools can only achieve so much and should be seen to complement and supplement what a good society already offers. In our schools we teach little linguists, budding artists, fledgling mathematicians, growing scientists and emerging historians. We teach future engineers, architects, lawyers, performers and journalists. Schooling can *help* society to do its job and secure all our futures but it is not the sole provider of that education.

By their first birthday, 70% of this month's babies will have learned to walk and, in the following few months, only those with special needs will find walking difficult. Similarly, by the age of two, most will be talking and by five this talk will be fluent with extensive vocabulary (though a sizable proportion will be struggling to talk easily). Most parents take naturally to their role in helping their child to walk. The child sees nearly everyone doing it, wants to join the club and grown-ups make it a good game. Early toddles are supported and encouraged, failure is brushed aside and effort is praised. The spotlight shines on the successes. So it is with talking. Babbling to babies comes naturally and the child mimics the noises it hears. Supported by focused repetition, a delight in books, endless commentary on experiences, praise for trying and a ready audience, the child will soon enjoy being able to communicate.

Can we capitalise on this natural urge to learn and encourage the intellectual, physical, emotional and social aspects of development in the same way that we might encourage walking and talking? Where walking and talking appear to come naturally, involving much effort on the part of the *individual* – not to mention the nurturing on the part of the carer – we seem to think other types of learning need more effort on the part of the *teacher*. In the development of walking and talking parents don't stand and instruct children: 'Shift your centre of gravity, lift one foot, place it down ... good, now the other.' No, the parent moves obstacles, teases and tempts by placing enticing treats just out of reach, cheers and celebrates, gently coaches and opens up many opportunities for practice. The parent does not outline a learning objective and set up success criteria. In teaching, however, there is a belief that structure, often linear, is necessary in order to speed progress towards our goals for our young. Yet often this progress is not speedy. There is a lot of repeated content. Children forget and need to be re-taught the same skills or knowledge over and over. We feel that a lot of time is lost where there is no time to lose. Nevertheless, the time is there to use and use well.

When we watch very young children learning it is almost as if they cannot help it. They explore, set themselves an impossible task and often apply themselves until they achieve it, failing endlessly, delighting in small discoveries and applying one idea to a new situation to test out possible solutions. They do all of these things without being told to, although the guiding adult will sometimes offer a helpful model or put a stepping stone in place or add a twist of confusion at just the right moment.

Leapfrog forward to the university years and the same process gets repeated – exploring, setting tasks, trying one idea in a new situation, experimenting, discovery.

At both ends we see self-structured learning, hypotheses being tested, conjecture and discovery. What do we see in-between these ages as children travel the school journey? Too often they experience learning which is linear rather than rounded, incremental rather than expansive and tested rather than testing. The most obvious difference though is the way the learning is set by others rather than the learners themselves. Is this because the learner cannot determine their own paths or because we, the teachers, know the best route? Is it because the learners need their experience to be channelled to save time? Is it because the learners suddenly lose ideas and imagination which return after they have passed the necessary examinations? GCSEs and A levels seem to become indicators of promise rather than achievement. So it is with SATs, and there is a danger that the Early Years profile will also become a predictor of potential. The point of schools is to accelerate learning so they need some incremental structures. The challenge is to use those structures to complement what we know about how young people learn.

The fact is that many schools feel inhibited about using the interests of the learner in designing and building learning experiences. We listen to central government for guidance about what and how to teach rather than believing or trusting the professionalism of teachers, or the consensus among stakeholders or the pupil voice.

Many would argue that schools are for the 'whole child' and fundamentally should address the list of hopes above. Others see the role of schools as providing that which lies beyond the scope of the home and family. They believe that the driving force for schools should be the knowledge and understanding of events and phenomena with a little bit of attention to affective experiences. When things wobble in society, and questions are asked about the outlook of our youngsters, the focus seems to be on schools to ensure that behaviour is good, which usually takes us into the realm of personal qualities. Some assert that the utilitarian purpose of schools is as a method by which children can acquire qualifications that will allow them to pursue an employment-related status in life.

Whatever schooling does it cannot do everything. Most schools in England seem to try to communicate what and how they do things by suggesting that they are adding to what parents do, trying to fit the child for their future and promoting the sort of society we would want to see develop. Most teachers appear to see their role as investing in the future and making a difference to the life chances of the children they teach.

Other so-called stakeholders have a range of views: business wants a workforce for the future, able to fulfil a range of demands from invention to production; universities want individuals who are ready to research and think; and parents, by virtually every survey, want their children to be happy, though how they define that varies from parent to parent ...

## What do our children need?

We don't have to listen to Radio 4's *Today* programme for many weeks to get a picture of what children should be learning. Personal finance, healthy eating, drug awareness, crime prevention, bereavement, sexuality, alcohol abuse, internet grooming, pensions, dementia, culture, parenting, voting responsibly, swimming and design all featured within a two-month period in 2012, with all the advocates asserting something like, 'Of course, it all starts in the school'. The fact is that all these claims will be appropriate for some children somewhere. There is a view that, since we have a national curriculum and if something needs to be taught, it has to be on the national curriculum, and so the lobbying begins. The problem comes with an old-fashioned perception of what schools are intended to do. Some hold the rather charming view that schools should teach lovely and interesting things about our world and not foist the challenges of adulthood upon the young. Then there are those who believe that the list above is the province of the home, or at least 'pastoral' or 'incidental', and has little place or importance in what we should intend our schools to teach and our children to learn.

Few would disagree that our children need the basics, almost going back to the United Nations Convention on the Rights of the Child that enshrines the rights of survival, protection and participation. Schooling fits into our wish to provide well for our children. Traditionally, schools exist to offer organised, structured and accelerated learning. In striving to improve schooling we believe we are creating a better childhood. Successive education secretaries of all parties have been able to chant the terms 'social mobility', 'excellence' and 'equality'. In recent years they have also added 'accountability', 'diversity', 'choice', 'market' and 'autonomy' to their list. One problem is that putting emphasis on the latter set means that the first set is virtually unachievable. We cannot seem to balance the need for equality with striving for excellence for each and every child.

Social mobility has become an easy issue for politicians to discuss, but efforts to address it are tripped up by the stress on high-stakes accountability in a market-led system. Parents (an example of that collective noun problem) typically want to do the best by their children and support their schooling in the belief that the school is a guide for them as parents as well as for their children. Business and employers have grown used to criticising schools for not producing 'work-ready' youngsters. Culture, arts and sport judge that they also have something to offer young people and want to do it, in part, via schooling. Very few adults are in one particular group alone. We are parents and employers, we are teachers and parents, we are innovators and parents. What parents want for their own children is often different from what they argue children in general should receive. As a result, the picture of what we want from schooling is confused. Educationalists, spurred on by successive secretaries of state, talk of a 'moral authority' where we rise above all the arguing and do what we know is best for children and seek to convince the wider population. The pity is that what many of the policy-makers actually mean is that the profession should rise above the arguing and agree with them and their policies.

Into this confusion steps central government, utilising the general lack of clarity about what education is all about in order to be assertive about policy. Over the last twenty years, central government has convinced us that qualifications are the prime measure of school and individual success. The parent who might worry about a school's practice in regard to many of the hopes for our young people will be compromised by the 'you can't argue with results' conundrum. It might not be pretty but it does deliver.

A lack of credible examination results leads to a question mark over a school's future. Maybe that is right – most other things lead to results and therefore all is not well where results are poor. But should a school with good results be compared equally with a school with poorer results when the parents of the first have paid for private tutoring and the parents of the second could not? Do statistics tell the whole story? How do we know whether a school at the top of the league table is ten times better than the one in tenth spot? Are two schools with the same results comparable in every way? Where does children's happiness and experience come in?

Previous generations needed to be work-ready; ready for the world of toil manufacturing or mining, shipbuilding or car making, fishing or agriculture. They took up employment in these industries and accepted their lot or they learned on the job and made progress. Sometimes they needed to be ready to answer their country's call and be prepared to lay down their lives. Only a few needed to be 'checked out' and examined to see whether they could stand the test. Examinations were specific to a particular chosen pathway. Nowadays, examinations are taken by all to check on the growth of the child and, at the same time, to confirm the efficiency of the schooling.

Being efficient is not always the same as being effective. This system has led to considerable concerns about the notion of 'teaching to the test'. If the test were an effective indicator of capability there would be no need for concern. But it is not. It is a turnstile and, once through, children need to be able to navigate all manner of complexity that no exam could ever prepare them for. Since, today, all children take the examinations, it stands to reason that all cannot get through the chosen gateway with the same ticket. Hence the need for a broader school experience which addresses the wider hopes for our young people.

Politicians run with the tide for their own electoral gain. The euphoria over the 2012 Olympic Games led to announcements on competitive sport in primary schools being made compulsory. The politicians probably thought this captured a public mood but almost immediately various well-known people came forward to recount their purgatory in school sports as youngsters. Top competitors talked about the joy of sport being derived from its many health and social benefits. Leading coaches described enjoying sport for its own sake and then, gradually, specialising if appropriate. Yet the government grabbed the compulsory and competitive elements and waved the wrong end of the stick as if it were a javelin.

The politicians somehow failed to see the impact of arts and culture on the Olympiad; the acclaim for the opening and closing ceremonies should have led to an equally bold statement on the need to support creative and aesthetic disciplines. The ceremonies, which included classical and popular music, comedy, dance, poetry, ballet, circus, pyrotechnics and stunning visual effects, should have led to an exposition on the brilliance of the stars of the arts, design and technology, stagecraft and innovation. The Olympics showed examples of architecture, construction, journalism, photography, logistics, venue management ... and sport. The elements of internationalism, health, companionship and mutual respect were all potential influences on society.

But no, competitive sport was the message to come out of the Games according to the government. The fact that thousands reported the positive effect on them as torch bearers – as they were recognised, supported, celebrated, acknowledged and thanked – did not lead the politicians to think that a 'chance to shine' might be important. They did not seem to consider that maybe all children should have an opportunity for a moment in the limelight; but rather that we must end the 'all must have prizes' culture. Somehow they think that the prospect of a moment on a podium will spur on a generation. They should talk to the Games Makers – the thousands of volunteers who volunteered and for two weeks made London actually feel friendly. For them, the Olympics were a chance to be part of something wonderful, to come together in human endeavour and celebration. This was a collective, social motivation, not a competitive one.

Still, 2012 offered a more positive vision of Britain than 2011. That summer saw riots and looting in various English cities. The political statements that followed the awful scenes centred on the need for better behaviour in schools and the requirement for effective discipline. But schools were out when the riots were on and most of the rioters were past school age. Ofsted has actually observed that discipline in schools is good, but what does evidence matter when it doesn't fit? If there is a problem that government is unsure what to do about, it is easy to place the responsibility in the lap of the school system. If there is a great achievement in our society, then the credit goes to government but the responsibility for making sure the good times continue is still placed with schools.

While the Olympic Games were taking place, the *Curiosity* rover was successfully guided to Mars and began taking soil samples and transmitting analysis to scientists on earth. At about the same time, the English astronomer and architect of Jodrell Bank, Bernard Lovell, died. Within days the passing of Neil Armstrong was also announced. Politicians were silent on these matters, but they might have asked how we inspire youngsters to emulate great scientists in the same way that they are inspired to emulate athletes at the peak of their performance. The opening ceremonies of both the Olympic and Paralympic Games made this connection with celebrations of the achievements of Sir Tim Berners-Lee who invented the internet and Professor Stephen Hawking. The creative directors found the connections that our policy-makers struggle to make.

Politicians often select a focus of schooling in order to catch a public mood that will fit in with their overall need for election. They rarely seem to see a big picture or question their own policies. For example, if schooling is intended to address society's issues, different measures of quality and success will be needed rather than relying on the crude measure of exam and test results.

Exercise and diet are major health concerns, while the declining impact and involvement in religion, anti-social behaviour and the lack of participation in elections and community activity worry many. All of these are crucial social issues of our time and some would be addressed by having a better educated, more literate and numerate adult population. That said, interestingly, when the 2008 banking crisis occurred, few people blamed the school system in spite of the fact that many of the culprits had achieved the very highest standards in education. Perhaps it is difficult for politicians to cast the spotlight on the failings of those who have been, up to that point, the premier products of a testing and competitive culture.

The challenge is surely greater than all of this. If schooling is to play a part in transforming society, it has to be offered the chance to do it as a respected influence with a serious contribution to make rather than a mere tool of national politicians. If building character is part of the challenge for schools, along with raising horizons, encouraging positive lifestyles and broadening experience, then we have to promote this as a serious agenda rather than see it is an add-on or an imperative in a crisis.

Schools cannot do everything although most try. The majority of teachers come into the profession to make a difference and with strong core values about public service and improving society. Many have taken on a social care role in the communities they serve, trying to help set the foundations for the children they teach. Many are driving forward with innovative pedagogic and institutional development. Some are researching the impact of new techniques. Many are confused by the unending change to the system. Many are distracted from their core role as teachers by spending time and energy on strategic planning around elements of structure and restructuring. Many are working with employers and higher education to develop links which support the progress of the pupils they teach. Many live by the annual cycle of test results. Most are hitting the targets set by government. Some are driven by keeping at bay the fear of inspection failure. Almost all care about the children they teach but the drivers and pressures on their work are extremely varied. For so many, the base level is exam and test results, inspection outcomes are next and securing pupil numbers to protect the budget relies on the first two. Yet their professionalism desires better schooling for the pupils they teach than they feel they are currently receiving. Too many are frustrated and feel powerless which can lead to a dwindling sense of professionalism. The high numbers of those leaving the profession within five years of qualifying should be a source of great concern.

My experience tells me that the morale of the profession is generally good in front of the children but low elsewhere. For many years political posturing has created a set of tensions such that, even as results improved, new buildings were built, salaries increased and budgets rose, for many the innate joy and pride of being a member of the teaching profession diminished. This has accelerated under the current coalition government, not just because funding has been pulled from building projects and salaries frozen, but because the combative rhetoric from government has driven many teachers and school leaders to despair. The satisfaction of working with youngsters is outweighed by the political meddling which plays school against school, head against head, teacher against teacher and child against child.

## So what might be done?

▪ We need an 'education spring' – a rising of intolerance about the way schooling is being manipulated in a piecemeal and uncoordinated way to serve too many purposes with unclear measures. We need to build a rational, apolitical debate and ensure that schooling moves away from undue, short-term political influence.

▪ In turn, this means establishing some sort of National Council for Schooling to guide schooling, which is built on evidence and research and has agreed and clearly defined aims for our young people.

▪ The National Council for Schooling would drive us towards a different view of accountability and bring more balance to the market-driven approach to schooling.

▪ We need to build a sense of purpose for schooling into all parents and pupils and to help them determine their own responsibilities in education, which is wider than simply what goes on at school.

▪ As a society we need to see young people, particularly teenagers, as a positive group in our communities and part of the solution for some of society's challenges.

▪ We need real engagement from and with employers.

▪ We need clearer parameters for the important teaching of social and moral responsibility in schools.

▪ We need a better definition of what a 'rounded education' really is and clarity about where schooling fits into that picture.

# … on the search for equality

The English education system still presents itself as a race with the first past the post as the victors. It likes to portray this race as a fair test but the reality is very different. Imagine the 400-metres event with lane allocations according to wealth, with the most wealthy on the inside lane and the poorest on the outside. Then take away the staggered start.

Children are born into a family. It might be the most secure or fragile beginning in life but even as they enter life their educational chances are unequal. Imagine the 1,500 children born on any one day in England being placed on life's starting line. The children from the privileged upper classes would be on the inside lane. On the extreme outside, in what is often called 'the gutter', would be the children who are born into poverty and are surrounded by society's ills. Very few are in either extreme but the distance between the two is enormous. In-between are the other stereotypes: the hardworking families, those trying to better themselves, the deeply in debt but coping, people on benefits, the newly wealthy and celebrities. Their children are placed on the educational track in order of the wealth of their parents.

For most families, the aim would be to edge towards the left, to have a better existence and lifestyle and to move further away from the desperation of the outside lane. Some are happy where they are and content to play a middle course, satisfied with their lives and enjoying fairly modest ambitions. Edging to the left means trying to have some of what *they* are having and many believe that hard work will get them there. A few resort to cheating or making the system work for them; some do it simply to survive and others to make it into that next lane across. Whether it is fiddling expenses claims or taking copper wire from railway tracks, within the community of your lane, if you can get away with it there is advantage to be taken.

Children continue to grow up in this range of different circumstances. Those born into that outside 'gutter' lane grow up as part of an 'underclass' where traditional social norms disappear and a new set of norms take over. Few take the time to care. Camila Batmanghelidjh of Kidscape, for example, speaks out for the children who live off the scraps of society and castigates the blind eyes that have been turned to the children who need us most. Louise Casey, the coalition government's 'tsar' for troubled families, has spelled out the challenges that these dysfunctional families cause to society, not least in terms of cost. She talks of the need to break the grim cycle that continues from one generation to the next. Successive government initiatives have passed by these families; Neighbourhood Renewal, City Challenge and the like were targeted at local authority areas, with pressure put upon them to achieve results. Those nearest to the target became the focus of attention and action, the so-called 'low-hanging fruit' or 'quick wins', and those furthest away carried on as before, wreaking havoc on all they touch in society. Louise Casey's drive to understand the circumstances, and then address every aspect of family need at the most basic of levels, is long overdue.

As long ago as 1990, there was a focus on the new 'underclass' and a television programme focused on a big estate in Sunderland. At the time, I was working with a primary school on the estate and knew of the social conditions from which these children came. These were feckless households in terms of normative behaviours but resourceful ones in terms of survival against the odds. Many people pilfered as a matter of course; stole as a job of work; did business with fences as a natural course of events; treated their children as little more than pets and their pitbulls as trophies; wives were traded and sampled; drugs were used as and when available; and some individuals were falling increasingly under the control of the pushers and runners. Yet most of them sent their children to school. It became an oasis of calm for these children in a desert of neglect.

In our society, at the beginning of the twenty-first century, we have significant numbers of children who fit a category that puts them in those outside lanes. Think of the words and consider the implications for learning and schools: groomed, abused, addicted, neglected, raped, targeted, frightened, hungry. Social workers and youth workers can provide graphic descriptions of how this underworld operates, how some children are deceived into gangs and weaponry, how some are drawn into sexual abuse, how some look for excitement and get out of their depth. A number of schools will recount examples of children who don't eat between their school dinner and the following morning's breakfast club. What do these children eat in August?

These families, and their children in turn, become a problem for society, which typically applies 'inside lane' thinking to 'outside lane' people. The Labour government introduced anti-social behaviour orders (ASBOs) without realising that there would be a competition in some quarters to see who could acquire the most. Another 'tsar', this one responsible for looking at behaviour in schools, has proposed fining families £60 for their child's non-attendance. The thinking is that deducting the money from benefits will ensure payment. How will that keep children fed?

The official report into the riots of summer 2011 refers to the 500,000 'forgotten families'. The chairman of the Riots Communities and Victims Panel, Darra Singh, said: 'We must give everyone a stake in society. There are people "bumping along the bottom", unable to change their lives. When people don't feel they have a reason to stay out of trouble, the consequences for communities can be devastating.' The government is trying to come up with strategies to reintegrate these individuals into society. It is a bit late but anything would help.

The anecdotal evidence of pupils arriving at primary school unprepared for learning is growing. Teachers talk of children who aren't toilet trained, don't know how to dress themselves and, more worrying, can't talk and don't know even their names. These are children who are treated as little more than pets or toys to enjoy when it is convenient.

These are examples of early childhood at its worst. The proportion is not high, but 500,000 'forgotten families' probably yields twice that many children of school age, about 8% of the school population in England. On the nearby inside lanes from these groups are the families trying hard but who are unaware of what to do, the ones with aspirations but little idea of how to achieve them.

Jean Gross, the Communication Champion until the government decided to close her office, reflected in her final report in 2011 that 'Many practitioners have told me that parents want the facts. Speech and language therapists in one local area, for example, told me how when they provided information about the impact of indiscriminate television-watching under the age of two, and the prolonged use of dummies, the reaction from parents was "No one told us this before". Once given the facts, parents were all too happy to make changes to their interactions with their child.'

The coalition government is trying to address these matters through a range of activities. Alan Milburn's work on social mobility continues to highlight the dominance of independent school pupils in future success and to find ways to overcome it. He suggests that families with children in failing schools should be given a voucher to use in any school, public or state. His argument is that families do not lack aspiration; they do not know how to achieve it and schooling holds the key. Graham Allen's 2011 report on 'Early Intervention' warns that 'If we continue to fail, we will only perpetuate the cycle of wasted potential, low achievement, drink and drug misuse, unintended teenage pregnancy, low work aspirations, anti-social behaviour and lifetimes on benefits, which now typifies millions of lives and is repeated through succeeding generations.' Frank Field, the long-time parliamentary campaigner for action on poverty, and at one time another of the government's 'tsars', this time on parenting, talks of parents 'falling out of love with parenting'.

One of the better moves by the coalition was to establish the Education Endowment Federation, an organisation tasked with building equity and increasing social mobility. Its chair, Peter Lampl, advocates change to taxation policy and, when it comes to education, some key reforms to address the education achievement gaps that increase with age in our stratified school system. He proposes ballots for oversubscribed schools, democratising entry into independent day schools by introducing means-tested fees and means testing for university fees. These are structural changes, but he also promotes attention to teacher impact by working on 'rewarding the best' and improving the 'bottom 10%' of teachers to boost school performance in a way that would dramatically improve the nation's overall exam results. However, there could be confusion here between school performance and the 'best teachers'. The simple measures of school results can easily deceive us into thinking that the best teachers have been at work.

Iain Duncan Smith is driving forward a strategy to recalibrate benefit payments to try to make work worth it. A pilot programme to offer parenting classes to those most in need risks being seen by many as a 'nanny state' activity, but it could be the start of a much needed support framework for a task that is vastly different from just a generation ago. If we think about it, why is it that the most difficult thing a human being will ever do – being a good parent – is singularly missing from the curriculum? Why isn't it considered an essential life skill? Ask any new mother what she learned at antenatal classes and she will talk of breath and breast. But what of the importance of talk and reading and the development of a baby's brain?

The downside of all this is that Secretary of State for Education Michael Gove seems unable to keep up. Tony Blair's first Labour government used to talk of 'joined up government'. They soon dropped the strapline but the coalition could do with it now. As part of the coalition's efforts to deal with the outside lanes of society, Gove has proposed a suite of academic qualifications as an alternative to his original EBacc (English Baccalaureate) proposals and reduced the value of vocational qualifications. He has set floor standards for schools regardless of their intake. The cap on housing benefits might have decent motives in terms of housing policy, but the reaction of some London boroughs – by shifting their tenants outside the capital – will have impact elsewhere. Stoke-on-Trent, Sandwell and Nottingham Councils, for example, are being approached to house displaced families. Schools in these areas will receive the children. Nobody would say these youngsters can't achieve but it might be reasonable to suggest that they need a different slant on provision.

On the first day of the Key Stage 2 SATs for ten-year-olds last year, I was in a primary school on a big estate in Walsall. The head teacher was unsettled because a murder had taken place locally over the weekend – one of the children in Year 6 had lost his father. The eventual court case revealed that the victim had been restrained in a tyre and burned. What troubled the head was the matter-of-fact way that children in the school were discussing the episode. There was no sense of the shock or outrage that her own children had expressed. During the morning, police and social workers arrived to collect the child and take him into care following the arrest of the mother and an older teenage sibling. They allowed him to complete his SAT paper first.

I remember clearly being lost in Manchester looking for a school that was located in an area of back-to-back Victorian housing. While looking at the map, I spotted a little girl of three or four sitting on a kerb and playing with a plastic cup that was floating in a puddle around her feet. If I let my imagination wander, I could see a sepia tint and travel back a hundred years. The problem was that this was the twenty-first century and every house but one was boarded up. This little girl was just seeing time trickle through her fingers. I reflected that elsewhere a child with plastic cup would have an adult nearby who would be using vocabulary about splashing, mess, colours and translucence and giving the child a vehicle of communication to a better quality of life. This child had a puddle.

People who work in these circumstances need humour. At another school in Manchester, the remodelling of the building culminated in a formal celebration and a blessing from the church, followed by a Friday afternoon party on the newly laid lawn. After the weekend, the head arrived to find the turf was missing. After contacting the chair of governors, they set off round the neighbourhood to find their grass. Grass was commonly traded on the estate but this was a different type. In front of several houses were newly laid lawns upon which families sat in their patio chairs, enjoying their new gardens, beer in hand.

The calls for more social equity can be hollow because as some people become comparatively more affluent, others meet them coming the other way as they become comparatively less so. Back on my education race track, it is worth pointing out that almost everyone in the race recognises that they have to watch what is happening to their right and protect their lane, their territory. This makes it hard for anyone trying to move towards the inside lane, the fast track. To keep individuals where they belong we construct codes of behaviour that make entry to lanes on the left inhibiting. We call this protocol and etiquette and they become challenges for those moving to unfamiliar territories. Children may gain qualifications which become the tickets to open doors to the future but they also need support to enable them to take advantage of the invitation. They need the guidebook not just the ticket.

It is easier to veer to the right. The curve of the bend creates a natural urge to glide outwards. Sometimes this is dramatic: the son of a rock star might find himself on a protest march temporarily in the company of people from the outer lanes and behave in ways that are uncharacteristic; a millionaire's daughter might get caught up and become involved in looting. In such cases, the law comes down hard, not simply to punish but to remind those in the inside lane that they should hold their course. Of course, there are many on the inside lane behaving dishonourably but there are also many support nets that are not available to those on the outside. Many of the rogue bankers were on the inside lane. They were able to create such havoc because the system protected them, refusing to believe that they might be deviant or criminal. Accountants, lawyers and family contacts all allow those on the inside to be protected from the consequences that those on the outside face routinely.

The vast majority of people are in the middle lanes. They may be aiming left or veering right but they want an honest life, have a strong work ethic and believe in fairness. Many of those struggling to stay in the middle are folk who have had troubles and they and their children are trying to make it through: refugees, asylum seekers and carers. The number of children who are the primary carers for an adult is significant. The National Young Carers Coalition asserted, in 2010, that 'there are many more young carers than the 700,000 on record'.

The concept of the running track is at the heart of parental preference for the school for their child. Basically, most of us would seek a school which takes most of its children from the lanes on the left of where we are. For many, there is a fear of allowing their middle lane children to mix with children who are more than one lane to their right. This is a fear fuelled by the media that they may fall prey to drugs, crime and other bad influences. The fact that mixing children from different backgrounds can benefit all is undermined by the unrelenting belief that we must all move left. Added to that is the uneasy realisation that contacts matter. Sending your child to mix with children on the left might result in a leg-up. The old adage of 'it's not what you know but who you know' weighs heavily on parents' minds. The result is greater segregation and the statistics become skewed. The educational performance of the school becomes a quasi measure of social mix. Hence, school league tables serve now to indicate comparative house prices; estate agents quote the performance of local schools as a desirable feature of a property.

On the very inside track, school admission choice is almost guaranteed. It is passed down through the family line and children go where their grandparents and parents went, almost as a demonstration of old money. In the middle lanes, people jockey for school places and seek to move home or transport their children to the perceived better school. Some parents do not have the means to organise this and some do not understand the system. As a result, we have a stratified school system where pupils are jostled into schools based on their parents' perception of which lanes they would like to be in and away from others which they desperately want to avoid. Others get what they are given, believing that this is their lot in life.

Are the schools that take the children with whom no one wants to mix 'bad schools'? A quick look at the excellent grades for many schools in the most deprived areas would suggest not. Let's be clear. We are not talking about good schools and bad schools here; we are talking about social stratification that leads to an extraordinary level of desperation. Schools are just part of that scene.

In places where the Eleven plus is still the way to grammar school for those who cannot afford the inside lane of independent schooling, many parents put everything into helping their child pass the gateway test. Private tutors build reputations based on hearsay (there are no league tables). For those who fail the Eleven plus, there is, for many of their parents, a general acceptance that they still have to do their bit to get their child in the most left hand lane possible. This might mean stumping up for an independent school that takes other Eleven plus failures or seeking the 'best' state school on offer, the one with a middle-left intake, even if it means a long journey each day for at least five years. Some children travel 20,000 miles in the course of their secondary career, making socialising with other pupils after school very difficult. Other parents simply accept their offer and their children end up with others who did the same, in the school that those in the left hand lanes know is the one to avoid.

This practice of steering clear of those in the right hand lane develops in primary schools. There are many rural primary schools that would have closed but for the attendance of children brought in each morning from the local town, so that they can learn with children 'like them' and not with children from the estate who attend the school closest to where they live. A small town will see the school run taking children to outlying village primary schools each morning. Having had an idyllic primary experience, they then have to attend the local comprehensive school which contains the very children they managed to avoid for seven years.

The Labour government's Sure Start initiative was set up to support children and parents in the Early Years. The evidence was that those in the left hand lanes knew how to use the system and took advantage of the Sure Start provision. Those for whom the Sure Start centres would have proved the most beneficial either failed to take advantage or could not gain access because the resource was overwhelmed by those who knew how to make the system work.

Each time a youngster meets a challenge their place on the track makes a difference. For example, children on the inside lane will undertake very different work experiences from those towards the outside, where an impressive parental network will be at play finding a suitable placement for their offspring. Alan Milburn's work shows how internships exaggerate inequality. Towards the outside lanes, teenagers have less and less opportunity for the plum placements. Even earlier, as children face up to the learning demands of their primary years, their levels of articulacy dictate their chances. For children who have parents who talk to them, take them to places and show them things, these tests would have been interesting. For example, the 2012 SATs for eleven-year-olds focused on a sugar plum. In 2011, it had been a visit to the Derbyshire limestone caverns, putting the children unfamiliar with these terms and places at a disadvantage. For those in the outside lanes, the SAT is like entering a foreign country where, even if you can read the language, the cultures and customs can make little sense.

And the pupils? Most adults would want our children to enjoy school, to have the time of their lives and, at the end, be ready to leave as they set out on adulthood. Many children do enjoy school, as part of an enjoyable childhood. They could get even more pleasure from it but hearing adults talking endlessly about the trials of schooling, and announcing that much of what they learned was pointless, must colour their view.

Most children work out the system. They can tolerate what is offered and fathom out quickly what they need to do in order to make their way across the lanes to their left. Others keep their heads down and get what they can from the whole thing while never quite seeing the purpose. Some children realise that, despite their best efforts, they are sliding to the right and simply allow it to happen, sometimes crying or rebelling as they slip away.

There is an amazing amount of tolerance in the schooling system. Typically pupils put up with school; those able to do so exercise a form of deferred gratification, knowing that it will be worth it in the end as they can see the access to tracks on the inside. Most develop some loyalty to their schools and their teachers who they believe are generally on their side, hence the added effort when the inspectors come to call. This loyalty is sustained by schools who manage to add sparkle through one-off events and special occasions.

As they get older, though, a growing proportion of youngsters realise that school is a time to be served in a regime driven by factors outside the control of the people who run their learning. They recognise double standards in daily routines, they tolerate or rebel against trivial rules, they cope (or not) with illogical demands and genuine learning takes a back seat. They see the irony of politicians demanding that schools insist on attendance but close schools at the drop of a hat for an election in which only 15% of constituents bother to vote. They semi tolerate uniform rules that question the shade of socks, with their shirts out and ties undone, in institutions that talk of seeing them as unique individuals. Some don't care because it is a long way to the inside track. Some don't care because they are so far from the outside lane. In either case, it is not their quest for education that is driving them forward.

## What do our children need?

The problem is that we expect our schools to deal with all of our diverse children in the same way. Because we believe in equality, we profess to want the same outcomes for all children. But outcomes for children have never been anything like equal and social mobility has never been a reality for more than a few. In the last twenty years there has been an emphasis on schools as the prime vehicle in social mobility and equality; therefore the school system has to do its job. The move to get the school system to do its job has been promoted through increased accountability and the rise in a belief in market forces – choice and diversity. But we never seem able to work out what to do about the different starting points for children. Do we offer the backmarkers a better start, more intensive coaching and a bit of a downhill slope? Or do we offer all children the same and expect those at the back to be taught harder, learn faster or simply drop out when it becomes too hard for them and plainly obvious that they will never complete the circuit?

At the root of the problem lies the question of whether schools are enhancing parental efforts or supporting, substituting or compensating for what goes on elsewhere in the child's life. In just forty years, the outlook on schooling has changed from one where *some* pupils were expected to succeed to one where *all* pupils are expected to succeed. We now hear talk of a 'no-excuses culture' and schools are expected to deliver the required outcomes for all children without allowing for their background; not least because this is the only way to help pupils to overcome their backgrounds.

In the late 1960s, around 15% of all pupils took the equivalent of today's GCSE, the Ordinary level examination. This would indicate their aptitude for Advanced level study with the prospect of university or a future in administration and management. The other 85% did not take the O level examination. Another 15% were deemed educationally sub-normal (ESN) and were not even allowed into schooling. In the 1970s and 1980s, we moved through a period of expecting more pupils to succeed, to the 1990s where most were to succeed, and to the present time where we expect all to achieve. What was seen as the 'average' level for an eleven-year-old in 1988, with the introduction of the attainment levels of the national curriculum, is now seen as the 'required' standard for the end of the primary phase. Society's expectations have risen and schools have responded to the demands of society, sometimes under duress as the leverage applied has become more public.

Imagine the head teacher of a secondary school charged with ensuring *all* pupils achieve five GCSEs at age sixteen. What would be the most effective way of guaranteeing success? One answer is to get the intake right by devising some sort of examination to make sure the pupils admitted were fit for the course. Where such an entrance examination is not allowed, another device needed to be developed to attract the right sort of pupil. Kenneth Baker's 1988 Education Reform Act led to the notion of parents expressing a preference, which in turn led to schools 'marketing' themselves.

The arrival of league tables and inspection reports were a lever in the system and outcomes-led schooling emerged. Except that even the schools at the head of the tables or those independent schools charging for admission are held to account by parents who put increasing pressure on results rather than the experience of learning. Why do they do this? Is it that it is easier and quicker to understand results or that 'you can't argue with results'? When these are the only indicators available, how else might a parent evaluate a school? The market forces and accountability-driven system risks folding in upon itself because results are driving the children's experiences and creating a vicious circle and thus lowers expectations for learning in the quest for better test results. There are still those schools where parents feel privileged to be allowed to let their children have a place and 'let the school get on with it', but even in the prestigious independent sector heads talk about being under pressure from parents to deliver examination results rather than provide a decent education.

If the balance has tipped towards outcomes, accountability and the market, then our hopes for our young people become distorted. The majority of parents provide for most of their child's ambitions as part of a productive enjoyable childhood so simply want the school to top up the competences and enable their child to become qualified for the next stage. Those same parents want their children to enjoy being with other like-minded children from similar backgrounds and to share some 'beyond the family' experiences. The further from the inside of the track, however, the more the qualifications matter and the more they might become the primary focus. Suddenly the schools that received the pupils that the entrance exam rejected are expected to get the same results with a different intake. Now the market-driven accountability takes on a different hue and results become all important; even pupils get the idea and demand to be taught what will get the results rather than what might be worth learning. Those children that hardly anybody wants, towards the outside of the track, get it as well. Either we work for the image of the school, for ourselves and get results, or we just give up entirely. These are the very schools where the drive for accountability and market forces has become a synonym for professional embarrassment and the threat of being taken over by a 'successful' organisation.

The schools that get no choice of intake have had to change from a 'do all you can for these youngsters' to a 'minimum requirements' outlook. That is fine if the minimum is achievable – and that is the crux of the debate. Can pupils from undernourished educational backgrounds achieve the same performance by a given time? If we say no, do we condone excuses? It is easy to say that there is no reason why every pupil cannot achieve, but it has never been proved. Never has *every* child achieved. If they all achieve the minimum, what should the best achieve? If the best achieve more, should the worst not be achieving better? The gap in performance might be attributed to something we now seem able to recognise: social inequality, the 400-metre track without the staggered start.

One thing is certain: it is entirely erroneous to suggest that if all teenagers gain an EBacc, or whatever becomes the new marker, social inequity will be removed and we will be living in an equal society.

## What might we do?

- Set individual and specific challenges for some schools to take account of their circumstances. Nearly every school seems to be able to argue that *their* intake of pupils is much more diverse than it appears and that a fair proportion of its pupils carry the scars of deprivation. This is true but it is also relative. Some schools have a population which, because of the impact of parental preference, is almost entirely made up of children from an outside lane with no staggered start opportunity. Might it not be sensible to make these schools a special case when it comes to accountability? Shouldn't these schools have a different set of expectations and measures applied to them without its proponents being labelled 'enemies of promise'? Shouldn't the full force of multiagency working be based in these schools? This would see health, social, police, youth, voluntary and education professionals working each and every day to bring order and stability to the community, unfettered by distractions elsewhere. It would see an emphasis on getting order into the daily routine of some homes. It would see school as a refuge for children and their families with access to the relevant agencies guaranteed. It would see the building open all day every day. With a bit of structure we might see children start to read, write and manage numbers along with their parents. Since the system has already placed these schools in the lowest strata, it surely would not matter if they were simply classified in a different way.

- Building character. This is a phrase from the official report into the riots of 2011 expressing one of the priorities for action. Indeed, the Final Report talks of the need for schools to work to help pupils become responsible citizens. Typically, this is a given expectation for schools rather than a requirement or a measure. It is one of those things that only gets mentioned in a school when things are plainly going wrong. It goes right when schools have thought through their whole educational offering to pupils and understand that the lessons are only part of the learning experience. The problem is that what we measure in schools is a limited set of test outcomes and this, in turn, forms the basis of a school inspection. There needs to be recognition that forming responsible citizens is one of the key building blocks that will, eventually, help to open the door to the traditional images of success in school. If we are serious about developing character, we have to respect the schools for doing it and give it status.

- Improving parenting and family competence. There is much debate about the coalition government's introduction of the pilot programmes for parenting classes. Parents can gain access via vouchers to classes and to a sophisticated online support package. There are those who worry that this is an area that government need not or should not enter. Maybe it would be better organised at a local level but the principle cannot be bad. Many new parents find the prospect they face daunting – what can be wrong with a support network?

Could we go further and insist that access to school be dependent upon the child having reached certain stages of development, excepting, of course, those with special needs? Early on during pregnancy parents could be given a pre-school checklist outlining a set of skills and competencies that children must have before starting school. Along with the enormous bags of samples and leaflets given to all new parents, there could be a booklet or website with top tips on developing your baby's mind. This might make the parenting courses very attractive and increase the interest of some parents in the development of their young child from an early age. I believe that nearly every parent wants to do their best for their child; too many simply don't know what to do.

- Impose a levy for admission to schools further away. Successive secretaries of state of all persuasions have uttered the mantra about a successful local school for all children. The pressure to get to the left on the educational running track works against this. How about a levy system on school admissions? Parents are told which school their child has been allocated a place in – the one nearest to their home. If they reject this and gain admission to one further away, then fine, the cost is £1,000 per year for a school in the nearest three miles and £3,000 per year for a school beyond that. The money levied would go to the school the pupil should have attended, the nearest one. Basically, the children to the right of the running track get the benefit from the reluctance of other pupils to spend time with them.

- Maximise the benefits of the pupil premium. In their election manifesto, the Liberal Democrats pledged a pupil premium to support the pupils most at risk in the system, particularly those with difficult school histories such as those who have been excluded. These are the pupils that schools are reluctant to admit due to the potential impact on their league table position. The much-heralded version that transpired in government began as little more than a free school meals supplement. The amount of money is now significant and, in some schools, is a major part of the budget. However, there is only now a growing scant record of what the money is used for, although this will form part of the inspection system. Although some schools are deploying it well – targeting the resource on specific pupils – Ofsted's 2012 Annual Report reveals that many are simply using it to overcome budget reductions and maintain staffing levels. We could insist that pupil premium funding is to ensure a set of pupil guarantees that would enable the list of hopes for our vulnerable young people to be realised.

■ Make public the successes of schools with children from the outside lanes. The value of the league table measure of the successor to the EBacc speaks volumes about the attitude of the government towards social equity. By setting a school accountability measure that differentiates the performance of those already achieving examination successes, the government is making a statement about what matters. There was to be no measure in league table performance for the proportion of pupils gaining an EBacc who are on free school meals or who are Looked After or Carers. Do those children not matter? Are they not a group that the government espouses to strive for? If so, should they not feature strongly in the accountability ratings?

■ Properly address aspiration. Aspiration is more than simply telling people that they can all do it – whatever 'it' is. It is about making the 'it' more than achieving five GCSEs or whatever becomes the next future success measure. There is something very powerful about getting a 'we can show them' culture going in a school and its community which can seriously question old social orders and their pupils' place on the track. In the end, though, communities and pupils, often later in adulthood, feel cheated when they realise they were pawns in a game for the school rather than having doors opened for them through endeavour. We need a real commission to look into aspiration, and it should be backed up by research.

# … on marching to different drums

In those vague times of long, long ago, the rich and powerful knew how to bring up their children to inherit their wealth and status. They provided for their offspring and ensured that their entry into adulthood was secure in four main ways: self-image, experience, contacts and education.

The privileged knew that, first and foremost, their children must believe in themselves and so they were helped to understand that they were important. Next they gave their children worthwhile things to do – they took them around Europe and introduced them to fine art and music. Then there was the vital life chance of knowing the right people. These days we would probably refer to these elements as developing self-esteem and experience and building contacts and networks.

The privileged classes were good at these three undertakings. They knew how to do them because they had received the experience themselves. However, there was a further need for formal lessons and teaching and so it was common for the privileged classes to employ a tutor who would teach their children the things they needed to know so that they could have well-informed conversations with their contacts and acquaintances about the Classics, the Age of Enlightenment or the refined art and literature they would encounter. They would need to know how to read and how to do arithmetic. So the tutor would give the children lessons and, when there were several children together, they would gradually build a class and the children might see this as being schooled. In Dickens's novels, the wealthier classes ask of each other where they were 'schooled'. It was a mark of significant wealth if boys were educated privately and a matter of rank where they had been schooled.

The purpose of this teaching was to ensure that the children were rounded and finished, so that they would be able to continue their networking through shared connections to get to university and eventually to prove themselves in the adult world. They would, in turn, realise how important they must be that their parents had made such schooling provisions for them.

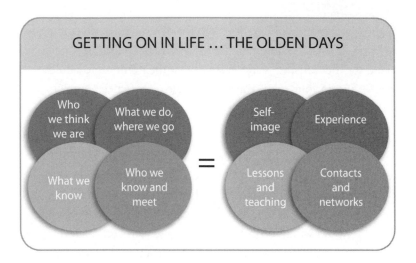

Once at university, and in those days only a few select institutions were universities, these privileged young people were primed to become leaders of men – trained for the church, the military, government or law. In all cases there was a requirement to be able to quickly assimilate a large amount of information and then succinctly reduce it to a speech, sermon, closing statement or policy. Even today, Oxbridge works with purpose – to create leaders who can read, think, distil, reinterpret and represent.

In the 1870s, mass education came to England. There was an urgent need to make sure that all children were schooled and gained some form of education so that the nation would become prosperous in the unfolding world of the empire and the industrial revolution. So it was that state schooling began and, in our effort to make the new schools work, it was natural that we would look towards the institutions that already existed – the public schools to which the privileged classes could afford to send their children. They taught the essential three Rs – reading, writing and 'rithmetic – which had evolved from a speech made by Sir William Curtis in 1795, alluding to the essentials of learn-ing in school. From their very beginning, state schools have offered one element of the education of the wealthy, the 'what you need to know' element. Despite calling the schooling process 'education', they have avoided the other three aspects that the privileged had taken for granted.

Britain wanted to ensure its economic strength and so we needed to develop work skills. Schools were organised so they would mirror the experience of a day at work: bells, signing in, regimented timetables and so on. We needed to manage individuals and make society work effectively ... if the privileged classes were to maintain their status.

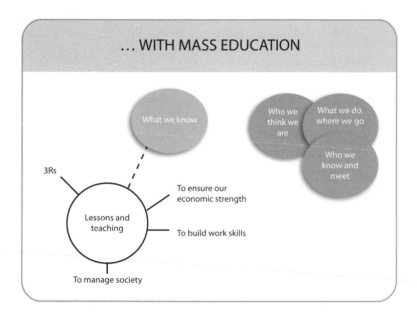

Leaping forward to the relatively recent past, we can see how this early image of state schooling has continued to dominate the way we look at success. We measure the achievements of schools through analyses of examinations and testing at various stages. Then we put the school results into league tables and carry out inspections based on those results in order to identify those schools that are succeeding or failing. And, all the time, the major emphasis in our analysis of success is lessons and teaching. We pay some attention to the experience the children have and to their self-image but give virtually no consideration to the contacts and networks they might build up – which is one of the key avenues to future prosperity.

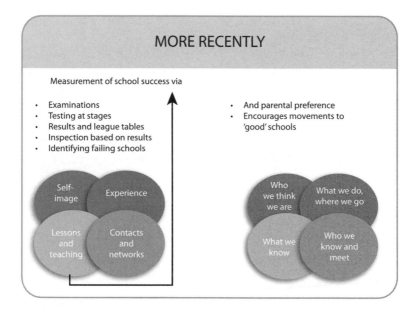

Of course, parental preference is influenced by the analysis that is produced. Parents know about exam and test results; they know about inspection reports. This encourages a movement to the so-called 'good' schools, which offer good lessons and good teaching. Because of the analysis we know which schools are struggling and, over the last few years, we have worked hard to make sure that those struggling schools are 'supported'.

First we call them 'challenged'. In order to address the challenge we adopt military language and then develop strategies to help them. A range of 'partners' are brought in to offer support and focus on 'deliverables'; that is, the lessons and teaching.

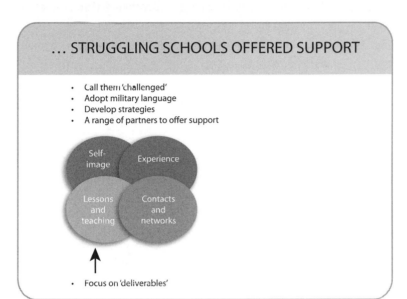

So much investment focuses on the 'problem', so we want to see incremental improvement in teaching and learning. We want to see focused accountability, so we target subgroups or we look at certain teachers to make sure there is progress. The Labour government offered new buildings and more resources for teachers and other staff and there was certainly an explosion in ICT. But all the time the emphasis was on lessons and teaching. Very little money was spent on trying to help children gain the sorts of experiences that might equip them for the wider world, to build their self-image or to understand how contacts and networks make such a difference in our lives.

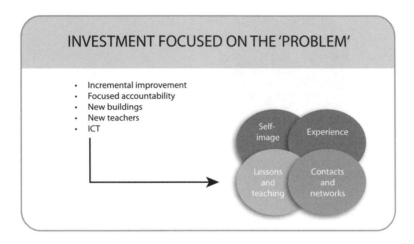

And what about successful youngsters? If we take the same four elements and look at those who are recognised as doing well, typically they are flourishing in the lessons and teaching circle. While the schooling system works for many young people, what we know is that many of them are simply playing the game. They can be successful in school because they understand how to do it, so they play along. At the same time they are increasingly intolerant of the way the system works. They recognise that they are exam fodder rather than individuals who can truly get to grips with scholarly pursuit. Politicians draw attention to a significant proportion of youngsters who are abusing their time outside of school by using it poorly and allegedly wasting aspects of their lives. There are some who are abusing themselves, and others, and there are many more who are disenfranchised. Surely what we want to see are young people who are thriving, engaged, independent, optimistic, challenged and entrepreneurial. That challenge and entrepreneurial spirit comes from a rounded education – one that takes account of all four circles in the diagram.

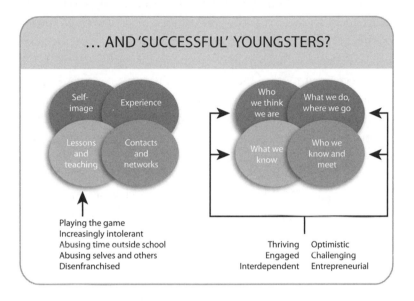

So what do we need in the twenty-first century? Well, first of all it is very clear that youngsters do need qualifications and these are a result of being well taught and being able to demonstrate the extent to which certain subject disciplines have been understood. But if we are really going to build their list of qualifications, they also need good assessment along the way which will help them grow as people; rather than simply informing them that they aren't good enough in certain areas or encouraging them to cram for examinations. They need an assessment system that builds self-discipline. They need to establish a good self-image and to understand the etiquette and tactics for success.

Young people need to understand that life is a game played out in different arenas and with each of us playing different roles at different times; they need to work out how to make the rules work for them. In terms of what we do and where we go, they need a guarantee of experiences – everything from culture, art, sport and the natural world to awareness of work and understanding the way the world functions. Lastly, and incredibly importantly, children need to know how to make contacts and use them to build up networks that they can enjoy, exploit and benefit from. This is the bit the public schools have always understood. The head master of one of the country's most well known, prestigious schools talks of having to recognise that the privileged pupils will learn as much from each other as they will from his staff. It is the secret that most of those who feel they have benefitted from a private education seem not to acknowledge as they go on about rigorous teaching and lessons. Most so-called 'successful people' will admit that the old adage is true: it is not what you know but who you know that matters. How else might we account for what Michael Gove calls the 'morally indefensible' prevalence of public school pupils in positions of influence? The easy bit is to pretend it is all about better teaching; it keeps attention away from the importance of contacts and networks.

... NEEDS FOR THE TWENTY-FIRST CENTURY

The etiquette and tactics for success

Rules of life game

Who we think we are

What we do, where we go

A guarantee of experiences

Assessment to build self-image

What we know

Who we know and meet

Learn to use contacts

Qualifications

Across the world, I have heard ministers of education extol the importance of a rounded education to enable their children to take advantage of the opportunities arising from the way the world is developing, one that is vibrant enough to help young people address the changes that are occurring. There is no time to waste they assert; we must strive for a new concept of learning and schooling. They talk of the importance of direct and authentic experiences. They emphasise skills and qualities such as problem-solving, adaptability, determination and resilience, and how these need to replace the rote learning of an older time. They also stress that these skills need to be better incorporated into examination and qualification systems rather than dismissed with the arrogance that simply states that traditional academic pursuit is 'harder'.

But they beat one drum and march to another depending upon who they are with. They are politicians with votes to capture. Within a very short while, the same ministers are explaining how they are going to make their schools more accountable with better testing and inspection. What will they measure as success? They propose measuring the things we have always measured; not the skills that might ensure young people are better set for a future world. They beat the drum of progress and march to the drum of tedious accountability.

## So what is urgently needed as the structure of schooling undergoes a seismic shift?

■ Whatever the school – free school, studio school, academy, faith school – the first aim is that the school fits in with, rather than isolates itself from, its community. This sounds so obvious and I know many schools state this as one of their reasons for existing. However, schools need to look particularly closely at what they mean by the term 'to fit in with', so that they start to explore more thoroughly how they can help their children and their families to have enjoyable and productive lives. Teaching, learning and qualifications are only part of the education success story. Many schools fall into the trap of convincing their school community that qualifications are the route to success. Indeed they are one route, but equally they need to teach their parents and children that there are many more aspects that people on the inside track already understand.

■ This means treating people as people and aiming high for pupils in a moral and ethical sense. In too many cases schools are setting their horizons very low. Success is measured by the next Ofsted inspection and so, as a community, we work to that deadline date as an important moment in the school's evolution. Some schools seem to work towards the next pause, the next term end, the next weekend or even the end of the day rather than seeing the unfolding life of their school community as a long-term development.

■ We need to see genuine tailored learning where young people's potential is analysed and supported. This means looking not only at their potential qualifications but seeing where young people are strong and weak in aspects of their development in the three other circles in the diagram, in order to help them to grow as genuinely rounded people.

■ An aspect that is often overlooked is the importance of exposing the true challenges facing the community that the school finds itself in. We are very good at talking about these challenges within our professional circles and to outside observers and scrutinisers (such as an Ofsted inspection team). However, the leadership of schools is less good at talking in educational terms about the challenge the community represents to the community itself. True, sometimes we hector parents and tell them to get their children to school or explain that they need to adhere to uniform rules, but too often we do so without providing an explanation. 'You must' should be followed by 'because', and 'because' should always be rooted in the well-being of the child. 'Please make sure your child has his PE kit because if he doesn't he becomes more isolated from the other children.' Or 'because if he doesn't, he spends an hour sitting in the cold, watching everyone else having fun' (then make sure the PE lesson *is* fun). Whatever the reason, parents are more likely to comply if they understand the benefits. 'Because we say so' doesn't really cut the mustard because, for some parents, the 'we' represents an enemy or a foreign set of rules and expectations that they simply do not value or understand.

It takes a certain sort of nerve to explain to the school community itself that one of the reasons their children are destined not to succeed is because they have failed to grasp the importance of the agenda that the families on the inside track fully understand. It is hard to explain to families that they need to give their children cultural experiences, especially when the parents themselves have never had this opportunity. It is even more difficult to explain to families that there are different etiquettes that hold in different aspects of life and that, unless their children are prepared to understand them, they will find it hard to exploit the opportunities that life can offer. Adopting these customs may demand that children break away from the social norms of their community and this can be very difficult to address. It is so easy to talk about people. It is less easy to talk with them. As a profession we must do better.

# … on national politicians and education policy

The relationship between politics and education reached an all-time low in January 2012. Secretary of State Michael Gove was reported in the media as condemning opponents of the government's policy on the conversion of schools to academy status. In a forceful and hard-hitting speech, he talked of 'ideologues' who were 'enemies of promise'. Whether that was true or not paled in importance compared with the context of the speech.

Much mirth has been expressed by viewers of the YouTube clip of the secretary of state delivering his speech at an academy in London. The camera initially focused on the serious and determined face of Michael Gove and then panned round to show the audience. On one side were the screen-filler characters who had little choice but to be there – school staff, Department for Education officials and educationalists who had received a late invitation to attend an important policy announcement before the attendant media. On the other side were pupils of the school, probably dragooned into being present and who were already looking bored, fiddling with their own and each others' hair, picking at bits of their anatomy and doing that heavy-head thing that adolescents do. It was funny but also very sad.

Here was a secretary of state who seemed to think it acceptable to deliver a political speech to teenagers, although the substance was clearly not for them and clearly not accessible to them. Many would find Gove's speech objectionable in its use of language and name-calling. There may be a function for such language in political debate, when you build up your opponent's argument (often into something that they wouldn't recognise) and then lampoon it. But Gove was recorded as saying that his opponents' views were a product of a 'bigoted, backward, bankrupt ideology of a left-wing establishment that perpetuates division and denies opportunity'. Such language does not help rational debate and understanding, and surely is questionable in a school setting.

Labour politicians have also been guilty of appropriating pupils for the benefit of publicity. A particular case was the launch of the Labour Party manifesto for the 2001 general election, which Tony Blair held in front of pupils at a school in Southwark and for which he was heavily criticised. There must be concern for the quality of our democracy when politicians can walk into schools and make unbalanced political speeches. School authorities, seemingly through their own lack of assertiveness on the role of education in a democratic society, cave in to what policy-makers want through flattery or fear or both.

These examples show the extent to which politicians have stretched their reach and tried to find the best backdrop for the announcement and promotion of their policies in an increasingly media influenced world. As the centralisation of education has gained pace, so communications from the secretary of state have developed from a few 'circulars' each year to a battle to present the right image to the press, often targeted at potential swing-voters. The needs of the audience sitting in front of them are secondary to those of the audience waiting beyond the camera.

It seems the best way to present yourself as the ideal candidate for election is against the backdrop of a colourful classroom, with children dancing or playing instruments to bring movement and melody to the image. Ideally the children are of primary age; their heads are still light and they actually smile. Many ministers are delightful in schools; even when the media have departed they are interested and helpful. Tony Blair was renowned for his ability to relate to youngsters and would spend time reading stories or keeping local officials waiting while he finished a game of football with teenagers. But the fact remains that too many national politicians use schools for their own ends. It wasn't always like this.

# The problem with national politicians

## Politicians seem to think that nothing good ever happened in the previous administration

When a new government moves in, everything in Whitehall is filed away and a fresh start begins. Often it involves a change of name: Department of Education and Science, Department for Education and Employment, Department for Education and Skills, Department for Education and Schools, Department for Education. At the same time comes the need for new signage, stationery and websites.

Worse, though, is the process of archiving and ignoring everything that was being done beforehand. As the last election in 2010 drew near, the new primary curriculum prepared following the Rose Review was pending. As promised in the Conservative election manifesto, this was jettisoned in the 'wash up' before the General Election. A very strong review of personal, social and health education (PSHE) carried out by Alasdair MacDonald at the request of the Labour government was also due to be implemented. This too counted for nothing. What a waste of resource and potential.

David Cameron placed much stress on the notion of the 'Big Society', including the establishment of a National Citizen Service for all six-teen-year-olds. The pilot programmes saw students undertake a three-week summer holiday experience where week one was spent on team-building, week two on designing a charitable project and week three on running the project. The intention was to build social respon-sibility. All very laudable, but no wonder primary school teachers raised their eyebrows. It is not unusual to see primary children doing boat-building, learning teamwork skills and running fundraising events in their local community.

The aim of the proposed National Citizen Service was to bring together young people from all walks of life to serve their community, and for this we apparently needed a new organisation. It seems the Duke of Edinburgh Award Scheme, Scouts, Guides, Sea Scouts, Air

Force Cadets, Boys' Brigades, youth clubs, boxing clubs, St John's Ambulance, the Red Cross and multiple other voluntary organisations can't be expected to build a citizenship service by working together. Politicians have to start again.

Labour was the same. Michael Barber's work on 'high performing systems' concluded that highly qualified teachers were the new silver bullet. The solution was a new qualification, a Master's Degree in Teaching and Learning (MTL). This would build the bridge between theory and practice and aimed to take the work teachers do in their classrooms as the starting point. For two years, the Training Development Agency (TDA) produced documentation, coordinated meetings with higher education representatives, negotiated regional consortia, sorted out the funding and approved prospective MTL programmes. There was not a thought that there might be something to build upon in the system already. There was. It was called the Teachers' Learning Academy and it had been incubated through years of negotiation, pilots and trials to ensure its rigour and effectiveness. It was just beginning to attract large numbers of teachers to the notion of having their school-based work accredited and gradually moving through a series of stages towards serious study, linked to practice, that would lead to recognition of their professional expertise and specialism. It was ignored. Whether it was because the General Teaching Council (GTC) had done the spadework, and by now the government was irritated by its own creation and didn't want to recognise aspects of its success, or whether it was about the TDA wanting to start afresh, who knows? It was a loss of several years of work. It didn't matter much anyway as the coalition quickly got rid of the MTL and, for good measure, the GTC!

## Politicians think everywhere is like London

It is impossible to overstate how London-centric our national politics has become. London is either seen as 'unique' or 'typical'. Things that happen on the London scene quickly translate to the rest of the country. What then happens is that policy oozes from ministers to address the growing media debate, which they have often fuelled themselves.

Steve Munby, when first CEO of the National College for School Leadership, used to joke that schools across the country from Bodmin to Berwick would receive policy guidelines from the London-based Department for Education for dealing with a problem they didn't know they had. Ministers picked up an issue near to Westminster, possibly through the *Evening Standard*, and would seek to solve it with a new policy for all schools everywhere.

## Politicians all have their own silver bullet

Every secretary of state seems to need a policy all of their own.

Keith Joseph was the first secretary of state to 'hold back' central funding from the schools' budget for specific grants. He established Technical and Vocational Education Initiatives (TVEIs) and the Low Achievers Project in the early 1980s with less than 1% of the total national education budget. Local authorities could bid for specific projects and they did so with relish. From there it was no turning back as the system moved through Girls into Science and Technology (GIST) and the Local Education Authority Training Grants Scheme (LEATGS) to the Standards Fund. Local authorities gained influence through securing and influencing the distribution of funding as the tide of control ran away from them.

Kenneth Baker created a sea change for schools with the 1988 Education Reform Act, which generated upheaval within the system the like of which has not been seen again until the arrival of Michael Gove.

David Blunkett nailed his colours to the mast over the national literacy and numeracy strategies. He predicted that Labour would ensure that 80% of all primary pupils would achieve Level 4 in English and mathematics. A better starting point would have been to say that within two years the results would improve by 5% and then set further markers from there. He seemed to forget the old adage to under-promise and over-deliver. With the results hovering at a glass ceiling just below the 80% target his team became more and more desperate, plus he could never do the one thing that needed to be done – revise the SATs process. If he had, his detractors would have cried that he had gone soft on standards.

Estelle Morris drove forward on teacher professionalism. As a minister in Blunkett's team, she had proposed several approaches to improve the image, recognition and achievement of the profession. The structuring of teacher pay with the threshold arrangement and the recognition of advanced skills teachers (ASTs) as people who might be tempted to stay within the classroom rather than seek promotion to management were ways of reinforcing the status of teaching. The establishment of the General Teaching Council was intended to mirror the General Medical Council (GMC) in its gravity but was seen as a threat to many teaching unions and professional associations. It always struggled to get away from the idea of a registration organisation with the power to 'strike off', rather than a professional body that could influence the way teaching was transacted (in a parallel with the workings of the GMC).

Charles Clarke recognised that twenty-first century schools would need to break free from the straitjacket that constrained them and saw technology as the way forward. He was a pragmatic visionary who sought to encourage schools to embrace technology and employ computer science to transform the way they would operate. As the Building Schools for Future (BSF) programme unfolded, it was he who was pushing for a dynamic and radical approach to the way we view schooling itself.

Ruth Kelly's big idea was parent involvement. Her speech to the North of England Conference in 2005 took place just days after her promotion and the expectant delegates heard her pronounce on the vital missing element: parents. After that she seemed not to have any policies unless the prime minister's unit told her so. The most notable announcement she made was during the 2005 General Election campaign to confirm that A levels would remain the gold standard qualification. In doing so, the development of diplomas, recommended by the 2004 Tomlinson Report, would always struggle for prominence.

Alan Johnson never seemed to have a policy.

With Ed Balls came the Every Child Matters agenda. Whether this was down to him or the untimely and tragic death of little Victoria Climbié, it was a significant policy. The five outcomes were attractive to the profession in the search for a rounded education that could be tailored to pupil needs: health, safety, enjoyment and achievement, civic contribution and economic understanding. It all made sense and, for the first time, removed the words 'I'm a teacher not a social worker' from the profession, but it hardly got going. It needed time and courage. They tried with health, but not too hard: a few worksheets on drugs and the removal of some chocolate vending machines in the corridors. They got stuck on safety, especially after some horrible high profile court cases. As for enjoyment and achievement, they could never get the balance. A Department for Education and Skills (DfES) head teacher conference would start with a ten-minute video of children in canoes, abseiling, clog dancing, playing violins, doing experiments, singing, building buggies, serving tea to old people and making pottery. That was the enjoyment. The next five hours of the day would be spent on why targets matter and how to improve achievement. They also forgot to tell Ofsted about 'enjoy and achieve', so they could never get past the security of their data and really look at the school. Yet all over the country enjoyable practice was springing up. Through initiatives such as Creative Partnerships, the freeing up of curriculum content and the determination of schools to develop more innovative practice, there was a sense that the tide might be turning. It just would not turn fast enough.

## Politicians want results quickly

Policy-makers want to reassure the electorate that their policies are working. Therefore they need policies which are measurable, short-term, eye-catching and appeal to their target voters. The current example is the mess over the proposed introduction of the EBC (English Baccalaureate Certificate) and the reform of GCSEs. While there had been mention of a baccalaureate as a way of ensuring a rounded education at the secondary stage, most believed this would be something like the International Baccalaureate (IB), so hotly discussed at one point in Labour's term. It might have been another programme long in development. But, no, it was much simpler. In autumn 2010, with the release of the school examination league tables for the previous year, a new classification was added. This was the new English Baccalaureate – the analysis of school performance in five particular subjects (English, maths, science, humanities and a language). In a stroke, Michael Gove had developed policy. The EBacc was to be a measure of school performance rather than a set of experiences for pupils.

As a policy it shouldn't fail. The introduction was unanticipated, the starting point was low (around 16% of pupils would have secured the new levels) and independent and selective schools would feature well. Moreover, within two years it is fairly certain that the overall result would be much increased as schools re-jigg their exam framework to hit the new target and ward off the inspection challenge. By the next election, a claim to have raised standards would be backed up by some statistics very easily absorbed by the media. Gove then went wrong by trying to incorporate the EBacc into his other reforms and, in spite of the climb-down, the use of particular subjects in league tables will still be seen as a measure of improvement.

So it is with phonics tests. There is a fair bet that the results of the tests of six-year-olds will show an upward trend over the course of the first few years. Whether it will translate into improved results in the SATs for eleven-year-olds in reading is debatable, but we will be past the next election by then.

Labour did try to do something about the deep-seated problems and published statistics on NEETs (not in education, employment or training), teenage pregnancy, school exclusion, truancy and the like. These entrenched issues, with hard-to-tell stories, have appeared less often in the last two years. However, they also played the statistics game. Labour presided over the upward trend in GCSE results with the acceptance of equivalent qualifications, such as the BTEC, which, in principle, was a good thing, but one wonders whether it would have been so readily accepted if the year-on-year results had been downward.

'It depends where we draw the line' is often the refrain when statistics are in doubt. The Libor scandal of manipulated interest rates was an example of people in banking deciding to set a line which suited them and would seem to make sense to onlookers. The outcome was the intended result. The coalition government, like many governments over the years, is busy redrawing constituency boundaries to give them the best chance of election success, while making out that this is to do with equalising representation. Drawing the line is a vital act. So it is in schooling. Move a line just a fraction and the SAT scores change dramatically or we have a fiasco (such as the one over variable GCSE English grading at different times of the year).

In my first month at the Qualifications and Curriculum Authority (QCA), as part of my induction, I was invited to sit in on the level-setting meeting led by the division responsible for managing the SATs. I had been around the education block in various guises but was as naive as many a teacher must be. I had no idea that the levels were set so close to the release of the year's results – I had somehow thought the tests were criteria referenced. I quickly realised that they were in fact norm referenced. Several weeks after the children had completed the tests, the spread of marks would become apparent and it was the time to 'set the levels', to draw a line that would split the 'borderline' and send thousands of children down or up a level. On a national scale this might be statistically valid, but in a classroom with just, say, fifteen pupils in Year 6, where the line goes matters in terms of a school's appearance on the inspection radar or a teacher's future. Should we be surprised that the SAT results remained static in the first year of the coalition government but rose in the second?

## Politicians get too much advice and like to be told what they want to hear

A secretary of state has a department full of civil servants committed to serving the government by offering supposedly disinterested advice and guidance through agreed policy change. In turn (until recently), the department is served by quangos set up to deal with specific aspects of the system. Education quangos grew under Thatcher's government, probably due to her deep distrust of the department from her time as secretary of state in the 1970s. The National College for School Leadership (NCSL), Qualifications and Curriculum Development Agency (QCDA), Training Development Agency (TDA) and British Educational Community and Technology Agency (Becta) all emerged from previous sets of initials to provide specific support and operational effectiveness to government policy. I was surprised when I joined QCA to find that the work of almost all of these quangos was mirrored and shadowed by a team within the department. These 'arm's length' organisations served a valuable purpose by virtue of the flexible length of the arm. When things are going well, the arm can be short and clutched to the bosom of government; when problems occur, the arm can be extended to allow people to be hung out to dry or used as whipping boys.

One of the machines of parliament is the select committee system where all-party groups scrutinise policy, call for evidence, interview witnesses and make recommendations. Recently there have been high profile inquisitions over issues like security for the Olympic Games, but the impact is minimal, as is the effect of final reports. In these cases, education ministers typically cherry-pick the issues they will address and select committee findings are side-stepped.

Then there is the prime minister's delivery unit. This was set up by Blair to 'do what it says on the tin': deliver. The unit included a circle of advisers close to the prime minister, each supported by very well-paid hand-picked people from the world of education who would help make things happen. Blunkett and Morris's years were characterised by Michael Barber leading and presenting education policy to schools. I recall receiving a phone call a few days after a well-received talk to a head teachers' conference in York shortly after I began my work at QCA. It was from one of the prime minister's delivery unit team who had also presented. He wanted to talk with me about some of my comments in answer to questions on assessment (SATs). I had said that the SATs served too many purposes and needed to be rethought. I was told that we need to stick together and hold the line that assessment was effective.

When Ed Balls was Secretary of State for Children and Schools he had a department, a set of quangos, a group of special advisers and a particular closeness to the prime minister's delivery unit due to his allegiance to Gordon Brown. No wonder there was confusion.

If that is not enough sources of advice, the secretary of state can appoint 'tsars' for particular issues and can commission special reviews. Recent examples include the Bew Review on assessment, the Tickell Review on the Early Years and the Wolf Report on 14–19 education, all designed to speed up the processes of government and ensure that outcomes achieve the intent of the government white paper on education. Sometimes these reviewers gain little more than a welcome for their efforts. Darren Henley's invited review of cultural education led to a national plan with Bridge organisations established but struggling to exert influence on the education of pupils in schools distracted by other priorities. The review of the national curriculum could hardly be said to have embraced Henley's intent. Louise Casey, the 'troubled families' tsar, has at least earned her spurs as a professional working in the most challenging of arenas and is totally focused on making the necessary difference. Even school meals get the same treatment, as Henry Dimbleby and John Vincent have been invited by Michael Gove to be commissioners for school meals rather than build on the considerable efforts of Jamie Oliver. While Vincent and Dimbleby have experience of running fast food restaurants, Oliver's commitment to healthy food for children cannot be doubted but it can be ignored. What was that Mr Gove saying about the 'morally indefensible' situation where people who attend private schools gain undue influence?

Into this mix comes another set of influences: the special advisers (or spads). These characters are there to help their ministers develop and enact policy. (The controversy over the special adviser to the culture secretary's role in the Murdoch empire's bid for BSkyB drew attention to the phenomenon.) The spads are there in education, often unnoticed in the background, testing the water, thinking about the presentation of policy and developing possible courses of action, all of which could be done by civil servants in the department or by arm's length appointed bodies. The role of spads seems to grow with each new set of ministers. They act as blue sky thinkers and suggest ideas, like insisting children wear school uniforms or stand up when their teacher (or parent) enters the room. It might be good for reducing deep vein thrombosis but hardly merits a salary.

One of the most influential of these advisers was Andrew Adonis. During the early Labour years he was to be found at the back of conferences, seminars and policy meetings, rarely speaking but carefully noting the tenor, tensions and opportunities.

After the 2005 election, Blair brought him into the department's ministerial team as Lord Adonis and he survived the transition to Brown, successfully building momentum behind the early academies programme. His commitment cannot be doubted and he has sought to make things better for the most vulnerable children in our society.

This growth of the unelected is hardly noticed by the working population actually running schools. Indeed, the status of adviser to the powerful is respected by those people who have little time to understand the machinations of politics and naively believe there is a bigger goal in education. There is a growing group of school leaders who seek to ensure their own professional future and listen to these characters only because they have the inside track on the rules of the game.

As the schooling of children becomes more centralised, as with the growth in the number of academies, it becomes less democratic. It becomes unduly influenced by certain individuals, sometimes unelected and not appointed by fair process. There is something wrong here which, as a democratic society, we might come to regret a few years from now.

Some individuals might become high-handed or too certain of themselves. One person's certainty then gets overtaken by another's and previous policies are decried to build credit for the new. When a review is needed, it is easy to turn to a lord with an interest rather than to an impartial appointed official; then there is a good chance of the review saying what the minister wants to hear. An invited review by someone steeped in the profession is another option and can help to soften any potential opposition. Elsewhere, Prince Charles has been known to express his opinion, including funding a summer school to promote certain approaches to teaching.

Occasionally it all looks very messy. The expert panel for the 2011 national curriculum review comprised four selected educationalists and was supported by an advisory group of around twenty. The publication of the early drafts of the programmes of study for a small part of the primary stage curriculum led to three of the panel publicly disowning the provisional outcome because it had veered too far from the principles that they believed had been agreed. There was a perception that the publication had been unduly influenced by close associates of the secretary of state, some of whom were on the background advisory group. There was support in some quarters for the general direction of the content and dismay in others that the proposals were seen as radical and might be resisted by teachers. Poor Tim Oates, the chair – left high and dry by everyone to explain the mess and try to finish a job half-done – was described by onlookers as exposed, bewildered and certain all at the same time, having been caught in the cogs of the political machine. The secretary of state's role is seen by many to have crossed the line that previously existed – where the detail of education and schooling was the province of parliament and unfettered by interference from ministers.

Which brings us back to Michael Gove. The current secretary of state is no doubt committed to education, but many believe he is high-handed and certain to a worrying degree.

Many scorn the gift of a leather-bound copy of the English Bible to every school in England to celebrate the 400th anniversary of the King James version. It will not have significant effects on school performance, but it is a nice gesture that could have been linked with the Queen's Silver Jubilee. Each bible is inscribed, not on the inside, but on the spine in gold letters, 'Presented by the Secretary of State for Education' – not 'presented by Parliament' or 'her Majesty's Government'. Years ago, every one of the pupils in my local authority was given a dark red copy of the bible as we made the step from primary to secondary school. It was the thickest, most expensive looking book I had ever owned. I had never held a book with such thin pages. I felt a certain pride in the knowledge that this book had been given to me by my county, with its crest on the presentation panel inside the front cover. How things have changed from the days of the humble local democracy to our current personalised and centralised leadership.

A Michael Gove speech to a conference is a masterpiece. He goes to 'safe' gatherings where the reception will be respectful. If in doubt, he used to send the Minister of State for Schools, Nick Gibb, who was viewed with bewilderment, disdain or even jeered. Since the departmental reshuffle at the end of 2012, the department now tends to dispatch a junior minister, an adviser or departmental official to conferences that the secretary of state would traditionally have attended.

In respectful surroundings though, Gove is a past master. The speech begins with gracious thanks to the host, an explanation of why he has the best job there is in helping today's young people to face tomorrow, and a reference to the people in the hall and how important they are in the quest. There follows some examples of schools he has visited that demonstrate the theme of his talk. The schools number at least six and balance faith, state, regions of the country and gender of those mentioned.

Whatever the theme, we then have a description of the progress and high achievements made thus far, followed by the 'but' ... there is more to do, we are not as good as the rest of the world, the variability is too great, the gap needs to close. This is laced with statistics and quotes from current bestsellers from the 'insight into society with statistics' genre. Then follows the section that explains what needs to be done and how, although it is a challenge, it can be done because some named people in the hall are doing it already. The final phase begins with a call to arms and a warning that there are detractors out there, but they are variously 'fatalists', 'ideologues' or ' enemies of promise'. The people in the room are then distanced from these awful characters through a set of compliments to their professionalism and the reminder that we all have the same commitment – the better life chances of our young people.

Who could not agree? I listened intently to Michael Gove's address to 1,300 leaders from schools at the National College Annual Conference in June 2010. He did all of these things and people left commenting that they were 'pleasantly surprised' or 'there was a lot that made sense'. The very next day he announced his intention to create a national system of academies and to open free schools. It just might have been relevant and polite to the head teachers in the room to have included it in his speech.

Mr Gove is an eloquent speaker. He is always brilliantly prepared and can quote easily from a vast range of literary and historical sources. He is free with compliments and praise and can relate to agendas personally. He can hold an audience. Anyone who heard him at the Royal Shakespeare Company's celebration and launch event for their work in schools, in March 2012, could not have been but impressed and touched by his passion and commitment to bringing Shakespeare's work to every child. He did not just want it 'embedded' but 'embodied'. It was an entirely positive speech and left the invited audience with a belief that they could continue to reach new heights.

The secretary of state could use his talents to bind the entire country behind the improving schools agenda. He could galvanise effort and bring the profession together with all partners on a shared course for good. He could do these things. But he doesn't. Instead he has driven in wedges and created factions. It is very sad.

On 5 February 2013, speaking to the Social Market Foundation, the secretary of state vigorously defended the EBacc against the criticism heaped upon it. In that speech, Michael Gove deployed his logic about the children from the most successful families (those on the inside lanes on the track) electing to send their children to prep schools that offered what he refers to as 'academic rigour'. As an aside, he suggested that some of the celebrities he listed could have found what they sought in good state schools near to their homes instead. He is probably right but, as I argue in the section of this book concerned with the search for equality, parental choice of school is often about with whom their children will mix as much as what they will learn. Gove once again polarised argument. However, he also talked eloquently about the beauty of learning with scholarly intent and his frustration at the lack of ambition in the school system. In what he called 'a spirit of proper candour', he asserted that 'this government's educational philosophy is not really conservative at all – but rather uncompromisingly radical'.

He addressed the criticisms of the EBacc head on: elitist, squeezing out creativity, restricting options, backward looking, narrowing the curriculum. He staunchly defended his position and scorned opponents, insisting that 'the EBacc is only a performance measurement. Its introduction does not mean anyone is mandated, required, obliged or statutorily commanded to do anything. It no more prescribes a menu of subjects that must be digested than a set of scales can force-feed anyone who weighs themselves. Measurements can influence behaviour. But the act of measuring does not mandate.'

Therefore it was, for many, somewhat surprising that two days later Michael Gove appeared before the House of Commons to announce a change of policy. Having consulted widely, he had concluded that 'one of the proposals I put forward was a bridge too far' and 'I have decided not to make the best the enemy of the good'. His EBC was to be abandoned.

So what caused this dramatic turnaround? Was it the lobbying by the 'creative fraternity' or the highly critical report by the Select Committee? Was it the doubts about whether proposals for a single awarding body for each subject of the EBacc contravened European law? Was it the concern of the regulator, Ofqual, about the speed of change? Was it the pressure from Liberal Democrats? Had Michael Gove lost his nerve?

Tellingly, the last sentence of the 5 February speech contained the phrase: 'I suspect that even if not every Conservative agrees with me …' Along with several other setbacks over issues such as parliamentary constituency boundary changes, MPs are concerned about their seats at the next election. Michael Gove is a politician and sometimes even the darling has to eat humble pie.

There can be surely no doubt about Michael Gove's personal commitment to a better life for young people. There is also no doubt that he is a political fighter. He is like all the others who become secretary of state; they are driven by the best of motives for children and young people, but they are more driven by the need for power and votes. That is one of the reasons why national politicians need to assume a different role.

## Can anything be done?

First, teachers have to believe they are part of the system. Over the years I have listened to heads, teachers and governors bemoaning the influence of national politicians. Yet their overall reaction is benign and there is a growing tendency towards greater compliance and less questioning, especially with the threat of inspection always hovering.

Sometimes school communities are active, such as the take-up of academy status, but often these responses are led by tactical rather than strategic motives. 'We decided to get in quickly because the funding might go down' may well be an honest explanation or a rationalisation, but it hardly suggests a course of action built on educational principles.

There are some simple things that the profession could do:

■ Clarify the role of national politicians in schools. We could prohibit MPs and local politicians from being filmed and photographed in schools. They would be able to visit but not for the purpose of being in front of the cameras. Many politicians do excellent work behind the scenes; let's make them all do that. Schools have become used to being flattered because their local MP or a Cabinet minister wants to do a walk-about. The photographs help to 'market' the school. But it has become a silly, fringe effect demonstrating the malaise that has brought politics, the media and public life too close to one another.

■ Heads and teachers should engage in debate and express opinions. Local MPs regularly hold surgeries in constituencies. A group of head teachers could monopolise their MP by booking surgery appointments on a rota basis to make points about national education policy. If every MP were hearing a consistent message every time they opened their door, it wouldn't be long before the secretary of state was hearing the message from their backbenchers.

■ Schools should take part in consultations. People from school communities take only a small part in consultations at a national level, probably because they believe they can have little influence. The typical response to consultations on the national curriculum is very low; the last one elicited 2,000 responses from all sectors. Given that there are over 20,000 schools, and many of the responses were from other sectors, it is a surprisingly muted reaction. Consultations on changes to an Ofsted framework secure even fewer responses. Perhaps everyone has got used to local authorities responding on behalf of schools or sheltering within the union umbrella, but debate needs to be more dynamic and less resigned and wearied.

■ Heads, teachers and governors could write letters to MPs or ministers. Secretaries of state have developed the technique of writing to individual schools to congratulate them on a whole range of successes: being on a list of the best schools, the most improved schools, the fastest improving schools and so on. Schools naturally feel flattered and the letter gets used with staff, pupils and parents. Schools fall for the spin and use the letter as part of their own marketing. They rarely write back.

Years ago, John Patten, a particularly beleaguered secretary of state, wrote to every school in the country to thank the head and staff for their efforts in a period of change and upheaval. In doing so *he* received good publicity as opposed to the schools themselves receiving good publicity. This was the first time that people could remember such an act. If every school had written back to say thank you for the letter and, while they were in touch, they would like to raise a particular matter related to their own school, followed by a few pertinent and detailed questions, the Department for Education would have been occupied for years with seeking and providing the answers. Currently, very few heads and governors write directly to the secretary of state. As each becomes a partner in the contract, it is important that they do so.

■ End the use of special advisers. Politicians should be able to set policy based on the advice of appointed officers within the Department for Education. The patronage of spads and the ennoblement of individuals for specific posts should end. The former are often on their way to a safe seat with little experience. The latter are ennobled for life yet often serve their purpose for only a very brief period. Let's have officials properly appointed and treated with respect by being given proper tasks rather than being regarded as administrative staff.

■ The nation could vote for 'specialists' and 'reviewers'. There is much debate about reforming the House of Lords and the possibility of elected representation. However unlikely this is to happen, it would probably be an election of the old-fashioned type: locality based, oppositional elections with the main parties funding candidates. MPs in the House of Commons are elected to represent their electorate. Some of these MPs become government ministers, where decisions are taken and policy made. Given that the route to government seems to be a path from special adviser to safe seat to government department, it hardly feels representative to many voters. The link between local representation and national policy is not clear. MPs typically work for hard their constituents. Now and again they serve on select committees but they rarely get engaged in policy direction; hence, the invited advisers.

What about an alternative? In these days of technological sophistication, couldn't we elect individuals to represent the nation on specific areas: education, culture or employment? Basically, if an individual could secure 40,000 votes from anywhere in the country they could become an elected special adviser to represent the nation within the specific remit of their manifesto. To get that many votes would be no mean feat and certainly the volume would exceed the size of parliamentary constituency majorities. True, there would be no opposition as such, but I have never lived anywhere where my vote would have made a difference in a parliamentary election. If we tried it, we might get interest, vision, expertise and passion at a national level of government without having to invite celebrities to become lords.

▪ We need a National Council for Schooling. Education policy should unfold regardless of party politics and in the interests of all pupils. Above all, we need to push national politicians away from the detail of schooling. Ministers of defence or health make policy but tend to pull back from the meticulous decisions about the point of attack on a guerrilla stronghold or the stitching technique after an operation. They recognise where the professional knows best and where the line should be.

# … on school autonomy, markets and competition

Once upon a time schools were autonomous. Head teachers were autonomous and teachers were autonomous. They just didn't realise they were.

In the immediate post-war years, the education system operated on a 'high trust, low accountability' model. Education was seen to be a good thing and we needed to get as much of it as we could, at least until children were aged fourteen and able to enter a buoyant blue collar job market. Those with the potential to enter white collar employment enhanced the basic literacy and numeracy skills offered to the majority with O levels or practical skills such as typing. The tiny minority destined for the professions went on to do A levels and fewer still to university where a successful and highly paid future in a high status job was guaranteed. There were jobs for all; the type of job was linked to the level of education the child received. The consideration that a school, or indeed an individual teacher, might bear responsibility for a child's aspirations and achievement was relatively rare.

Equally rare was interference from central government. There was a state of balance between central government, local government, schools, teachers and their representatives, and the churches. Most schools were 'maintained' by local education authorities and a significant minority by churches. Those so-called 'voluntary aided' schools could operate separately from a local authority, working directly to government.

Head teachers ran their schools with little interference from outside. Indeed, in many schools class teachers ran their classes with little interference from the head teacher. Teachers could teach what they thought was important, what they knew about or what they were interested in. The Schools Council promoted discussion of the curriculum and this was picked up locally. Universities were in charge of school qualifications which were available for the minority. Teachers of older pupils who were to be examination entrants had a syllabus, but other teachers could devise their own pathways for learning. Her Majesty's Inspectors (HMI) were rarely seen by most schools.

Education was a relatively minor government department. The secretary of state had very few powers and, if he wished to send a circular to local education authorities, the expertise of HMI would be called upon to provide advice, supported by civil servants who expected the profession to exercise its independence. Local education authorities took responsibility for offering the best provision that they could in their area. This usually amounted to ensuring enough school places and securing money for new school buildings. Occasionally the government would bring in a new policy, such as the tripartite grammar, technical and modern system of Butler's 1944 Act or the move to comprehensive secondary education instigated by Crosland's Circular 10/65. These were systemic structural changes with far reaching effect.

Inside schools, though, the pace of development was up to the head and the staff of the school. Changes in approach to the management of schools and the way teaching and learning took place grew from occasional and important 'reports' – the outcomes of Royal Commissions. Here, a committee would meet under the leadership of an eminent individual and discuss a matter of national education importance, carefully researching and consulting, independent of government. Their reports were heralded as the way forward. They were often better known by the names of the chair of the commission rather than the title of the report itself. The Hadow Report (1931), the Crowther Report (1959), the Plowden Report (1967), the Bullock Report (1975), the Warnock Report (1978), the Cockcroft Report (1982), the Swann Report (1985) and the Elton Report (1989) all brought forward recommendations for how education could be improved. There was an assumption that, at school level, recommendations would be accommodated if possible, but the autonomy of heads and teachers meant that they could simply 'disagree' with the new proposals or the proposed way forward. Hence, Plowden's call for more involvement of parents was heeded by many and ignored by others. Bullock's appeal for 'language across the curriculum' was dismissed by many. At the same time, trends developed as a result of the reports; for example, so-called 'discovery learning' spread after Plowden, though not always effectively. It was for the school to justify its own practices, and usually to itself, for autonomy meant that there were few questions asked from elsewhere.

As austerity receded throughout the 1960s, there was a growing demand for better education. People wanted improved lifestyles. Middle class managerial workers started relocating to different parts of the country on a larger scale than previously. One development in the finance sector had a significant effect upon the autonomy of schools. In 1971, the Bank of England relaxed its rules on lending for house purchase and allowed high street banks to offer mortgages along with the building societies. Home ownership became a real possibility and the concept of the attainable housing ladder began for many young families. The boom in buying and renovating old properties, with the prospect of a swift resale, meant families with children were relocating more often than in the past. With each move of neighbourhood for the family came a change of school for their children. Schooling, which had previously been seen as a service provided near to home, quickly became seen as a commodity. Through experiencing several schools, many upwardly mobile parents realised that schools weren't all the same. Their children were being taught things that they had previously covered elsewhere and expectations of teachers and standards of behaviour differed. There was increasing questioning of the education service.

Simultaneously, there was a gradual erosion of trust in the teaching profession and a call for greater accountability. The raising of the school leaving age to sixteen, which had been promised by Butler in 1944, took place in 1972 and examinations opened up to take account of the need to offer opportunities to a new segment of the pupil population. CSEs, and particularly Mode 3 approaches for which the syllabus was devised locally, gave a broader spectrum of pupils the chance to take away something from the education system in terms of an acknowledgement of success. At the same time, as more people 'passed' something, doubts emerged about the quality of education on offer and the 'Black Papers' – written by people like Kingsley Amis and Iris Murdoch as an attack on Labour policy – voiced concerns that became 'evidenced' in the Risinghill School scandal and the related example of William Tyndale Primary School. These schools were reported to be in disarray and under a total lack of direction and discipline. Fuelled by the media at the time, the chaos of these schools sowed seeds of doubt on all.

This erosion of trust culminated in the prime minister of the time, James Callaghan, voicing concerns in a significant speech at Ruskin College, Oxford in 1976, in which he questioned the value of the education service and called for a 'great debate'. This was the first time that a prime minister had taken a big step into questioning the value of our education system. It also coincided with a faltering economy. In times of full employment and stability the education system had been considered important as long as it served its purpose. There were enough jobs for all; whether or not a child working in a mine had the potential to be a doctor was a moot point; the world was ticking along. In the late 1970s, facing a global oil and monetary crisis and industrial disputes, questions began to be asked about the role of education in servicing the needs of the economic future of a country. When education systems were first established they had altruistic motives; education was a moral right and a means to a secure future for the child and family. Now education was being seen as a means of securing a future for the nation. By some, the speech was seen as a way of diverting the press from the economic woes of the time, but by others it signalled a shift – one that can still be seen today. If there are too few jobs, if school leavers are unable to secure employment, if the country is failing to compete economically on a global stage, who is to blame? Previously it was the government. Now, for the first time, there was the suggestion that it might be the school system.

Callaghan wondered aloud whether there shouldn't be a 'core curriculum' and so began the 'great debate' on education, led by the Secretary of State, Shirley Williams. Local authorities were asked how they supervised the curriculum and state control was on its way. The debate about our school system was shifting markedly away from teaching professionals taking the lead. The Taylor Report of 1977 proposed that each school would have a governing body made up of parents, local communities, businesses and school staff representatives in equal proportion. It was nicknamed 'the busybodies' charter'.

Low trust and high accountability then became the outlook. As Margaret Thatcher's government came to power in 1979, the questions of value for money started to appear along with the Conservatives' desire to reduce the influence of the state. Yet, as we have seen, Keith Joseph was the first secretary of state to begin the allocation of budgets to specific grants with TVEIs. It was only a small percentage but local authorities could now bid for funding and the culture of ministerial pet projects began.

Oliver Letwin was a young political adviser at the time of Thatcher's government and he was instrumental in the move towards parental preference in school admissions. The 'sink school' was dismissed as a fact of life in a new order that put power with the consumers. Individual schools started to 'market' themselves to demonstrate to prospective parents how they should be preferred over other local schools. Competition was eroding autonomy. Families with access to information and funds began to move house in order to secure their child a place at a 'good' school.

Those areas then became more affluent. Rising house prices and shrinking catchment areas led to increased segregation in residential districts. The 'good' schools became populated with aspirational children pushed by parents with high expectations – many of whom had been successfully schooled themselves. The 'bad' schools were populated with the children of parents who may have been no less hopeful, but who were less well informed or had little choice about where they lived. Or, in many cases, whose own experiences of school had been so poor that they did not believe that it mattered which school their children attended.

Local authorities who maintained the old grammar school system found themselves with an influx of middle class families – whole wards became more wealthy. In other areas, a glut of private schools appeared – old grammar schools appealing to the fears of a reasonably affluent generation of parents afraid of the scare stories of comprehensive education. Many equated comprehensive with secondary modern – substandard and socially contaminated. For a time, there appeared to be a danger that any child whose parents were unable to afford to pay for an education, either through the fees of an independent school or by virtue of location, would be consigned to the scrapheap. Suddenly it was necessary to reassure the population that state education was safe and effective.

Kenneth Baker's Education Reform Act (1988) heralded a swathe of measures designed to ensure the quality and value of the system. Significantly, the role of local authorities was reduced through the local management of schools. Funding went directly to schools to manage their own budgets and take responsibility for their own premises and staff costs; autonomy that significantly restricted the influence of local authorities. The later Thatcher years brought about the establishment of grant-maintained schools – schools which decided to 'opt out' of local authority control and work directly to government. Schools were being offered more autonomy as a means of loosening the influence of local authorities but it was autonomy of a managerial kind: it simply enabled governance of systems rather than leadership of vision or philosophy.

Within schools, the invitation to consider and respond was still there. The 'Three Wise Men Report' on primary education in 1992 ended with the expression of belief that readers would 'readily accept the invitation we now extend to discuss and address these issues'. The then Secretary of State, Kenneth Clarke, had commissioned this work to be done in one month by three eminent educationalists: Chris Woodhead, head of the National Curriculum Council; Jim Rose, Chief Inspector at HMI; and Robin Alexander, professor of education at Leeds University. There had been much media interest in the supposed 'trendiness' of primary education and a call for back-to-basics was to be emphasised, following some research by Robin Alexander into primary schooling in Leeds. Clarke, in his no-nonsense way, decided a month was enough time to review the system. The upshot was a report that still became an invitation to schools, local authorities and teacher trainers to think about the issues and act as they saw appropriate. This would change a very short time later with the appointment of Chris Woodhead to the role of chief inspector when the job was advertised. The establishment of Ofsted to lead a national inspection system was the beginning of the very end for school autonomy.

Central government involvement in teacher appraisal, a national curriculum and nationwide assessment had led to central control like never before. The development of a national curriculum took away from teachers the debate over what should be taught. The establishment of an Ofsted-led inspection process for every school and the availability of emerging additional data led to accountability and competition through league tables which have became a rich source of controversy for the media. Later, central government used this data to focus on floor targets, challenged schools, coasting schools and any other category which would put schools under pressure.

The Conservative government harmonised the examination structure in 1988, establishing GCSEs as the 'examination for all' sixteen-year-olds and the control shifted from universities to market-driven awarding bodies overseen by Ofqual, a regulatory quango and just one of many educational quangos established at this time. There was an initial trickle of schools 'opting out' through the new grant-maintained status, but it never became a flood. Nevertheless, the culture of competition in schools meant that there was less collaboration. Chronic underfunding led to countless media reports about leaky roofs, shared and outdated textbooks, shrinking school fields and large class sizes, all of which served to drive more and more frightened parents to the independent sector – a sector now flourishing with increased autonomy.

Following the 1997 election, the Labour government attempted to balance accountability with support and managed autonomy.

Grant-maintained schools became 'foundation schools' and, at the same time, the government brought in the requirement for schools and local authorities to ensure 'fair funding', inviting questioning and a reduction in local authority influence. Through these authorities the government created Education Action Zones, Excellence in Cities, Specialist Secondary Schools, the London Challenge and similar efforts elsewhere, all the time encouraging the growth of decision-making at a school level and leaving local education authorities as arbiters and coordinators rather than the drivers of education in their areas. These were all funded through grants which came to schools via their local authority, but these emphasised still further the gradually expanding central government agenda. The Department for Education, which had assumed a status within government which would have been hard to believe in the 1940s, now sought to claw back control from the quangos.

The Labour administration made much of the vital importance of head teachers and established the National College for School Leadership. While allowing collaboration to develop, it also aimed to create a consistency of skills through the creation of a leadership quali-fication. At the same time, at the classroom level, it brought in a national strategy for the teaching of literacy and numeracy. It was the first time that a government had moved from telling a school not only what to teach but how to teach it. The first incarnations of the strategies broke teaching time into fifteen-minute slots and prescribed content for each block. There was an outcry from teachers and national bodies, such as the National Literacy Trust and the National Association for the Teaching of English, that the prescription was killing enthusiasm.

The 2009 Cambridge Primary Review criticised the overzealous crea-tion of objectives, which removed even planning from teacher control, and claimed this had resulted in dull, formulaic teaching and learning. Education had become a franchise, with Secretary of State Estelle Morris talking of the concept of 'managing over 20,000 outlets'. This centralised model of teaching and learning was a far cry from the autonomy of just thirty years previously. Gradually the national strat-egy extended from literacy and numeracy to other areas. An Ofsted report in 2010 identified 111 different elements of the Secondary National Strategy. Teachers will recognise the emphasis on areas like attendance, social and emotional aspects of learning, Assessment for Learning and Letters and Sounds, which all became part of central government's influence on the teacher in the classroom.

Where previously the minister was often hard to name or someone in the last throes of their political career, with a few notable exceptions, the secretary of state of the twenty-first century is usually a big hitter within government. The department has gradually eroded the role of the quangos and, at the same time, because of the stature and perceived political importance of education, the prime minister's delivery unit has a direct line to policy. On top of that, the growth of the special advisers, whom we met in the previous section, means that policy can emanate from many sources, although relatively rarely from the system itself. This is policy that is enacted either though the leverage of funding or inspection. It is a demonstration of how the trust and accountability axis has shifted. Autonomy for schools has virtually gone and in its place is a market-driven competitive business model with enormous central control.

Many now suggest that the challenge is to explore whether England could be the first country in the world to develop a system that creates trust while retaining accountability. To do so will be difficult because the incidence of perverse incentives is great and changes to teacher pay, along with the end of the traditional school governance structures, mean that the ecosystem of schooling is wobbling.

The coalition government has used words like 'freedom' and 'autonomy' to spearhead its agenda. Michael Gove has pushed the notion that structural change to the system is a way of giving schools this autonomy and freedom. The expectation is that all schools will become academies or free schools and, with an annual funding agreement, will be in the direct control of the secretary of state. These schools have freedom in terms of staff salary and are excused the nationally devised curriculum. Over time they might devise courses for their pupils that would see them funded through their agreement to be innovative in approach. In this way, diversity in the system would become a reality on the back of competition and market forces working in tandem with autonomy.

As an aside, much of this has resonance with the beginnings of state education in Forster's 1870 Elementary Education Act which brought schooling to all. School Boards were established and local people of influence and power acted in the public interest and set about working with government for the common good. However, the complexity of the system and its legislation and funding led to confusion and to the unintended financial culpability of many of those who had come forward to offer their support. Such was the mess uncovered by an official named Robert Morant, that the free-for-all of school boards was abolished after thirty years. The 1902 Education Act placed financial responsibility with the then newly created county councils, while agreeing to contribute to the costs of ageing church schools. This tier between central government and schools, the so-called third tier, is the one that many now believe needs to exist. Can central government control all schools individually while also encouraging diversity? In the case of Morant's findings there was concern over financial controls. These are mirrored in the findings of the House of Commons Public Accounts Committee in April 2012, which assert that the Department for Education should 'implement measures to improve its understanding of value for money in schools and ability to ensure that it is achieved'.

Faced with questions of value for money, the debate is now shifting to questions of local accountability. Where the 1970s saw notorious school cases being influential in leading to questions of quality, we are now seeing high profile examples of school communities questioning and challenging whether what schools and government do matches what they want. One such case is Downhills Primary School in Haringey where the secretary of state is forcing the school to become responsible for its own destiny and take academy status against the wishes of its community.

School providers nationally and locally might start to worry about facing their own 'shareholder spring' if they do not get right the need to account for themselves. There is a general acceptance that the centralised model of accountability cannot hold. Will the market sort it out? In a world of independent state schools, those that are strong will grow while those that are weak will go to the wall. However, with growing numbers of primary pupils there is limited scope for government to fund the creation of surplus places to allow a market based on quality to function effectively.

There are serious concerns with the current level of government control. The secretary of state, not parliament, can decide whether a school remains open or closes and what it should teach. The individual contract between secretary of state and schools provides what Thatcher's chancellor, Nigel Lawson, always wanted: exact Treasury control of expenditure on every English school.

So what we now have is a difference in outlook between the new and old players on the pitch which will lead us to some challenging considerations in the coming months and years. The major difference is in the perception of what is on offer. The new arrivals – the academy sponsors, trusts and owners – grasp the challenge of running schools as units to deliver required outcomes. Much as a retailer or cinema would measure sales or footfall, so they set targets for their schools. The continuum from education to schooling and public service to private enterprise sees a range of outlooks. They all believe that their approach will benefit communities, build a work ethic and encourage civil responsibility, all of which will lead to national prosperity. But they carry different starting points for values into the task.

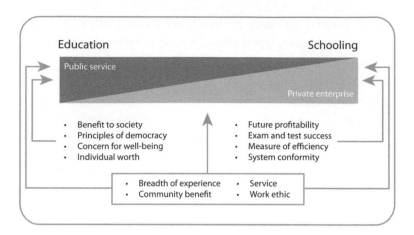

The experienced players still seem to think they are running something called 'education' and schools are part of a bigger set of outcomes. The newer private enterprise players typically believe the bigger prize will come from the more simple measurable outcomes. This fundamental difference in outlook leads them to consider and question the very heart of their working world: the notion of being a 'public servant' that many teachers have lived with throughout their careers.

This brings to a head an often unspoken aspect of the debate of the last few years. Blair's 'education, education, education' really meant 'schooling, schooling, schooling' and the target-driven approach has beaten the Every Child Matters agenda to a pulp. While we softened it up with the use of 'learning' as a cosy word, the league tables, the floor targets and the inspection judgement placed the emphasis on how well children were schooled rather than how well they were educated. Pupils became a currency as test results grew in importance; although nobody is saying that reading, writing and numbers are not vital.

The coalition government has extolled the virtues of choice and competition. In a speech to civil servants soon after taking office in 2010, David Cameron asserted: 'One way we can bring in real accountability is through choice. Wherever possible, we want to give people the freedom to choose where they get treated and where they send their child to school – and back that choice up with state money. Because when people can vote with their feet ... it's going to force other providers to raise their game – and that's good for everyone.' He continued, 'Another tool we must use is competition. By bringing in a whole new generation of providers – whether they're from the private sector, or community organisations, or social enterprises – we can bring in the dynamic of competition to make our public services better.'

Typically, the new players simplify the task; no bad thing. They respond to centralised control and deliver the required outcomes through their pupils and they do it in the most attractive ways they can muster. Collectively they might miss the bigger picture of English education which is at the heart of the system, though rarely recognised: that education, rather than schooling, is part of the democratic fabric of society.

Of course, there are people caught in the middle of the pitch as the game changes; the true public servants who suddenly find themselves in the market-driven team. Some adapt and accept the new game. Others wonder whether going along with it is fine but might there be something more sincere and honest about the old game. Is education about results and measurable outcomes? Or is that schooling?

## Where next – schools for profit?

Are the concepts of the market and competition to be taken to the next level with schools being run for profit? The free school model is built in the image of the charter schools in the United States, where half are run for profit, although they school only 3% of the nation's children. Another much quoted success story is Sweden, where 60% of free schools are run on a for-profit basis by business. Could this develop here? Secretary of State Michael Gove has declared himself to be a pragmatist; he is prepared to see what happens and move in response to developments.

The concept of profit has been within the education system for many years. In the late 1980s, an early assault on local authority spending saw the arrangements for supply staff being taken into corporate hands. In the 1990s, catering slid away, and since then school improvement has found its way into the private sector along with aspects of IT provision, music services and outdoor education. The examination system sees considerable profits accruing to awarding bodies. To a large extent school inspection is a contracted out activity, with Ofsted being augmented by 2,000 additional inspectors employed by profit-making regional inspection providers. The Labour government outsourced the running of education services in several local authorities to private limited companies, beginning with Islington in 2000.

Where education meets children directly, there is more uncertainty. Learning in the Early Years has long been accepted as a profit-making enterprise and children with profound educational needs have often needed to be found places outside their local authority, often at considerable outlay to the authority and profit to the provider. Children with persistent and dangerous behaviour difficulties, frequently excluded from schools, find themselves in pupil referral units, sometimes so specialist that the independent owners make profits from the service provided. Many parents pay private tutors to help their child achieve the necessary examination grades or SATs results to guarantee access to the desired destination. Some secondary schools faced with a pupil who cannot cope with school, and with a tendency to cause problems for others, will seek out 'alternative' or 'complementary' provision, again agreeing contracts that provide service and profit. All of these examples deal with those children on the fringes: the early starters, the special needs, challenged and stretched. What about the mainstream and the school system itself?

It is often held that schools are not like railways or power companies. The revenue yield and assets would be slight, plus there is the challenge of convincing a sceptical public that profit should replace the public service ethos. Yet the first signs are there. Leading UK think tank Policy Exchange, described by Michael Gove as 'the formidable regular army on the think tank battlefield' has proposed for-profit provision based on the 'John Lewis model', which has become the latest way to describe something unpalatable in a way that feels reasonable, given the popularity of the chain of stores and their adverts at Christmas. Policy Exchange proposes 'social enterprise' schools in 'deprived areas', which is seen as sensible middle ground on the way to all-out profit making schools. It is a nice way to blur the distinction in the public's mind of the journey from social to private enterprise. The prime minister's early pitch for a 'Big Society' suggested that substantial funding could be released from charitable giving and endowment revenues for social enterprise models of schooling. The spectre of takeovers and asset stripping, and the notion of pupils carrying a price tag, is looming and the momentum is starting to build.

The motive for extending for-profit provision is the pressure to provide a wider range of selective schooling for the relatively well-off who might not be able to afford private schooling and who see the range of options positively, particularly as the differentiation in examination provision begins to bite. Sponsors, shareholders and CEOs make the same demands that governors and local authorities made previously, but now with more powers and more options for change.

From autonomy, schools, head teachers and teachers have been slowly dragged first towards conformity and then compliance. Now accountability, competition and market forces have edged into the agenda under the guise of autonomy and freedom.

Once upon a time schools, heads and teachers really were autonomous; they just didn't realise it. Nowadays they are told they are autonomous. But are they living happily ever after? Whatever comes to pass, our increasingly autonomous schools don't have quite the freedom that they anticipated. Some sponsors call the tune in a way LEAs tried to do before the changes to school governance at the end of the 1970s. Indeed, many head teachers seem to feel very isolated and uncertain about their capacity to act as senior professional educators.

## So what might be done?

There is much that is good about the whirlwind that is blowing through the structure of schooling. There is re-thinking, re-branding and re-awakening for communities. This is renewing the system but it is too hand to mouth, and it is the coherence that is lacking.

How do we avoid some children falling out of the system? It was bad enough before but now that children are a currency in terms of examinations and tests, rather than a currency because of their presence, those that have no perceived value risk being jettisoned by the very system that purports to protect them. The prospect of Ragged Schools, established for urchin children in the 1800s, looms again.

Changing the status of a school and rebranding it in its local community is shown to have an impact. There is no doubt that, where parents passed by a school with their children on the way to somewhere better, they stop and take another look once it becomes an academy. While there are critics, most seem to accept that academy status brings a fresh look, a new impetus and a renewed sense of optimism and purpose. Eventually, though, the academies will have been in place long enough to genuinely compare each with the rest and then the concerted criticism will begin. How long will it be before the term 'bog standard academy' will start to be used?

We need some extended research to monitor and secure the school system as a provision for all children.

■ Councils, as designated champions for children locally, should assertively demand of central government some clear answers and approved strategic plans for the schools that are failing any of their children. The boot is now on a different foot. After years of central government calling to account local authorities for the struggles of their schools, councils should now be strident in calling to task central government for any perceived failure. They should do it loudly and make their actions explicit to their own constituents. The newly published league table of Ofsted inspection outcomes offers all the plaudits and brickbats councils require. If this process is to be credible, it needs to include academy chains in the analysis rather than lumping together all schools in an administrative region. Many pupils of urban councils find their way to the nearby rural communities for schooling to an extent not seen in London.

■ Furthermore, councils should define the measures they expect to be accomplished for the children in their area. They should set the targets to government for reduced teenage pregnancy, NEETs, richer and broader experiences and work experience. If a local authority has any power, it is the right to call central government to account on behalf of its children.

# … on business, industry and other professions

It always amuses me when education is told that it needs to be more like the private sector and that schools should learn from business.

Schools in the twenty-first century are businesses. In fact, the head of a school or the chief executive of a chain of academies is usually leading a business bigger than many others in their community. The changes in the management of schooling over the last thirty years have seen heads become involved in a market, controlling significant budgets, dealing with complex personnel issues, managing premises, dealing with crises and handling logistics as complex as any company.

## What is a business outlook?

Which parts of the private sector should schools copy? Maybe they should mirror the banking sector by gambling with money that doesn't exist and earning from bets that were works of fiction in the first place? Paying back something that didn't exist shouldn't be complicated. Or perhaps schools should adopt the ethics of the hacking media enterprises? Or the efficiency of the company contracted to deliver security personnel for the 2012 Olympic Games?

Which practices would make schools more professional? A glimpse at one of the hotels I stayed in recently near the National Exhibition Centre in Birmingham would be instructive. As hotel guests tried to check out in the morning for their day's exhibition, the queue trailed around the reception desk as two receptionists slowly processed their bills. This happens daily but the management doesn't seem to notice or address the matter.

Or would schools be advised to mimic the scripted conversations of a chain of restaurants, such as the French one in which patrons are asked, 'Is there anything else I can get you?' A diner who asks for mint sauce is told it is not available, but a waiter still arrives a few minutes later to ask if everything is alright with the meal. A sorbet from the dessert menu then comes dressed with fresh mint. That will be what the business sector means by customer service.

On the other hand, there are good examples of the private sector getting it right. An excellent example of how to run a business is Chiltern Railways. Over a very few years this company has taken a couple of lines from the Midlands to London with Hornby-like stations and made it work. Trains run mainly on time, they are clean, the logistics mean that small stations are well served and connect with trains that stop at major stations. There is a clear programme of line upgrades, station refurbishment and car park construction. Beyond all that, there must be a good programme for helping the staff develop customer service skills because they are unfailingly polite and helpful. There is an air of professional informality, including the absence of announcements found with other companies about station arrivals and endless talk from train managers who fill the carriage with noise to announce that coach B is a quiet coach. Instead, on Chiltern there is an in-carriage electronic sign and the train driver simply says which station is the next stop. At peak times fares might feel expensive but there are numerous efforts to encourage people to travel on special rates and enjoy their journeys. There is even a book club at some stations.

So how does this connect to schooling? If Chiltern were a school, communication would be clear between management, staff, pupils and parents. Technology would assist in ensuring the sharing of speedy and effective information. Community values of respect and treating people with dignity would be upheld. The drudgery of learning the basics or sitting tests would be offset by exciting and motivational developments in the curriculum which would encourage children to enjoy school.

There are good businesses and bad businesses; good business practices and bad business practices. To lump business into a single entity creates a false image (another collective noun problem) but business has no problem with doing this – it has no problem because the image it projects is the vision of the people in charge; the people who know what this country needs. When it suits them, politicians assert that business knows best, especially the so-called 'business leaders'. Several of these regularly berate schools for allowing young people to leave without adequate qualifications in English and mathematics. Primary schools are castigated because some children cannot read at the age of eleven. Enquire as to what these business gurus mean by 'being able to read' and they explain that children failing to reach Level 4 in national tests can't decode. In fact, reading tests are a bit more complex than that. The charity National Numeracy published a report in March 2012, showing that 49% of all adults of working age are unable to manage the mathematics expected of an eleven-year-old. Given that 85% of pupils leaving primary schools in the same year achieved the expected level in mathematics, there are arguments for saying that primary schools are doing a pretty good job and standards are better than they have ever been. Instead of that, leading lights from industry, spurred on by national politicians, criticise present practice.

Business leaders bemoan that we are falling behind other countries without understanding the tests that suggest this might be true. If they looked at them properly, they would discover that it is not our pupils' literacy and numeracy knowledge that causes problems, but their ability to apply knowledge flexibly in problem-solving circumstances. More rote learning in the basics will not help with this difficulty.

Typically, business leaders want to help schools but struggle to know how. They are convinced of one thing though: schools should have sports days. Whenever I am with business people they always get round to it: the need for competition and the importance of sport. They seem not to know that most schools hold a sports day or that all kinds of competitions are regularly held in schools, not only sporting but Accelerated Reader programmes, inter-form enterprise competitions and tests. Do we really believe that schools will improve and our business future will be secure if children have an annual sports day?

It is easy to lampoon industry, but we should remember that education is incredibly confusing for anyone sitting outside of it. This has been greatly complicated by the pace of change over the past twenty years. Many of these perceptions are based on an employer's own experiences of school; but this is like assuming the computer you used in 1995 is the same as the one available in 2012. Times have changed and communication between the education sector and business has been poor. Head Teachers for Industry (HTI) has been established for twenty-five years and done sterling work to improve communication but it has never had the funding needed to build the infrastructure necessary to enable real understanding.

Employers explain that they have, for example, 150 applicants for each apprenticeship. They have to make a choice, so they take five GCSEs as a first cut-off point since they cannot make sense of all the other information they get. For employers, five GCSEs is shorthand for a good rounded education and reasonable potential. Why shouldn't they think that? They have been told this for years by politicians. The proposed EBacc Certificate measure might have given employers a new shorthand for the segment of the cohort that are a cut above the rest, even though the cut might not have been what employers really need. The problem is that most of the youngsters will be heading for the university sector and not seeking jobs. Most of those apprenticeship candidates will have stayed on at college until the age of eighteen too but may have taken a vocational route instead. The problem is that the route is not vocational if their future employers can't understand the qualification, the variety of which can be bewildering. NVQs, BTECs, AS levels, A levels, Extended Projects ... how should they know what all this means?

# Performance targets

Many in industry do not understand the education system, but educators are told to use business models to ensure quality of provision. One of these examples is being held accountable for performance indicators. The problem is that these indicators do not lead to the same oppressive accountability in business and politics as they do in education. For instance, when a major supermarket group saw profits fall significantly during 2012, the reasons offered included customers having less money to spend and a 'hostile trading environment'. The store implemented a number of measures to update the image of the brand with a more thrifty customer in mind. There was no naming and shaming, no special measures and no suggestion of no-notice inspections for stores resulting in reports that could be made available to the general public. How many head teachers might like to cite a 'hostile learning environment'? Why no intervention board from the world of the public sector to offer guidance to unprofitable stores? Similarly, there is hypocrisy in the politics of economics. Chancellor George Osborne has many times announced that he is revising his forecast due to uncertain economic conditions. How many head teachers would like to revise their forecast for exam or test results based on 'conditions'?

# Comparisons with other professions

Comparisons are continually made between schooling and other professions, but only when they suit the agenda of the latest initiative. If we make some real comparisons, we see absurdity in the disparity between the institutional trust afforded to other professions in contrast to teachers.

In medicine, patients first meet a GP, the one responsible for their general allotted group – the equivalent of a class of pupils. Of all the patients they see, the GP treats or prescribes to perhaps 80%. This means there are 20% of cases that are beyond the GP's level of experience, knowledge or skills and these are referred to a specialist. The specialists receive the patients referred from GPs and treat 80% of cases but find their expertise and experience insufficient for 20% of cases. These are referred onwards to a consultant.

On this estimate basis, the consultant is dealing with 20% of the 20%, which is just 4% of the total; these are the extreme cases, the challenging, rare, complex or unusual. When the consultant arrives, others stand back and watch the 'best in the business' and learn from the experience as the consultant treats the patient directly.

In teaching we work in almost the opposite direction. Those who are 'consultants' rarely meet pupils face to face in order to teach them. Typically, education consultants are being strategic – working with head teachers, the specialists or middle leaders (the equivalent of registrars in the health service) – to support the classroom teacher, the equivalent of the GP.

Pupils present themselves to their teacher, who finds that 80% are eminently teachable but about 20% present challenges beyond their scope. This group is then allocated extra support which is arranged by a special needs assistant – often someone who is not a qualified teacher, but who is asked, on a lower salary scale than the teacher, to attend to the child's needs. If there are extreme needs, a one-to-one provision might be made with someone assigned to support the pupil through the school day. Typically, in the normal school, the more complex the need the more likely the child is to have a less qualified person, such as a higher level teaching assistant, helping them.

It is a simplistic comparison but the parallels are fascinating. In teaching, promotion takes us away from the classroom. Efforts to ensure there is leadership of learning rather than 'management' have tried to ensure a focus on the classroom, but there is still a gap between the rhetoric and practice, which tends not to exist in other professions. In law, for example, the most complex legal cases are the ones dealt with by the head of chambers and the team rally round this person who assumes command of the professional agenda. The head of chambers is not too busy planning strategy, managing budgets or organising transport; those jobs are done by someone on a lesser level.

The main reason for these differences, of course, is that in teaching we are managing 'arenas', whereas in law and medicine individual cases receive attention. In education we manage a class, then a faculty or department, a school and, after that, who knows. In law and medicine, cases finish; the accused is freed or jailed, the patient recovers or dies. In education there is no limit to learning, no end to the challenge of making progress.

However, in teaching the system has concentrated significantly on the achievers. The sixth formers were always allocated the best qualified teachers and only in recent years have Early Years qualifications been seen as valid and respectable. Exam classes still claim prominence and in most secondary schools the high status posts are head of departments in English, mathematics and science. The proposed introduction of the English Baccalaureate had elevated languages, geography and history (and recently computer science) to baron status and recent government policy has ensured that PHSE and citizenship, along with aspects such as primary/secondary liaison and work experience, are too often reduced to peasant status. Despite evidence to suggest that focusing attention on building autonomy and articulacy in Key Stage 3 reaps dividends at GCSE, the teachers allocated to Key Stage 3 classes are often the least experienced.

Should children be taught in group sizes that reflect their age multiplied by two (i.e. a four-year-old is taught in a group of eight children, a ten-year-old in a group of twenty and a sixth former in an A level group in a class of thirty-six)? The tradition of A level students being in very small classes and closely tutored comes from the time when very few pupils indeed took A levels and therefore allowance had to be made to enable these individuals to gain access to our universities. Times have changed and schools now teach older students in bigger numbers. At the youngest end, though, we still talk about ensuring no class has more than thirty children. Of course, one problem is that we build all our classrooms the same size; Building Schools for the Future was a chance to think again but rarely was the chance taken.

The latest comparison area is the success of the British team at the Olympic Games. Immediately there was the hope that education could capitalise on the achievement in terms of medals gained and enthusiasm generated. The prime minister swiftly emphasised that we needed to see more physical exercise and sport in schools coupled with more competition. This might lead to more medals in the future and could address the fact that private schools were 'winning more than their fair share'. It might be easier to produce Olympic rowers if there is a river or lake on your school grounds but they are few and far between in downtown Derby.

Worse, he attributed the perceived imbalance between state and private schooling to the fact that there are too many teachers in state schools that are 'frankly too lazy to get involved in after-school activity'. This from the politician whose own secretary of state for education boasts that 'if there were Olympic medals for chillaxing, the prime minister would win gold every time'.

It is the collective noun problem again. No doubt there are some lazy teachers, just as there are lazy people in every walk of life, even politics. However, most teachers are busy being asked by their school leadership to complete volumes of paperwork to keep their scrutinisers at bay, yet still find the time to commit to the school through drama, dance, visits, clubs, music, special events and sport. All this for little thanks or recognition, although the pupils typically appreciate the effort. To extend the Olympic metaphor to the school inspection, the inspected lesson assumes the importance of the last lap of the keirin, the final vault or dive of the set, the last fence of the round or the last lift of the weights. As the sport commentators often say, 'It all boils down to this. All those years of effort, the lonely preparation and sacrifice. All those years of supporting pupils with their career advice, visiting science fairs, gaining a degree, taking pupils on residential visits, taking part in musical performances, organising work experience, helping the struggler to keep up, pushing the strider to stretch for the top, those hours of planning and writing reports, this is it ... Can she hold it together and deliver an outstanding lesson on density with Year 7 on a wet day just after lunch? Can she turn it on when it really counts?' While there are many decent, committed national politicians, there are still too many who are (collective noun-wise) self-serving, cheap-shooting, media-managing, main-chance spotters.

The current government jettisoned the highly successful School Sports Partnership programme within days of taking office. Indeed, the sell-off of school playing fields began with Tory Kenneth Baker as secretary of state. He was also responsible for insisting on directed time in teachers' pay and conditions and his requirement that teachers be 'enforced' to work for 1,265 hours per year saw the end of much voluntary sport and other pursuits in schools. The high-stakes accountability regime has meant that schools need to play the game and deliver what is measured: a narrow range of test results in a limited area of learning.

The London Olympics saw many examples of superlative performance from the athletes of many countries in a commitment to sporting excellence. The GB cycling team was heralded as a 'long-term project' that had born fruit. The coaches and managers had sought every opportunity to shave percentages from the times of their team's performance. They pursued the marginal gain. They resisted the simple instruction of telling their team to 'ride faster'. They explored the aerodynamics of equipment and constantly modified the Lotus superbike first developed in 1992. In schools, the instructions are often to do the old fashioned better, faster or stronger, usually around some silver bullets of practice, rather than look for every possible incremental gain or the equivalent of the superbike design.

Sadly, though, our sporting achievements are a bit like our much quoted PISA (Programme for International Student Assessment) rankings. Our finest performers are on a par with the best in the world in sport or schooling. But our overall sample would see us a long way down the international league table. Achievements at the very top are depressed by the tail of underachievement; indeed, our much publicised concern over obesity and lack of exercise is probably a place where we could build best on the Games success. For every medal winner, there will be a thousand overweight, fast-food munching couch potatoes cheering them on via the TV during a month of inactivity. Like so many aspects of improving performance, there is a much broader challenge than the one described so simplistically by policy-makers.

How has the tide of opinion turned so easily in the last five years? When the economy went into meltdown the bankers were vilified. The MPs' expenses scandal added to a growing disaffection with politicians. Somehow the media was managed in order to show that the root of the country's problems lay with public sector versus private sector polarisation. Private sector companies now linger around education, health and housing looking for the next stream of public funding. The idea that the private sector generates income is only partly true.

In any case, working in schools is not public sector but public service. Many people have devoted their careers to a better society through their work in health, education, social care and the emergency services. To blame them for the failings of others in seeking political gain is to demean the efforts of hard-working professionals, and this is dangerous. When teaching professionals are vilified and demeaned they lose passion and purpose, and the only people who suffer in that scenario are the children. The politicians who accuse teachers of being lazy, the jeering attacks in the popular press, in the letters and comments pages, and the accusations of business all combine to potentially destroy the very thing they claim to protect: the quality of the education of our young people.

# What might be done?

■ Make teaching professionally regulated. In the medical profession, the General Medical Council carries great professional weight. The power to 'strike off' is the action for which it is best known outside medical circles, but within the profession the GMC is a touchstone for good practice. Medical treatment and surgical procedures are regulated through the GMC. A complex but fair system of peer review accompanies a career progression pathway which is clearly understood. Professionalism is respected and an overall forward-looking ethos has seen practice change for the better over time. Surely teachers could operate in a similar way? A teacher should be seen as a professional, suitably qualified for the range of tasks they are asked to carry out. This should be a given but open to question and scrutiny by fellow professionals. It should be confirmed through relevant further training, the presentation of papers at regular intervals and observation by colleagues in the course of their practice. The Teachers' Standards offer real possibility and they should be taken seriously at every level as a chance for the profession to control and develop itself.

■ Take national politicians out of the arena of schooling. Let them debate and decide the systems of education but keep them away from the structure of what goes on inside schools. Instead, as I mentioned above, elect and appoint a National Council for Schooling which would seek to enhance the educational experience and outcomes for all pupils. The Council could be elected via public mandate and therefore would not be politically driven by the parties of government. It would be for any prospective member to secure 40,000 votes and to serve for up to ten years. The remit would require: the definition of aims for schooling; consideration and recommendation of schooling practice; calling for evidence-based solutions; setting up appropriate good practice trials; and the holding steady of school requirements so that practice can be stabilised over time, and changed only when there was proven improvement to be gained as measured by the achievement of aims.

- Similarly, build a body of business, professional, media, industrial, cultural and sporting leaders who could genuinely influence the National Council for Schooling with their experience and evidence from other facets of working life. Again, these could be elected rather than selected.

- These two bodies could produce a tri-annual report on the needs of schooling and make recommendations to parliament, regardless of the election cycle.

# … on professional integrity and game theory

Previous sections in this book lead to an inevitable question about notions of professional integrity and expose an underlying fault line in our society at the present time: game theory. The explanation of how we have reached the current situation should urge us to consider possible ways forward in terms of preserving educational integrity into the future.

There is a current vogue among policy-makers to quote from pseudo-sociological modern texts, such as *Bounce* by Matthew Syed, *Outliers* by Malcolm Gladwell or *Luck* by Ed Smith. These get cited by politicians in speeches as evidence and background to support government education policy. Indeed, these books do shed light upon certain social trends and raise important questions about the way in which we organise aspects of society.

In the same vein, maybe we should think about game theory. This is a set of ideas which emerged in the 1950s and developed extensively in the 1970s to the extent that several game theorists have since won Nobel prizes. The principles are very simple. Basically, game theory relates to our capacity to take the rules that we use within games and apply them in everyday life. So, for example, chess involves capturing the opponent's king but equally defending our own. For some people the importance of out-thinking their opponent means they become ultra-defensive, protecting their own king rather than seeking to attack. In the end, the very purpose of the game is forgotten, as each strives to outdo the other by not losing rather than seeking to win. Similarly in bridge, while the purpose is to work with a partner to defeat the opposing pair, it is very easy to slip into the pattern of judging what the opponents are seeking to do and subverting them rather than playing the game for its own validity. The essence of the game gets lost.

This notion of tricking the tracker can be seen in other aspects of everyday life. It occurs when those under pressure seek to make the system work for them rather than suffer the consequences. We see train companies, threatened with targets and penalties for punctuality, simply extending their timetabled journey times in order to arrive on time. In fact, railway journeys seem to have become a more pleasant experience as the leeway creates less tension for passengers and staff alike and the early arrival into stations is met with a triumphant announcement from train managers. Similarly, hospitals threatened with penalties for long queues in outpatient waiting rooms are given targets for when patients should be seen. Hence, when we join the crowded waiting area it is not many minutes before we receive an initial consultation which usually consists of little more than being weighed or producing a sample. Similarly, in A and E the triage system ensures we are seen at speed. Regardless of the hours we then spend waiting, at least we have been seen; the process has begun and nobody can catch the hospital out.

Police forces with responsibility for traffic speed erect speed cameras, so motorists immediately slow down prior to reaching the location of the camera. Local authorities, faced with the knowledge that motorists reduce their speed when they are made aware that a camera is in the area, simply erect road signs warning that cameras may be in operation as a traffic-slowing measure. This works for a while, until the regular motorists work out whether the cameras exist or not.

In supermarkets, shoppers are given the opportunity to use an 'express' lane if carrying a hand basket rather than a trolley. It is not unusual to see people with enormous amounts of shopping in their basket, defying a test of strength, just to get out of the store quicker. We go to pizza restaurants that invite us to 'eat as much as you like' from the salad bar and it is not surprising to see students of architecture constructing the most amazing cantilever framework with celery sticks in order to load on as much salad as possible. Insurance companies have a direct link to police forces for information on traffic accidents linked to premium rises. Footballers dive to gain a penalty. In the Olympic Games, two pairs of badminton players achieved notoriety when they all sought to achieve defeat in their doubles game in order to progress to a perceived easier tie in the next round.

We can see how game theory has triumphed over integrity when the chief nursing officer calls for nurses to demonstrate more compassion in their work. After years of target-driven external measurements of efficiency, it now appears that many nurses are distracted from their primary purpose. Should we be surprised? In the end, game theory takes over and perverse incentives mean we lose purpose and integrity as we seek to respond.

## The real drivers in the school system

The reality is that schools and teachers are driven by some very simple practices that suck them into the tactics of game theory. Schools are driven by data (which is often suspect), their league table position, ever more complex hurdles (such as the proposed EBacc subjects), inspection (again often suspect), market-driven awarding bodies and ministerial favour. This simple list says so much about what is creating pressure on schools at the present time. The evolution during two decades of all of these drivers has made schools very different places from just a generation ago. While schools, heads, teachers, governors, parents and even pupils respond to the new rules, many professionals question whether their fundamental values are being compromised.

As game theory takes hold, schools engage in practices which might make sense at the time but which, from a distance, seem to have questionable validity. We see 'cusp chasing', where children are identified as potential Level 4s or as being on the D/C borderline for GCSEs. This small group of children represents a significant percentage in the school's overall results and therefore its league table position. In order to help the children on the cusp, schools offer a simplistic syllabus and extended courses. In the secondary sector pupils are offered, through the awarding bodies, 'short fat courses' or 'long thin courses' so that they can be spoon-fed their learning as effectively as possible. There are schools that have identified the four children in the Foundation Stage who, if worked upon throughout their school career, will make the significant difference to the school's capacity to hold its league table position as these four-year-olds eventually leave Key Stage 2. All of these things make a certain sort of sense and, for the children that are the focus – the potential Level 5s, Level 4s or five GCSEs candidates – the outcomes might justify the means.

The truth is though that, in all of these tactics, the pupils gradually become the currency for the school rather than the beneficiaries of education. We know pupils benefit because the results count. However, many young people come to realise that they achieved their results for the school rather than because they were of benefit to themselves. Many teenagers feel cheated as they realise the world does not open up in the way it was promised. Within this system we get that 'Ofsted tweeting' I mentioned above where, because of the importance of inspection outcomes, practices run around the system, often built on myth, because it is felt by teachers that these are the things the inspectors want to see. So many people in the school system are dancing to the tune that is being played for them. They're playing the game but the question is whether they're dancing the right dance. Or, if we shift our metaphor from the dance to the game, it is important to work out tactics. After all, we are all trying to win. And by win I mean survive.

The ruses for passing the Ofsted inspection have become urban myths, apocryphal stories, the stuff of staffroom and training day legend; the things that everyone knows happen but everybody says somebody else does. There is the constructive use of work experience and educational visits that just happen to occur on the day of the inspection so that certain pupils or groups are not on the school premises. There is the way we say 'We're in a collaborative' or 'We've formed a working group' in order to show that we are dealing with a serious issue the inspectors might have noticed. How many schools produce their own statistics, developed by 'our own data manager', which are more valid and powerful than anything that we can get from RAISEonline or the Fischer Family Trust? Of course, every school would deny that they borrow good staff simply for the inspection but it does happen. Nobody admits it and as soon as the inspection has been a success the staff and leaders of the successful school tend to forget that they were helped by neighbours down the road or long-term educational pals. What school does not have contingency plans in place – the local vicar on standby, practising the parent workshop in advance, asking a local sculptor or the police to be available at short notice? If all else fails, send for a travelling circus.

Much is made of such subterfuge; however, in game theory terms, the nagging worry that these things happen have led Ofsted to suggest 'no-notice' inspections. Of course, the very notion that you need a no-notice inspection implies that some things are escaping the eye of the inspectors. It's all game theory; the trickers and the trackers. The pity is that it all becomes self-defeating.

The game theory problem is at the root of professional and political tensions. Nobody seems to deny that we want a good education for our young people. Politicians have assumed the upper hand in so much of teaching that they enact change in order to see improvements. They then seek to measure that improvement so the electorate can be reassured and, of course, they need to do this by the time the next election is called. Schools themselves want to see children enjoying a rich education but because of the activities of policy-makers they feel incredibly pressurised to achieve what is required, and therefore they compromise their beliefs and practices in order to meet the perceived demands. And this is where they push on allowable tolerances within the system and exploit game theory.

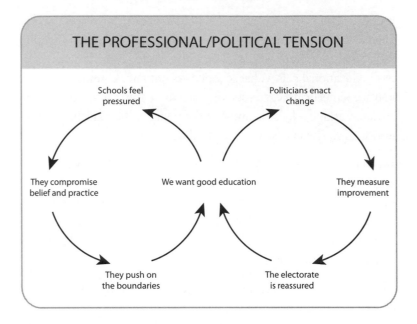

THE PROFESSIONAL/POLITICAL TENSION

Schools feel pressured

Politicians enact change

They compromise belief and practice

We want good education

They measure improvement

They push on the boundaries

The electorate is reassured

An interesting perspective on game theory is currently operating around the learning diet of pupils. The secretary of state espouses that the national curriculum constrains schools and one of the incentives offered for becoming an academy is deregulation and freedom from the national curriculum. The implication is that this will allow learning to flourish and schools to become more innovative.

It is a clever sleight of hand. One of the interpretations of the term 'freedom' is that schools will no longer have to fulfil obligations. The early evidence is that, while some schools are exploiting their freedoms and becoming more imaginative about the range of learning on offer, many are simply using their independence to abandon that which is not measured or is difficult to teach. An Ipsos MORI survey in 2012 reports that of the 27% of schools that have withdrawn courses since the introduction of the EBacc as a league table measure, drama and performing arts have been removed in 23% of schools, art in 17% and design technology in 14%. As the messages about freedom permeate, the pressure within the system ensures that practice becomes even more restricted.

As the government changes the school accountability measures in the new league tables, following the fall-out from the EBacc debacle, there will be yet more readjustment in schools as they come to terms with the new game. This is to be expected and who would blame schools? What matters is that the accountabilities are agreed by a greater consensus than has existed for some time. Moreover, the government could engage more deeply with the general public, employers, business, civic leaders, parents, teachers and even pupils themselves in trying to define what matters most in learning and how our hopes for our young might be best realised and measured.

## So where has game theory led us?

Many people would continue to argue that schools are becoming better places, that leadership is better than ever, that our teachers teach better than they ever did, that teachers are leaving initial training better prepared than ever before; the basis of their claim is so often because 'the Ofsted inspection tells us'. This is an example of game theory in action. Ofsted has made inspection such a key driver in the system that, in order to persuade ourselves we are making progress, we use the 'evidence' from Ofsted inspection reports to show that we are winning. I am not so sure that inspection is making the school system significantly better (see pages 133–135). There is no doubt that there are fewer poor schools than in the past but it is questionable whether our best schools are as good as they were previously in the all-round educational sense. We have become so excited about playing the game that we are falling into the trap of using the categories employed by Ofsted, even though they change so frequently and the criteria that create the categories are amended on a regular basis. What was 'outstanding' last year is now only 'good', what used to be 'satisfactory' now 'requires improvement'. If we went back seven frameworks and inspected schools on the criteria being used ten short years ago, we would probably find more schools nowadays would be described as good. The problem is that we have upped the ante six times since. Each time, we have raised the standard and given the public the view that our schools are getting worse.

If instead we think about schools at the very beginning of the national inspection process in the early 1990s, we could categorise them in very different ways. Yes, there were many ropy schools, schools that did not have a sense of direction, did not know what they were doing, did not strive to do the best for their children and sold them short. At the other end of the scale there were many schools that were absolutely splendid, where results were good, where expectations were high, where young people left with a sense of fulfilment and a commitment to taking on the world. These schools exuded good education. Their whole being was built around engaging with their pupils and creating the right environment, experiences and opportunities that would set them fair for life.

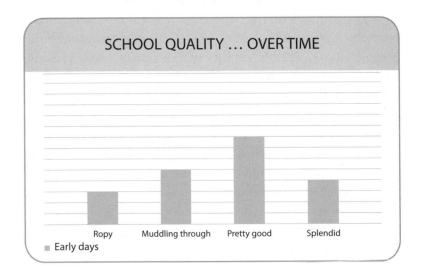

Two decades on there are virtually no ropy (by 1990s standards) schools. Ofsted has seen to that and, to its credit, has identified and challenged those who are holding the education system back. However, at the other end of the scale, the need to strive to meet the criteria to be what is now called an 'outstanding school' has meant that schools have compromised practices and beliefs that have stopped them being what would have made them splendid schools twenty years ago. Many of the schools Ofsted have identified as outstanding do exude education in its broadest sense. At the same time, we see schools that are classed as outstanding but have achieved this status by playing the game. Why shouldn't they? And should we criticise them for doing so when they are successful?

The sad thing is that there are also many schools that are really splendid except for the fact that they cannot hit one of the key drivers in the system and so fail to produce the requisite data. This is where the concept of the outside and inside tracks, discussed in the first section of this book, starts to really bite home. There are many schools dealing with children on the outside of the track which offer a splendid education but can never be recognised as outstanding.

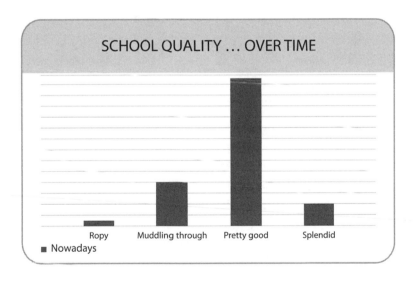

Ironically, a stream of HMI reports on themed inspections around aspects of schooling or particular subject disciplines has drawn attention to the narrowing of teaching approaches, the lack of width in coverage of curriculum, the play-safe lack of practical approaches and the lack of flexibility in schools. HMI are typically champions of effective teaching and learning but they are let down by the foot soldiers of the school inspection regime who scrutinise teachers fighting to achieve the school results by narrowing the risk. In his speech on the 2004/5 HMCI Annual Report, David Bell, the then HMCI, drew attention to the lacklustre experience of pupils as teachers taught to the test. Who could blame them?

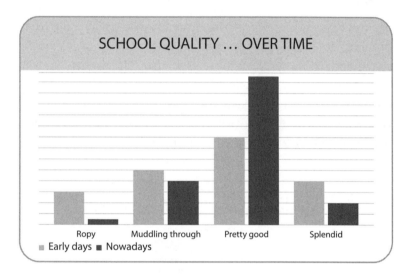

When I worked at QCA, we were keen to help schools to learn from the best in terms of curriculum and learning for pupils. I commissioned researchers to visit thirty primary schools rated outstanding by Ofsted to interrogate the curriculum design and learning offer so that we could build confidence in schools generally. The schools visited were the usual cross-section: rural and urban, faith and non-denominational, big and small, new head and experienced head – every variable we could manage. The outcome was fascinating. The researchers, all very experienced practitioners in the primary sector, found very few examples in these schools of a dynamic curriculum. Out of the thirty schools, they found just four that were providing a curriculum that pushed the boundaries or offered the children a rich and powerful learning experience. Most were fine but not particularly inspiring – they had simply cracked the 'inspection code'. Many spoke powerfully about how they had done this and prefaced their comments with statements such as 'What inspectors want to see is ...' Some of the schools were downright disappointing in terms of the learning offer. Our researchers concluded that the common characteristic of the thirty schools was that they were *outstandingly efficient*, but not splendid in the learning sense.

A former chief adviser in a local authority in the south of England reported to me that he had been persuaded back to a temporary headship after retirement. It was a school struggling to appoint a new head teacher because it was small and outstanding; not a good bet for a new head – these are two negative factors in the game theory of careers. His view was that the children were not getting as good a deal as when he had left his headship twenty years previously. His new school was outstanding on outcomes, much of which could be attributed to home circumstances, but way below outstanding on provision.

Another example of inertia within the system – and game theory in action – relates to the examination process. About fifteen years ago, some individual schools began approaching the regulator to accredit qualifications that most readily suited the needs of their own pupils. The regulator applied the formula that was agreed with the government to the proposed examination. In the main this related to the concept of 'guided learning hours' – the amount of time the pupil would need to follow the course of study in order to be ready to take the examination. As these examinations took a considerable amount of guided learning hours they were credited with being the equivalent of up to four GCSEs.

Other schools that were subject to questions about how many pupils gained five GCSEs saw this as a potential way to beat the tracker and approached the initial schools to see whether they could also offer the examinations. Awarding bodies saw a new opening and gradually exams were crafted that would 'do the job'. It was beneficial that many young people were now taking courses that mattered to them, made a difference and showed a realism with their daily lives. Unfortunately, these courses were often simple to follow and made little intellectual demand on pupils. But who was complaining? Results in schools went up and the government could claim there had been year-on-year progress. Game theory was winning.

Of course, what really happens is the bean counters win. First it was Fischer Family Trust Data (FFTD) that quickly became the watchword on standards. Then the DFES produced graphs, complete with stickmen, as a way of dissecting the data. RAISEonline grew in importance and still carries weight in inspections. Ofsted gradings became enormously significant as schools sought to justify their existence and performance. It doesn't stop there. Individual children now carry around with them their levels and target levels. Teachers are required to identify the progress that children at every level will make by the end of and during the lesson, now, even more absurdly, in twenty-minute blocks. There is little attempt to scrutinise the wisdom of all this. Maybe it is possible to show that a child has made progress in hitting a shuttlecock within fifteen minutes or learning an equation, but in understanding democracy or evidencing empathy?

In order to make sure that the case for the defence is firm, schools have developed the concept of scoring the equaliser first (i.e. heading off the criticism). While contextual value-added scores were part of the league table mechanism, it was not unreasonable for schools to identify aspects of their context which would enable them to show the tracker just how well they were doing. Hence, the emphasis on special needs and the urgency to achieve a statement, or the importance of identifying every child with English as an Additional Language (whether they were newly arrived refugees or the children of academics from the local university).

Junior schools complain that teacher assessments from the feeder infant school are often over-inflated, making it more difficult for them to achieve the required levels of progress for their Key Stage 2 pupils. Comparatively more junior schools struggle in Ofsted inspections and are seen as needing to improve than other school types. It could be that there is some truth in the contention that in primary schools Key Stage 1 results are suppressed in order to allow required levels of progress to be achieved. Or it could be that infant schools over-inflate their assessments. What does Ofsted inspection reveal? Secondary schools suggest that the test scores achieved by Year 6 pupils do not equate with the performance of Year 7 pupils. They might blame the primary schools, but they also know the summer holiday might have had an impact or that difficulty in adjusting to a new school, class, teacher or set of peers is affecting progress. Game theory leads to blame theory.

For some schools, while contextual value-added data was part of the formulaic assessment, the ideal position would be, ironically, in the most deprived circumstances that could be imagined. I have lost count of the number of schools I have visited which are in the bottom 10% of all deprivation indicators, have the highest teenage pregnancy rates, are in the worst employment black spots in the country, are on the biggest council estate in Europe or are under the flight path for an airport. Finding justification for poorer results or taking pride in overcoming difficulty rests on proving that you are worse off than others to begin with.

Parents, teachers and pupils all get involved. The new framework invites evidence of how well children are learning to read and the inspectors are expected to talk with children about literature. Schools are bringing in friendly 'men in suits' (CRB checked of course) to hear reading with Year 2 pupils and talk about phonics or discuss authors with Years 5 and 6. Parents are being prepared for impromptu conversations with inspectors when the inspection is imminent. Photographs and comments from children and parents are catalogued, websites updated with commentaries on progress by parents and archives of good literary experience assembled. All of this is worthwhile in itself but it is being driven by the need to play the inspection game, and to achieve the right judgement, as much as by the quest to meet the school's mission statement.

Day after day, teachers are observed by senior managers who say 'What Ofsted want is ...' in order to secure better judgements. Would it not be better if the dialogue centred on the words 'What these children need is ...'?

## Examinations

We need to rethink the purpose of examinations and tests. There is still a lack of clarity about whether we are testing the pupil, measuring the school or recording national progress in performance over time. The vicious circle of game theory means schools have to use any tactic they can to improve results year on year rather than implementing a properly motivated strategy.

When I was chief education officer in Manchester, I supported a group of local business leaders in the establishment of the Food 4 Thought scheme. I was told that some pupils had limited space and opportunity to study and revise for examinations at home and, with the city always being in the relegation zone in the local authority league tables, any tactic was always worth a try. Working with a group of community leaders and schools, we invited local Year 11 pupils to the upstairs room of a curry restaurant for a weekly two-hour study period in science and mathematics, the target areas. The tuition was managed by students from local universities who prepared work based on the requests of the Year 11s. At the end of the two-hour session, the pupils enjoyed a meal which we paid for. At the first meeting we were delighted to get nineteen pupils attending. By the fourth meeting, we had sixty-nine from four schools, plus one from a nearby independent school. Exam results improved but, probably more importantly, the pupils asked whether the system could carry on in order to allow them to continue working together around the hard-to-understand aspects of learning.

As one local authority caught up in the game theory of results, the expansion of Food 4 Thought was all too obvious and it spread to eating venues around the city with the added involvement of local police community support officers, social care and youth workers and employers. It became a sort of youth club with a purpose – and always with food. This was an example of game theory that did good. The pupils were complicit and knew that their results were tickets to a new set of possibilities. Crucially, there were wider gains than simple examination results – being fed, developing confidence in ordering and choosing food (many had not eaten in a restaurant before), socialising, peer learning and building trusting relationships with adults. There was more to be learned than simply how to pass the exam.

The whole concept of exams strikes me as archaic. Instead of the age-old papers, we could encourage a connectedness through time trials: the student enters the room, is given a problem with three hours to solve it and told that they can use any device or any system they want but must reappear within the agreed time with the solution. Then, like most people in business and industry, they would contact others, hold small meetings, get on the web, talk to people in other places, send messages for help, gradually provide solutions, test out their solutions with colleagues and eventually work towards the best answer possible.

Game theory is also at the root of SATs practice. In many schools, pupil enjoyment, engagement and enrichment in Year 6 takes an annual nosedive as practising for SATs begins in earnest; the richness of learning reappears only in June. What a tragedy, when this is the very year that pupils could exploit all they have learned in primary school, when they could become leaders of others, develop the skills for transition into secondary school and reflect on and celebrate the rich journey from reception class to this final year. Instead, they find the curriculum narrowing to English and maths. They sit endless pretend tests. Imagination and creativity in their writing is ignored and all emphasis is redirected to VCOP (Vocabulary, Connectives, Openers, Punctuation).There is nothing wrong with VCOP; it is the reduction of the enjoyment of English to short-term gains that is the problem.

And why are we not using old SATs papers? Each year we spend millions of pounds developing new questions to test our eleven-year-olds. If we are really using this as a screening device, as a way of measuring progress over time or testing one school against another, surely we can use papers from previous years at random, saving millions of pounds annually. Doing so would enable us to check our progress, say in 2015, against the achievement of eleven-year-olds in 1994. Of course, one of the problems is that the children of 2015 will have practised the tests from previous years so extensively that the results might be distorted.

Practice is a fundamental part of game theory. What we need to question is whether teachers and their pupils should be jumping through hoops or whether they should be following learning in a natural way and exploring the avenues that it opens up. At the moment, too many teachers are bent double trying to make sense of the requests and demands upon them. Head teachers constantly adjust their school in order to respond to the latest meddling government initiative, and often not in meaningful or innovative ways but more to meet what they see as a new requirement. They twiddle and tweak, rebrand and rename old ideas. Starters become hooks, objectives become outcomes, lessons are chunked up and little really changes.

## Ministerial favour

People advertising and speaking at conferences seem unable to resist the tendency to justify their message with isolated extracts and quotations from ministerial speeches in order to persuade teachers and others that their message is in line with government requirements. To sell places on a course, give credibility to a product or validity to a conference speech it is easy to isolate a small section of a ministerial speech to offer justification. At times, this is surely done with fingers crossed. The speaker will find a scrap of positivity in a ministerial speech promoting the arts or another area of learning – when in fact coalition ministers have led an assault on the arts, culture, sport, design, technology, ICT, religious education, health education, citizenship and countless other aspects of learning. To find threads of support in isolated sentences uttered by a minister is not the right way to engage with the profession. This is game theory again – the double bluff. It plays on the fears of all those at risk in the game: those who are in danger of finding themselves in a weak category and those who need to maintain their place in a strong category.

# Game theory and the learner

We can generally understand how game theory affects the system and how it starts to manipulate the professional behaviour of those involved. It is where game theory meets the pupil that its effect is most telling. It is here that the concerned professional has the most nagging doubts about the practice they need to demonstrate to be seen as doing the job well.

If you want to more fully understand the futility that game theory creates in educational terms at the point where learning meets the pupil, just think through these conundrums.

■ Is it easy to observe teaching? There are some fundamentals of good teaching but any good teacher will admit that there are no guarantees. A change in the make-up of a teaching group makes a difference: a new pupil, a significant absentee, a particular pairing. Then there is the weather, the room, the resources, the time of day and a multitude of other variables such as where the group were in the previous session. Even with the most amazing preparation and planning, a perfectly honed exposition, captivating explanations and tasks with real archives, the appearance of a blackbird on the crossbar of the goalposts outside still seems to have a magnetic ability to draw the eyes of the pupils. If just occasionally the brilliant teacher falls flat, what of the rest of us?

■ Is it really possible to measure your progress every twenty minutes? The current vogue seems to be that teachers have to talk about developing progress every few minutes in order to satisfy possible onlookers. Do we really believe this? Can anybody truly say that it is possible to learn in an incremental linear way so that progress is achieved in such short spaces of time? If we make progress in twenty-minute spans for the rest of our lives, do we realise how good we'll be by the time we're sixty-four? It used to be that schools expected pupils to move up two sub-levels in a year. Now teachers report that their senior managers are demanding at least one sub-level every lesson. By the time they are twelve these children will all have doctorates!

■ Remember what you gave up for lack of practice. There is a difference between practising and rehearsing for tests. If there is one thing that is lacking in schools at the moment in terms of children's learning, it is the opportunity for practice. There seems to be no time allowed for children to simply practice, practice, practice, rehearse, rehearse, rehearse, until they get better, better, better. Instead there is a mantra of meet it, learn it, move on, as though all learning can work in this way. Try thinking about your own learning, maybe another language or a musical instrument. So many of us give up learning things that we think will offer so much joy. The problem is the investment feels too great for the perceived or imagined reward. The amount of practice needed is significant and we tend to quit because the pace of the expected progress is greater than the amount of practice possible. How else can children build confidence if not through consolidation and practice?

■ See how long you can keep on working through a pupil workbook. Workbooks dominate classrooms for children, even though sometimes they are part of an IT resource. If you want to see just how tedious life is for many pupils, set yourself the task of working through some of the activities they have to undertake. They are often incredibly banal and mind-numbing. However, if you know the game and need to get the marks, then I guess you can stick at it. But what have you actually achieved and who is the workbook for? I suspect that for many teachers the workbook allows them to say they've done it. Look! Evidence! The reality is that the workbooks go home at the end of the year and, unless there is something funny or endearing in it, they find their way straight into the recycling bin. If the learning is not in the child's head, it is lost forever, hence the repetition of content as they move up through the school. Workbooks do not provide evidence of learning. They provide evidence of busy-work. And busy-work does not necessarily stay in the mind.

■ Try writing for ten minutes in every thirty minutes in legible script with no doodles. We seem to expect our youngsters to write enormous amounts during the school day. Most of the writing is unnecessary. Even then we expect it to be presented neatly, coherently and legibly. I look around meetings where I find myself with adults who are at a high level in their organisation and very responsible. The writing they are doing is usually scrawls, mind maps and scribbles all over a page and there seems to be an incredible amount of doodling. We should be teaching our children properly about the importance of purpose, process and audience in writing so that they understand when their writing needs to be a thing of beauty and when it needs to be perfunctory.

■ Compare three pupils on their birthday in terms of weight, height and foot size. It is self-evident really. They will vary enormously. If they vary enormously in these simple physical measures, why should we expect them to perform equally in terms of mathematical achievement or linguistic capability? We place too much emphasis on age and performance and not enough on development.

■ Keep a list of the tactics you use when you can't do something. Most of us who see ourselves as successful have found ways to duck and dive when we can't do a process, don't know the answer or feel lost in an explanation. We have tactics that we employ in order to help us survive. Most children have not yet developed these or their parents have not taught them. The children feel there is no hiding place, especially when asked challenging questions which are really 'on the spot putters' and likely to cause embarrassment. Because they do not have the necessary techniques, children are most likely to do something to save face with their friends – and move one step away from pleasing their teacher.

If this is touching a nerve, think about other aspects of the way schools have changed over the past few years. If we combine the quest for progress with better performance management, the school leader might set a series of focus points with staff for discussion. A walk around the school might address some of the list of questions below.

- How much pupil 'work in progress' is evident? The novel being read (or written), the model, sculpture or painting, or the on-going experiment are all examples of work that pupils have 'to get on with'. This might seem to be the natural business of learning – of getting on and making progress – but the emphasis upon the staccato lesson as the sole unit of learning means that pupils are expected to 'finish' their work by the end of the lesson to achieve the learning outcome.

- How much equipment is being used? Are pupils using scales, measures, maps, test tubes, saws and screens? Or does the pencil dominate in search of evidence of the written word? Numeracy lessons always used to involve a significant section of applying mathematics through practical insight. There seems less of it about these days. If equipment is being used in a limited way, what does that say about value for money in terms of all the purchases made?

- What is the evidence of extended and incremental practice? If pupils are going to become proficient then practice is vital. Is it evident or is the requirement for evidence of progress somehow stopping pupils making progress in terms of quality and confidence?

- How much singing can you hear? Tick a chart every time you hear singing. Then ask whether the learning diet of pupils is rounded.

- What is the on/off ratio for computers? Was the expenditure cost efficient?

- Is the whiteboard interactive? Or is it simply a white electric version of the old-fashioned blackboard used in the same way?

- Where are the interactive learning platforms? Are pupils engaged in activities using learning platforms that make them interact? The artist's palette, the piano keyboard, the bookshelf, the cooker hob, the ordnance survey map and the dance mat are all true platforms for learning interaction. Are you seeing them in use?

All of this relates to game theory. They are examples of where the psychology of learning and teaching give way to the tactics of getting the results for the purpose of survival at whatever level we are in the schooling game. This is the sharp end of all the games we play to 'make the system work' and achieve the successes we are pressed to achieve, even though some of those successes fly in the face of the educational values we hold. Of course we should seek the best standards and performance for all pupils. Of course we should strive for year-on-year improvement. Of course schools should improve as public funding is invested. The challenge is to ensure the improvements we make are genuine, that the success for pupils is worthy and that we are offering education in its widest sense to better the future of our society.

## What can we do?

The issues covered in this section permeate everything in this book. They sit at the heart of our schooling difficulties and so, instead of listing what we can do, I would point to the proposals in the rest of the book and suggest we need them all.

The suggestions listed at the end of other sections that apply to the school and the teacher, or to the system and the nation, are the ways forward for a system led by game theory.

Many aspects of our society are now mathematically modelled and controlled by readily amassed data, such as quotas and performance targets. Schooling is in the grip of game theory and we need to recognise its impact. Our integrity is challenged when we find ourselves chasing perverse, often arbitrary, performance indicators and questioning our own professional behaviours. Instead, we need to pursue new ways of bringing to life the values that motivate us. In other words, we need to innovate with integrity and create the conditions within which young people can flourish. We need to be technically proficient, operationally efficient and effective at making evidence serve its purpose to enact procedures that will drive up achievement. We also need to be morally and ethically good and hold on to the integrity of the job of teaching.

# … on Ofsted inspection

Few would disagree with the need for school inspection. Overall, inspection has been a force for good these past twenty years. Sadly, though, one with side effects that has at times done more harm than good. The ideologies of changing ministers and Ofsted chiefs can have a significant impact on the effectiveness of the inspection process and there are times when this inhibits genuine improvement. Are we in one of those times at present?

Appointed in 2011, Sir Michael Wilshaw, Her Majesty's Chief Inspector, has attracted a good deal of media attention with his statements about what society should expect of schools and how they should operate. He has ruffled feathers, in the way inspectors tend to, with his questions about the relative and comparative performance of schools in different local authorities, and the need to look at school performance in conjunction with performance management and pay arrangements for teachers. At least he is asking questions and setting out to find answers rather than rushing to judgement, as one of the previous incumbents of his post was prone to do. While many in schools and local authorities will bridle at the new intrusions, Sir Michael might, over time, be an HMCI who will be respected for addressing the complex, long-standing challenges with simple, principled questions and a drive to propose something tangible about the answers. Nobody can doubt his commitment and drive. What will be essential will be to deliver actual results in terms of the quality of schooling for pupils, rather than allow game theory to produce a more pleasing set of statistics without justification.

# Can every school be a good school?

Well, anything is possible in theory and Sir Michael insists that every school should be a good school and that the changes to the inspection framework allow that to be possible. It is just that when theory meets practice the reality bites.

Sir Michael has eased the link between attainment and inspection outcome and states clearly that it is still possible for a school to be good when attainment is not high but progress is strong. In theory then, every school can be a good school and those head teachers in schools below the floor now know they are not condemned before the inspection begins.

So, is it realistic in practice to think that all schools can be good? There is certainly more likelihood now that there are only three categories (outstanding, good or requires improvement) and the margin for error is reduced. The only thing that has ever been consistent about Ofsted inspections is that they are inconsistent. With three categories the spread is more contained. Doubts remain though.

There should be a calling to account of schools and a regular check on whether they are good enough or not. If not, action needs to be taken. If the school is good enough then it is surely for the school to demonstrate that it is outstanding to its own community, including parents, employers, neighbours and pupils, rather than wait to receive an accolade from Ofsted. It is when the inspection system attempts to reach fine-grained judgements that questions should be asked. When the mass inspection of schools began just twenty years ago, there were seven categories of school; now there are to be three with the expectation that all will be in the top two. A simple 'good enough or not' judgement would make inspection valid. Having three levels leaves us aiming for two tiers. 'Can every school be at least second tier?' is surely not the question we would be asking in a world-class system.

## What are the problems?

First, we need to remind ourselves that inspection is not an isolated phenomenon. There are ripples of effect. From the big picture of the political imperative of the time, alongside the localised picture of the school in its community, coupled to the personalised picture of what inspection does to people, Ofsted affects lives on many levels.

We live in interesting political times. The drive to increase the number of academies and to break any remaining bonds of local democracy means that the unwilling have to be offered no alternative. Many schools that have been working with their local authority to improve, often against the odds, know it is now only a matter of time before Ofsted brings its next framework and the almost inevitable prospect of being in a 'negative category'. There is a resigned acceptance as they wait for the drop and possibly the chop.

The secretary of state, in a long line of those intent on school improvement, states publicly that head teachers have autonomy and freedom. Yet many heads smile wryly and see only their freedom to be afraid. Fear for themselves, fear for their school and fear for its community being labelled a failure. With the wolf at the door, they focus more and more on trying to generate the data that might give temporary reprieve, knowing all the time that their school is becoming something that their pupils do not need and is far from their own belief about what education should be for. In some cases, integrity is replaced by increasingly desperate measures to meet and cheat the stats. It is a brave head who sticks to what is known to work in the long term when the pressure for a short-term fix is mounting.

The accolade of the 'outstanding' school opens doors to teaching school status and national leader status. Who would criticise the system if these prizes might be theirs? And anyway, who would complain when 'outstanding' means the process won't happen again for years? Of course, the 'outstanding' schools are on a short rein since one blip in the data and a new inspection might be triggered. Don't get too comfortable; stay on your toes. Indeed, Ofsted report that a significant proportion of requests for school inspection come from 'outstanding' schools. Are they more nervous than most? Does the leadership need to keep pressure on the staff from outside? Or is the stacking of 'outstanding' judgements seen as a way of scoring the equaliser in case the results dip?

Ofsted is now intending to use heads from 'outstanding' schools to work on inspections of poorer schools. This implies that all is good in an outstanding school and all is bad in an unsatisfactory school. But, of course, there are plenty of splendid schools that are not outstanding and plenty of ropy ones that have outstanding aspects. The terminology of judgement, though, implies reliability and validity.

## From descriptor to judgement: the downward spiral of the reliability dream

One of the positive aspects of the arrival of national inspection all those years ago was the beginning of a shared vocabulary. The Ofsted framework created a set of terminologies that were seized upon by the multitude of inspectors, many of whom had previously worked as local education authority advisers. Where previously they had often struggled to define their observations, they now had common descriptors, definitions and gradations of quality. This shared vocabulary was, in turn, used by staff in schools and so the school improvement agenda had a common parlance that focused action within schools. It can't be a bad thing that conversations centre on the same definitions of 'progress' or 'teaching' or 'leadership'. We have to be sure, though, that we are talking about the same thing in the same terms.

I recently spent a morning at an annual primary head teacher conference prior to my own contribution in the afternoon. The morning was led by the training director of one of the national agencies who introduced the new inspection framework. It was excellently presented and appreciated by the head teachers. There were short talks, videos and opportunities for discussion. At one point the group was asked to consider the criteria for teaching judgements and a PowerPoint slide showed two lists, one for 'good' and one for 'outstanding'. It was explained that there was no other descriptor since anything else was needing improvement and, being not good enough, did not need description. On four occasions the presenter had to stop the group to explain which column listed the good features and which the outstanding ones. The irony seemed lost on everyone. If it is difficult to spot the difference in an explanation on a slide, how will we be able to tell the difference between the actual practices in a school?

The descriptors have the same problem that the national curriculum attainment level descriptors and the Early Years profile have always had; as the described feature develops we have to resort to comparatives. We talk of *more, greater* and *additional* and as we do so our description becomes woolly and the definition subject to interpretation. This leads to the possibility of inconsistency. To avoid inconsistency the agencies develop pseudo-formulas for their inspection teams. 'If you state X, then Y follows.' 'You can't say A, unless you say B.' Quantities start to be defined: 'By sufficient, we mean 77% or more.'

The agencies employ 'readers' to ensure consistency before the reports are submitted to Ofsted. When challenged by head teachers, lead inspectors use phrases like 'I'll struggle to get that past the reader.' In order to make the judgement fit the criteria, evidence is vital. This is where inspectors have leeway. What do they look at? Where in school do they go to see what they need to see? Where do they need a blind eye? What can the school show that proves their point?

Now the inspection risks moving from valid, impartial scrutiny towards negotiation. When it becomes a negotiation, the credibility drops. Suspicions of hidden agendas, of motives or being part of a bigger story dominate some head teachers' thinking.

In a few short steps, the process of inspection has moved from the comfort of the printed framework to the discomfort of the final report, even where judgements are good. One part of the process leads to the next and people with integrity get caught in the game of making each step of their work match a notion of consistency that takes the spiral downwards.

The inspection process is not a consistent impartial scrutiny. The only consistent aspect of an Ofsted inspection is that it is an inconsistent mechanism. It is a negotiation between the lead inspector and the head teacher based on their relative assertiveness, with the inspector holding the all important data. Most inspectors are diligent, experienced and committed educationalists who try to act with integrity. They want to see splendid schools. The pressure to 'deliver' is on them from their contractors: 'We are not allowed to write that', 'I'm going out on a limb for you', 'I dare not argue with the data'. The pressure they fear from their own contractor's 'quality assurance' means that they will always be looking over their shoulder in case *they* are reported for being inconsistent. While the image of HMI remains high, freelance Ofsted inspectors often portray themselves as little more than foot soldiers, with no decisions to make and plenty of orders to take.

The reports themselves are very consistent, the readers ensure this is the case. Many an inspector uses the reference control of the quality assurance reader as a justification for not awarding an 'outstanding' judgement. Who are these readers? They are people employed by inspection teams or inspection agency contractors to provide the back-covering service of scrutinising reports before they go forward. This helps to ensure that future contracts are awarded; future contracts for the company, the inspector and members of the team. No wonder they comply.

## Perceptions and validity

Many head teachers talk of their perceived unfair treatment by ill-informed inspectors. Often these schools are in lower categories. Others talk of highly professional forensic inspectors. Often these schools are in the higher categories. There is a trend here. Ofsted points out that evaluation of their inspections is almost wholly positive. Would anyone with a good outcome complain? Beaten to submission over a few days, most head teachers would concur with the view that the sharks were nice really and only doing their jobs. They also know that you cannot argue about data and evidence that has been made to match. There is no decision review system and who would ask for further inspection when at least the prospect of the next visit is a while away.

## A personalised inspection

We also cannot ignore the personalising of the process. There are some head teachers who now live by the day, waiting for the call from Ofsted that will decide their fate. If they know that teaching needs to improve then some carefully resourced and well-rehearsed lessons for each teacher need to be literally on the shelf. Websites are readier than ever. Plan A and Plan B are in place. These are good, honest professionals often doing a hard job in difficult circumstances. Eventually they will lose heart and accept that the core purpose, that easily stated 'moral authority', has gone. What we know is that there will always be others ready to step forward, especially if the incentive of salary is good enough. In due course there will be sufficient numbers of schools that are good at playing the game, and enough time lag between recurring political need to criticise, that all schools might be deemed good. At what price?

Thankfully the new Ofsted framework acknowledges that judgement on teaching is about more than observing lessons and emphasises that formulaic lessons are not what is required. Nevertheless, inspection feels intensely personal. A lesson described by inspectors as 'outstanding' or 'good' very quickly becomes assimilated by the teacher as a comment upon themselves as teachers, and sometimes even upon themselves as human beings. Things get lost in translation and heads start describing their teachers as 'good' or 'outstanding' based on inspection or observation 'evidence'. It is noticeable these days how even teachers describe one another in inspection terms. 'Mr H is an outstanding teacher.' 'Mrs K is good with outstanding features.' 'Ms D', whisper it, 'is only satisfactory.' Of course, they overstate. Ofsted inspects lessons and reports on teaching. From saying that the *teaching* was good it is a simple but mistaken leap to say that the *teacher* was good. True, an outstanding teacher leads good lessons for the most part. But the outstanding teacher is more than that. It is the teacher who notices the lonely pupil on the playground and engages in a casual conversation to check all is well. It is the maths teacher who the plays trumpet in the school jazz band. It is the reception teacher who joins the Year 6 residential and the art teacher who gives up a weekend to help a group with a charity project. The teacher who adds to their skill in the classroom by contributing fully to the routines, events and wider life of the school is the truly outstanding professional. Outstanding teachers seek to achieve the aims of the school, subscribe to them and live the purpose of their vocation – and they teach excellent lessons as well.

A positive feature of the new framework is the emphasis on the effectiveness of performance management. If all staff are at the top of the pay spine, the hypothesis goes that pupil performance will have shown a continuing upward trajectory. Here is one of Ofsted's dilemmas: hypothesis becomes a search for judgement. However, the search always seems to find the evidence it seeks, with slight modifications achieved by the game theorists who manage to negotiate alternative starting points.

Whatever we may think of the process, the personalising of inspection leads to the sad but understandable state where heads are ringing local radio stations to be wished luck with their inspections, to thank their whole community for their support during this stressful week and putting in a request for 'Good Vibrations'. It is an inspection but, at the end of it, we need to have a party because we've seen off the bullies and we need to let everyone know that we did alright. We're not failures after all – at least not yet …

Many a time I have received texts from heads whom I know and respect for their endeavours telling me an inspection is looming. After what seems an interminable wait for it to actually take place, with all the attendant stress, it has come and gone in a blink. I then get a text with the message, 'Ofsted says we are outstanding'. I send back a simple response, 'You knew you were'. Validation is a good thing and it is reasonable to feel pleased when so much personal commitment has gone into the intense work of the school, but professionalism should see a stronger conviction in itself.

Over time, head teachers have changed the way they describe their schools. Have they also changed the way they see them? There was a time when, if you asked a head about their school, they would refer to the size, setting, history, its strengths and the challenges they were facing. They would talk about their hopes and some of the ambitions they had for the future. Nowadays, the simple question 'What's your school like?' seems to elicit an answer something like, 'It's good with outstanding features.' It sometimes feels that they are not part of it but sitting beside it, pushed out of place by the machine they seek to feed.

While the 'no excuses' outlook on behalf of the pupils is understandable and great rhetoric, we have to accept that some pupils present a greater challenge than others. Just as we know the top inhibitors for health are smoking and obesity, so there are inhibitors for learning. While the medical profession is now starting to say that an operation can be performed only when the patient has lost sufficient weight, so the school system might throw some of the responsibility onto parents. Inspection reports might state clearly that the school is not good enough and the most significant reason is that the parents generally are not offering sufficient support for the school's efforts. In many communities this might be a wake-up call, sufficient to galvanise the community into a 'let's show them' attitude, rather than yet another report that adds to their feelings of being let down by all around them and blaming the school. Taking parental responsibility does not mean simply moving the child to a school with a better reputation. The government's intent of making people take charge of their own lives surely has to start with spelling out parents' duty to their own children.

Then we get the flaunting of the outstanding outcome by successful schools. Why not? It is hard earned and hard won, so let's make sure people know we are outstanding – on letterheads, straplines and signs. There are schools with banners proclaiming that they are 'an outstanding school' and I know of some that have had the words painted onto the school building in metre-high lettering. It sometimes reminds me of seeing a plaque in a village celebrating a third prize in the tidiest village competition four years ago. It is easy to see why we do it and, indeed, many parents see the accolades as vindication of their own choice and the efforts of their children. In other walks of life, the very best do not go on about it. We know without saying that the Royal Academy is the tops when it comes to art, that Covent Garden calls the shots on ballet, that the Ritz is deemed top class for afternoon tea and that the RSC is the bee's knees at Shakespeare.

## The question of evidence

Let's not fall prey to the myth that inspectors can only judge what they see. There are too many discrepancies from report to report. According to Ofsted reports, it is likely that a newly appointed head teacher knows what they are doing, has a clear vision, a strategic plan and is taking the staff and community with them. Open any hundred reports where the head has been in post for less than a year and see such 'evidence'. Hence, leadership gets judged 'good' and, by inference, the governing body is recognised as having first-rate procedures and clarity of vision.

Yet, the incidence of criticism of head teachers in struggling schools in the second year after their appointment is higher. Now how can this be? Is it that the new leader suddenly loses all that foundation after being recognised as good? Or is it that the inspector couldn't spot the inherent weaknesses in the first place? Or that they too easily give the benefit of the doubt? Or that the second inspection team misjudges the progress made? Whatever it is, there is something that seems too difficult to spot, or there is something that gets ignored, or both.

Another example of why questions might be asked about the validity and reliability of inspection relates to the sad court cases where accusations of financial irregularity are punished. So often the accused head teacher argues that the school was recently judged outstanding by Ofsted and that its financial management was a model of good practice.

HMI subject and theme reports, now called Survey Reports, consistently and constantly state that the quality of teaching in subjects needs to be better with more practical approaches, less textbook use and more application to real life and the working world. They want to see pupils enjoying the beauty, big ideas and power of subject disciplines. The much respected HMI regularly complain that the richness of learning is being sacrificed in the pursuit of test scores. How can it be that HMI say there are so many concerns in subject disciplines when Ofsted school inspections fail to spot them? This is a serious contradiction. It could be that some of the schools that are being categorised as good and outstanding are playing the game of defeating the inspection, while not actually improving the learning for pupils. Maybe some of the schools are being classified as good while becoming worse at education.

## Effects on the schooling system

Then there is the sort of 'Ofsted tweeting' that happens as different practices run through the school system because a rumour goes around that this is now what Ofsted are looking for – so give them what they want to see. After all, inspectors are always keen to find evidence to put in a report to validate their judgement. For example, an inspector refers to the use of 3D replicas that bring learning alive. While checking the Ofsted website for reports submitted by the lead inspector of the team due to visit their school next week, the head teacher sees the reference to 3D replicas and, within no time at all, they are part of the fabric and routine of learning.

It gets worse. As inspectors prepare for their inspection of a school they check previous reports and find references to 3D replicas. This suddenly becomes food for thought on their own inspections elsewhere and they find themselves enquiring whether 3D replicas are regularly used. Teachers tell each other of the conversations with inspectors and, before we know it, the 3D replica trade is booming. They call it evidence.

The 'judgement' industry means that the school helps the inspection team to write the report by spoon-feeding them the 'evidence' that is needed. Schools are often told at the halfway point that the judgements indicate a level lower than that which they hoped to secure. The school then produces a volume of 'evidence' to show why the level should be the one they claim. They do the job for the team by laying it on a plate.

The problem is that inspection has become a big industry and one that is convinced of its own validity. As an industry, it is also necessary to convince the public of its authority in order to secure its survival. By attempting to strike the balance between reassurance ('We are effective because schools are improving') and the need to feed our fears in order to ensure continued viability ('You need us because things are simply not good enough'), the industry creates confusion for parents and teachers. The fact is that judgements supported by examples of a certain aspect of schooling do not constitute evidence. The failure of the education system to embrace research means that the historical growth of school inspection has acted as a large-scale pseudo-action research programme prone to shifting more in response to the ideology of the paymaster than to the needs of the consumers – the parents and children.

If we were so certain of our evidence and judgements would we have needed seven inspection frameworks in ten years? It is strange that when children end up with roughly the same solution to their work, we suspect and often assert that they have colluded. When the grown-ups copy each other in preparation for an inspection, we call it learning from best practice. Just as with our need to cover all the bases in exams and tests, so we strive to make sure that we are ready for inspection. There are web-based products, books and courses to help the school leader feel confident in their capacity to take on the inspection team. Inspectors sell their 'secrets', amassing significant status because they can tell others how to beat the system. One such course advertises a new approach to school self-evaluation as having the solution that will 'make the inspector tingle'. If only our outlook were to make the children tingle with the excitement of learning.

## What could be done to improve inspection and its image?

We might trust inspection if:

■ It was a requirement that, as a condition of registration, all school inspectors should teach for a minimum of half a term every year. Not just spend time in a school, but actually teach, full time and paid. This would have the effect of helping inspectors to be respected and it might lead to a more human approach, with a little more humility. It would probably result in fewer inspectors. There is something rather tasteless about inspectors making judgements on the work of a supply teacher who is doing a job they would struggle to do, while being paid twice the rate of the person they are observing.

■ Practising teachers were included on the inspection teams as a vehicle for continuous professional development as well as bringing reality to the insights.

■ We inspect simply whether a school is good enough or not. If not, let's set about improving it. If it is good enough, let's leave it to the school to convince its own community that it is outstanding by working with parents, governors, local employers and pupils to demonstrate that what the school offers is worth it.

As I mentioned above, there are many splendid schools which have been graded by Ofsted as outstanding. There are many other splendid schools that are not graded outstanding. There are some schools graded outstanding that are not splendid. The fact that Ofsted is the only show in town when it comes to governmental inspection services gives it great public credibility, but it is not necessarily correct. Is it really possible to sit in a lesson, with all the nuances that make up the dynamic between pupils and teacher, and reach a judgement that the teaching was 'good with some outstanding features' but not quite 'outstanding'? Especially when we know that the observation is often done to corroborate and build the evidence base to support an already hypothesised judgement on the school. The new inspection framework is a step in the right direction. The big step will be when there are only two categories and only one set of descriptors. If the school meets the descriptors it will be good enough. The descriptors will be clear and unequivocal rather than subject to interpretation. They will be about the overall effort of the school rather than a few arbitrary and dubious statistics.

■ We stop changing the framework and giving the impression that there is a new target group of scapegoats. This is where the politicians pull the strings. We need more schools in certain categories, so change the rules. If 'evidence' is what drives inspection, might Ofsted stand accused of bending with the wind and following fashion as it changes its 'evidence base' so often? Let's stop pretending that what Ofsted sees is evidence. What inspection does is spread its own notion of good practice and then recognise it.

■ We make the inspection team review the school before it reviews the data. Time in a splendid school would make the data itch in a different way.

■ We stop spreading the notion that the lesson is the only unit of learning and teaching. Pupils learn through the whole of their school experience – lessons, events, routines and what takes place before and after the formal school day.

■ We make the inspection team watch the middle of lessons or, radically, even whole lessons! Teachers are now so attuned to the demands of the framework that lessons are more formulaic than ever, despite what Ofsted claim they require. After the stunning opening and the ritual writing of learning objectives come the swift questions with a touch of group discussion, on maybe an exposition using the whiteboard (when did it stop being interactive?). By now the inspector has usually gone ... but might return for the finale with the revolving stage. The new framework states that there is no expectation of model lessons. So how will inspectors know what judgement to make?

Good questions in some of the schools waiting for the drop might be: How long since you saw a child playing a glockenspiel? How long since a numeracy lesson included the children using apparatus like they did when the numeracy hour first began? When did the children last paint?

■ Ofsted itself could work to break the myths and legends. There are lots and they must come from somewhere. The one about 3D models is a good current example, as is the one about all pupils needing to working independently within ten minutes of the start of a lesson. It would not take much to produce a web page about what they do and don't need or want to see. Ofsted could clarify the rumours every month.

■ We are sure whether we are inspecting for all the rules or just the flavour of the moment. Safeguarding is important and is rightly prominent. However, many heads feel aggrieved when they are caught out by a minor blemish on the grounds that rules must be stringently applied. If we inspected strictly on the law about an act of collective worship at the start of each school day many schools would fail. How do schools know which rules are being applied and to what degree?

■ Head teachers who have been leading a school on three occasions when a school has been judged successful are credited with knowing what they are doing to a greater extent than inspectors who have not had that experience. These individuals could become the leaders of a self-regulating and monitoring profession.

■ Head teachers felt confident enough to ask for an inspection to help identify points of development as a part of a strategy to deliver the best for the pupils – and without, as Sir Michael states, fear or favour.

■ We set up an independent complaints authority. It cannot be right that complaints about inspection are dealt with internally.

I took my car for an MOT recently and when I collected it I was told it had passed. I was dismayed that there was no mention of outstanding features.

# … on teaching, pupils, and classrooms

It is all very simple, yet all very complex.

Teachers try to help pupils learn. That's the simple bit. The complex bit is created by the overlap of many of the issues discussed in this book. There is so much available for pupils to learn about and that the teacher could assist with in their chosen learning adventure. Yet society wants schools to teach certain things because it is more economic, more certain and more straightforward to 'leave it to the school'. The purpose of schooling has become to teach to pupils those things that society sees as important and beyond the scope of natural learning within family and community. The teacher therefore becomes a trans-mitter of prescribed learning. Tests and examinations measure the reception and from that we judge the effectiveness of the transmission.

Some pupils seem more able to receive the same transmission, due to aptitude, interest or ability. Society then wonders whether every pupil should learn the same things; whether we should offer a national enti-tlement or whether that is not relevant for all pupils. There must be some things that are relevant to every pupil – these are called basic expectations. As teachers transmit these basic expectations there are still those pupils who cannot seem to learn them. So how do we improve the transmission – the teaching? How do we improve the pupils and their readiness to learn?

We examine and test our pupils to check they are learning as they should be. We then make a cognitive leap in assuming that those that do well in tests and examinations are well taught. Those that do less well (in a group that generally does well) are deemed have particular needs because, after all, the group was well taught. Where a significant proportion does less well on tests and examinations, it is often argued not that they have more needs but that they have been less well taught. At the same time, society inspects its schools to check that they are as good as they could be at teaching. From this emerges a set of techniques that define good teaching – the things that teachers do to secure good results and inspection grades. Teachers are shown and implored to mimic these techniques yet still some pupils seem unable to learn sufficiently.

If all pupils improve year on year, then it is argued that the examinations must be getting easier. If we try to demonstrate what pupils have achieved by developing new courses and qualifications, it is thought that 'dubious' qualifications made the difference rather than the teaching. No one seems to apply the same illogical reasoning to sport. If the 100 metres record is broken it is seen as an achievement. No one accuses the track of being shorter than it used to be or the clock of ticking slower.

The result of game theory around testing and inspection is that what teachers are expected to teach narrows. Their successful practice becomes more closely defined. They are expected to teach to the test and perform as the inspection system requires them to. They become technicians rather than crafters; deliverers rather than nurturers. The true meaning of teaching is lost.

In truth, the role of the teacher in the schooling system was never that of the worldly wise counsellor who mentored the young on their serendipitous journey through life. The state, as a funder of schooling, believed that teachers would provide the learning necessary for its citizens and workforce, though not necessarily in that order. Over time, the teaching profession has promoted the view that the 'essentials' would emerge from their rounded approaches. It is only in the last forty years that the essentials have been questioned and refined and only more recently that we have accepted that some pupils are more advantaged than others. The solution to the lack of success in learning for many pupils is to ensure better teaching – the narrower, more technical sort. The way to ensure that is by accountability through examination and test results.

In recent times, the notion of accepting 'no excuses' has gained strength, as has the idea of putting pupils who could do well with teachers in schools that achieve better results, almost tacitly accepting that they should be separated from their fellows on the outside lanes. For teachers who work in the outside lanes, their daily challenge of inspiring the self-proclaimed un-inspirable pupil from the low aspirational communities they serve is a million miles away from those who work on the inside lane, inspiring the self-proclaimed certainties who will do well and see their learning as a bit of a chore but necessary to pass the wretched examinations. These teachers do important but different jobs, with different sorts of pupils, work from different starting points and background experiences, with different advantages and disadvantages and different images of success.

The job they do inside the classrooms is vital – teaching is 'the noble profession'. Seeing the work of the teacher in terms that move beyond the next lesson, the next examination or the next year, towards realising that pupils will, thirty years on, bring to mind moments of teaching in the blink of an eye, shows how crucial the role is. To influence positively a person's life many times over is surely the greatest challenge and accolade for educators.

Yet, immediately, here we move into the uncertain territory of the work and role of a teacher as defined by government and society. In 1862, the government brought in 'payment by results' where teachers were measured on pupil test scores, attendance and behaviour, and were paid accordingly. This was abandoned within twenty-five years because there were few teachers prepared to work with the poor and because of 'teaching to the test'. In general, teachers were trusted until Callaghan's Ruskin College speech of 1976 and their big pay rise of the same year. From there on the role and perception of the teacher in society changed.

As mentioned above, as secretary of state, Kenneth Baker decided that teachers would be made to work 1,265 hours per year. In doing so, he subtly made them into hourly paid workers. Margaret Thatcher later insisted that no teacher should be trained without a degree in a subject on the national curriculum. This did away with those free thinking '-ologies' and '-osophies' but it also did away with civil engineers, lawyers and architects who might have transferred to teaching as a career. Blair's 'education, education, education', really meant 'results, results, results' and, while resources improved dramatically, the Labour government got stuck trying to hit their own targets. Now we have Michael Gove stating that a high-level degree is essential for anyone seeking admission to a post-graduate training course, while simultaneously allowing academies to employ teachers without a teaching qualification.

The secretary of state does not seem to need others to contradict him as he is more than capable of doing it himself. His pronouncement that a teaching qualification is not essential in schools, while insisting on some very banal and obvious basic learning for pupils to be measured in tests, implies that teaching might require little more skill than the role of a machine operative. At the same time, David Cameron wants teachers to lead more clubs and after-school activities so that we produce more rounded citizens who won't riot and will win Olympic medals. As a teacher, the way to job security and career progression is through success in high-stakes assessment and inspection accountability. 1862 revisited?

Yet somehow the profession keeps going because it wants more than simply career progression. To be at the start of a conference for Warwickshire, Leicestershire and Coventry secondary school teachers as they embark on a weekend of dissemination and workshops to share their own classroom based learning and endeavour to improve their own practice, is to be in the furnace of professionalism. The Improving the Quality of Education for All (IQEA) programme that had been the original funded catalyst has long since gone but something stirs these teachers to try to move forward in their professional commitment. It is Friday evening, there are 200 teachers and dozens of workshops, all self managed. The enthusiasm is catching and heart warming.

If society could find a way to thank its teachers better, we might see a more valued profession and one that values itself a little more.

## ... on pupils

Again and again, the conversation about being a 'qualified' teacher is muddied by confusion about what knowledge a teacher needs. In secondary schools the emphasis falls on subject knowledge delivered by subject specialists, yet we all know that being knowledgeable in a discipline does not necessarily equate to being a good teacher. Too little is said on the importance of the subject of children, on the physiology, psychology and neurology of the child. This should be the specialist subject of all teachers. And this brings us to children.

In 1952, Virginia Apgar developed a very simple method of screening newborn babies to check whether they would thrive during the first few minutes of life. She took five basic vital signs (appearance, pulse, grimace, activity and respiration), measured the baby against each of those on a two-point scale and came up with the Apgar score – a score out of ten. If you ever see a documentary about childbirth set in a labour ward, within a minute after birth you'll hear someone say 'seven on the Apgar' or 'eight on the Apgar'. If the baby scores below four the staff know that they have some urgent work to do to enable the baby to thrive. This simple method was instituted across the developed world and has had a remarkable impact on the survival rate of newborns.

If we were to apply the same principles to children in school, we would identify five key vital signs that would show whether a child was likely to thrive or not. Try it. Think about the five things that would indicate whether a youngster, say in Year 5 or Year 8, was likely to flourish in school. The natural tendency is to think of those obvious factors like 'safe', 'be healthy', 'well-fed' and 'good sleep'. Let's take those for granted and leave them to one side and consider the five key areas that will help a child to thrive *in school*.

The next inclination is to think about things like 'independent', 'curious', 'take responsibility', 'enjoy themselves', 'be happy' and 'have high self-esteem', all of which are absolutely correct. But these are, in fact, second-order elements of thriving. They come about because other, more basic vital signs are in place. Just imagine talking to a Year 5 child who is not doing so well in school and saying, 'Now, if you want to do better, you need to be more confident' or 'Try to gain a little bit more self-esteem in order to do well' or 'I know you're not doing very well, in fact you're failing, but you need to try to be happy'. Now, all of these expressions are essentially correct but they are still second order. They come about because of the five key vital signs that *do* indicate whether a child will thrive as a learner.

First, there is the vital sign of *articulacy*, of literacy and numeracy. Without these key elements of competence children are unable to attack the curriculum. In fact, the curriculum will leave them behind from about Year 4. Articulacy is the key to opening doors to literacy and numeracy. If we look at the very youngest children in school, we see how the limits of their vocabulary, brought about by the constraints of their life experience, really come into play. Articulacy is the vital sign. Literacy and numeracy are themselves second order; it is just that, since schooling for all began, the 3Rs have been dominant. And because schooling began with the rich, it was taken for granted that they were articulate. We never reassessed the starting points when everyone began to go to school in 1870. In our system, young people with silver tongues tend to do well; those with leaden tongues tend to do poorly.

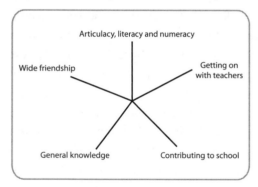

The second vital sign is a *wide general knowledge*. Children who succeed in school typically have a broad general knowledge. This has the impact of enabling them to be more articulate, literate and numerate, as well as giving them the confidence to engage in friendships. Equally, we know that children with a weak general knowledge struggle to build literacy and numeracy skills. General knowledge comes about through experience, conversation, reading and interests. It is fairly obvious to observe that the children who have the most experience are going to be the more successful.

The third vital sign relates to *wide friendships*. We know that children who do well in school are more likely to have wide friendship groups. Some children are loners and some children stick with their very closest friend. Families often remark on how some children are like 'blood sisters' or 'blood brothers' and how lovely it is. Well, it is delightful until the two children fall out and then neither of them has any friends. Easy friendships help children to thrive.

The fourth vital sign is *getting on with teachers*. Those children who do well in school have picked up on the subtle cues of how to succeed. They know that teachers carry enormous influence and, if you want to get on, it is a good idea to keep in their good books. Some pupils overdo it but most children who succeed realise that pleasing the teacher is one of the arts of doing well at school. If you think about going to a restaurant and having a good meal, one of the preconditions is quickly establishing some sort of rapport with the waiter or waitress. Upset them at your peril! Similarly, in the classroom some children do not realise that the teacher is somebody to get along with and work with in order to help you to succeed. Most children get it and hence they play the game of 'go along with the teacher', use the codes of classroom discourse and react appropriately to some of the more unlikely things they may be asked to do. Some don't seem to get it and react too honestly to the situations they meet. (How many of us tell the waiter that the food is average at best?) The children who don't cotton on are the ones who answer 'no' when asked if they like a story or ask why they have to do things; the reactions they get can gradually lead to them being seen as 'a problem'.

The fifth vital sign is *making a contribution to school*. Children who contribute are more likely to do well. Contribution can be taking part in school teams, choirs or performances – those bigger things that typically get recognised. Contribution can equally be participating in the school council, representing the school on visits abroad or taking part in residential visits. At the smaller level, contribution might be such things as getting the school hall ready for assembly, looking after the goldfish, watering the plants or tending the school gardens. Whatever it is, and at whatever level, those children who contribute will make more progress than those who don't get involved in school life.

Pupils who have all these vital signs will typically do well in most schools. They will thrive – whatever their social background, whatever their place on the track. Where the vital signs are less prominent, their chances reduce.

Taking forward this notion of vital signs for successful learning, consider the following profiles with the image of individual pupils in mind.

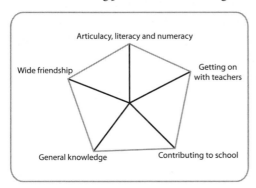

We will call them all 'he' for ease. Let's start with the well-rounded pupil, the one about whom there would be little concern. These are the thrivers, raring to go because the vital signs are in place.

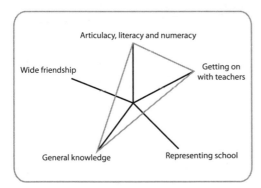

Then look at this one. He is very articulate, has lots of general knowledge and loves to please the teacher. As for friends, he is a loner and he doesn't join in very much around school.

Quickly these pupils are seen as different and acquire names such as swat, boffin, geek or teacher's pet. They are the compliant and able, happy to do tasks for which they get teacher praise even though they make little sense.

Next we get the pupil who struggles with knowledge and articulacy and, partly because of that, has fewer friends. He does like to please

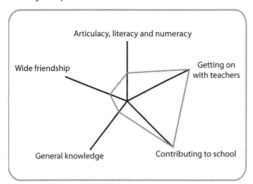

though and will always do any job required. These are the 'happy helpers': 'Please can I clean the art area?' 'Do you need the PE store tidied?' 'Any litter to collect?'

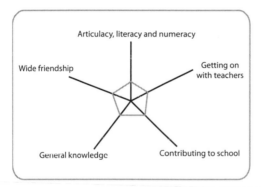

Here is the pupil about whom there would be enormous worry; the entire opposite of well-rounded.

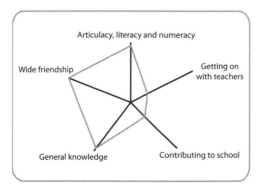

Last, let's look at the pupil who has endless friendships, is able in terms of general knowledge and is very articulate. He is, though, one of those who has no concern to please the teacher or any interest in contributing to school. These individuals offer a different sort of challenge. They are the 'in spite of' pupils who can drive their teachers to distraction. They seem perverse and can create mayhem with their ability to play on words, use innuendo and can start off their friends in convulsive giggling as they enjoy the poem for reasons other than those intended. Many would call these pupils 'trouble.'

Each of these profiles carries with it the need to think carefully about how we help individual children to meet their potential and develop their capacity to thrive. The child who has no friends should not simply be recorded as a loner and thereby treated as such. Instead they can be encouraged by the artful teacher to take part in activities with others in order that they develop the capacity to make friendships. The astute teacher persuades the loner to help another child carry a bench in the hope that on the way back from the activity they will simply talk to each other. The subtle management of groups in the classroom gives the opportunity for children to work together and sort out the organisation of the work they are doing amongst themselves. Clever teachers know that by moving their pupils around they can contribute to their growing understanding of their capacity to work with each other. Good teachers know how to help a pupil become more articulate – and it isn't by asking challenging questions in front of the whole class.

This type of profile creates a simple a way of assessing pupils and understanding why they might be thriving or not in school. We shouldn't read too much into the profiles or use them as anything other than a light shedder. However, it is possible to create a grid for every pupil in a class or form group on an A3 sheet of paper. Thirty minutes to complete a profile for each pupil will give a quick overview and highlight those individuals who need different sorts of help to thrive. Give the help and redo the profiles in eight weeks time and compare them with the previous set. A picture of ongoing strength and need quickly builds up without the necessity for endless sheets of record-keeping. Try it; teachers have found it illuminating, useful and worthwhile.

Of course, seeing who is thriving is just one aspect of trying to teach well. We need to *help* the pupils to thrive. So what can we do? The point about children having different outlooks goes back to the concept of the running track without the staggered start. The disposition of pupils towards their learning and their concept of school is a vital aspect of eventual success. The problem of labelling is well understood yet it persists as a negative phenomenon. Politicians and others are right to question the allowances made for children's backgrounds – the excuses for lower performance. Michael Gove talks of 'fatalists' who believe that pupils from poor backgrounds will not succeed. We categorise children (and adults) as 'bright', 'quick', 'sharp' or 'slow', 'dim', 'dense' – and the labels stick. The more our children are pigeonholed, the more they act like the label says they should.

Labels are often linked to attainment. I have been to many schools where results matter. As chief education officer in Manchester, I would spend time in schools where we were desperate for improved results to lift the city from the relegation zone in the league tables. Heads, for all the right reasons, would point out a Year 11 pupil and say something like 'He's a predicted five A–C'. We would then check ourselves and remind ourselves of important things like his talents, aspirations, personality and name. I know primary schools where children are referred to as the 'borderline Level 5s' or 'the secure Level 5s', which admittedly shows good knowledge of the children in terms of test outcomes and what we need to do to raise scores, but fails to acknowledge their unique qualities. These children then get appropriate work to lift their test performance. At the other end of the scale are the 'Level 3s' in Years 6 and 7. These children are Level 3 in terms of tests in *some* aspects of learning. What happens, however, is that they are given appropriate Level 3 work in mathematics and in English and, almost unthinkingly, Level 3 conversation and Level 3 opportunities. They start to live a Level 3 life and when they are tested again, guess what they score? Level 3. See, we were right all along.

One thing that marks out good hospitals from poor ones is the way staff behave towards patients. In poor hospitals patients are treated as though they are poorly; in good hospitals patients are treated as though they are going to be well. In schools we need to behave towards our pupils as though they are going to learn and achieve.

If you work in a school you might like to try one of my favourite sessions with pupils. Because labelling matters – and it is good for students to understand the concept – I go around the cupboards at home and find labels from packaging, tins and jars. I place the labels on tables in front of groups of pupils and ask them if they can remember feeling like this. The conversation is hard to stop. It is great personal, health and social education. Have a look at some of the labels and imagine the conversations.

Try it yourself. When have you felt fragile or inflammable? In this country we have an obsession with children being the 'right way up' to teach them. It started in Victorian times, when the confines of space and the need for stillness meant that children had to sit in a yoga position with arms and legs crossed. Teaching a group is still easier if the class sits still because it reduces distraction and enables the teacher to focus on transmission (we have all seen the infant assembly where the wriggler sets the rest off and the throng on the floor soon resembles a tin of maggots). Anyone with a teenager of their own knows that they can lie on the sofa, doing their hair, watching TV, working on their handheld and answering a phone call while reading a magazine. Turn the TV off and they get upset because 'they were watching that'. People today multi-task easily yet, for the most part, we still expect pupils to be doing one thing at a time, especially when *we* are talking. What we also know is that protocols matter and there are certain times when it is considerate to others to be 'the right way up'. At a concert or the theatre there are customs that help the performance to work. Similarly, in the classroom there are conventions that allow the teacher to transmit and others around you to learn.

A most telling label is 'best before'. Our education system seems built on the notion that people have a 'best before' date for their learning. Teaching is a strange activity: we start off with children who know little and then we teach them until they announce they can't do it. When children announce in Year 8 that they 'can't do history' or they are 'no good at art', or an adult says that 'languages are not my thing', they are labelling themselves based on their experiences. Most were alright once. They simply reach a point when they perceive they are out of their depth, when they believe they have reached their limit, when they fall off the greasy pole never to clamber back on again.

How many pupils have you met where the learning sediment needed to be stirred? Those children who exclaim that their learning is 'boring', rather than applying themselves to the challenge, are held down by that sediment.

How many schools have something in their mission statement about all pupils 'achieving their full potential'? If we want them to be the biggest learners possible, we need to 'pump them up'. Then they get 'bouncy'. Bouncy pupils are a challenge in many schools. Who hasn't sat in the staffroom and heard someone remark, 'The children are very bubbly today'? Someone else replies, 'That'll be the wind.' The instruction when they get bubbly is to 'keep the lid on' and 'hold it down'. We need to survive until the next pause and eventually get to the end of the day. But surely we need excited, bubbly, energetic youngsters who are striving to extend limits. We just have to use the labels to help them learn about protocols rather than themselves.

This use of labels matters because it can define whether children will succeed or not over time. Pupils usually exhibit the negative labels because of other factors in their life, not least their position on the track. Those in the outside lanes are likely to feel less confident about some aspects of life than those on the inside lanes. A teenager who cares for mum before and after coming to school might not carry the label 'effervescent'. When reprimanded for the wrong shade of uniform, the label might just turn to 'highly flammable'. The classifications need to help us to think how we can help youngsters to learn.

So, given all these different pupils and their many different outlooks, how should we teach in order to achieve our hopes for our young? What should happen in classrooms?

## ... on classrooms

If we stepped into an Early Years setting, most adults would be expecting to see the children enjoying and working with the sort of equipment mentioned in the panel below.

---

### WHAT NEEDS TO BE DONE BY THE CHILDREN

mirrors, material, plants, boxes, candles, wood, fish, mud, paint, sand, smiles, songs, space, pictures, hats, bricks, stories, friends, bubbles, dark, dragons, straw, silence, toys, sunshine, steps, dolls, letters, eggs, dough, puppets, tomatoes, tickets, balls, buckets, mobiles, maps, patterns, pedals, music, seashells, dinosaurs, wheels, lights, flowers, ladders, laptops, clocks, maps, rhymes, hats, bubbles, masks, flowers, words, books, words, books, words, books, words, books, worlds

---

This is where the school seizes on natural interests and brings learning alive in a context that meets the child where they are: in childhood. The adults know that it doesn't matter much whether the children meet straw before they meet mud, or sand or dough or sawdust. What we are doing is extending the children's sensory experiences. When children are asked what they are doing, they often reply with the name of the equipment: 'eggs', 'tomatoes' or 'worms'. The adults know that what we are really trying to do is extend the children in terms of the skills in the panel below.

## WHAT NEEDS TO BE DONE BY THE CHILDREN

appreciate, observe, record, measure, manage, hypothesise, test,
perform, discriminate, create, exhibit, illustrate, exemplify, compose,
serve, mix, investigate, connect, debate, discuss, note, argue, control,
present, prove, demonstrate, define, persuade, produce, differentiate,
design, practise, find out, make, argue, plan, devise, generate, mend,
try, connect, interpret, know, translate, wonder, reject, exercise,
books, words, books, words, books, words, worlds

These are all terms from the Early Years profile and national curriculum expectations. Good teachers know that we make the learning matter by associating with the age and experience of the child and exploiting the skills in context. As the children get older, so the skills might be made more explicit but, essentially, if we want children to learn skills they have to use equipment.

In the Early Years, adults know that steps and pedals matter because of the child's need to explore and feel new sensations, but also because gross motor skills encourage balance and have been linked to cognitive development. We are not asking children to do hammering because they are on the first rung of training to be a carpenter but because hand-to-eye coordination is vital; the understanding of the resistance of certain materials will develop over time. All of these experiences with equipment will extend the child and offer opportunity for that most vital area of development: language and articulacy.

Taking this forward into Key Stage 2 and 3, what equipment might we expect pupils to be using in order to extend the learning required in the national curriculum?

## WHAT NEEDS TO BE DONE BY THE CHILDREN

microscopes, xylophones, compasses, wood, brushes, mirrors, maps,
scales, plants, trowels, screens, rulers, charcoal, rocks, calculators,
stamps, pipettes, lenses, prints, stages, mats, glue, hammers, arenas,
pictures, spanners, pots, chemicals, creatures, dials, microphones,
tapes, eggs, aquariums, landscapes, relics, specimens, ladders,
costumes, discoveries, frames, cameras, keys, needles, balances,
books, words, books, words, books, words, books, words, books, worlds

Now comes the crunch. Where in the Early Years it would be common
to see various apparatus being used frequently, as children get older the
equipment comes out less. Given the aims of our schools, we might
expect that classrooms, laboratories and studios would abound with
activity – with equipment in use virtually all the time. But classrooms
are becoming drier. There is less experimentation, less mess, less paint.
There are fewer occasions when pupils naturally turn to equipment
and there are numerous reasons for this. The perceived formulaic
nature of each session means there is little time for the use of equipment by pupils, especially if they have not used it before. The need to
record work as evidence also means the time for doing anything practical reduces. After allowing for learning objective writing and a couple
of plenaries to discuss progress, what time is left for actually doing
anything? Yet in the so-called real world, people turn naturally to
equipment and less towards writing – and the writing they do is of
many different types. Should we typically see pupils using equipment
for most of the time if we drop in to a classroom? Classrooms are not
as busy as they might be because two things happen as children grow:
they sit still and they learn to write.

# The clerical burden

I often think that, if I had my time again, I would pretend that I couldn't write. Once teachers know that you can write they make you do more and more of it. The clerical burden takes over and other doorways to learning seem to close around you. Not that there is anything wrong with writing; it is just that it should serve a real purpose.

While visiting a secondary school in the south of England to lead a discussion about approaches to teaching and learning, I was given a whistle-stop tour of the school by one of the senior leadership team. We set off twenty minutes after the afternoon session had begun and we peered into many classrooms through the windows in the door, popped into others or passed through some on the way to others. Nobody seemed to mind, though it was hardly an in-depth observation; less of a learning walk and more of a learning sprint.

At the sixteenth classroom we ground to a halt because something unusual was happening. This was the first classroom on the journey where the pupils were not engaged in a clerical task. In every classroom until now they had been either writing or reading or both. Now, the proportion might not have been representative; it might have been just that day or the fact that another route would have revealed a different picture. We had, though, passed through music, food technology, drama, physics and art. Whatever, in that twenty-minute spasm, the 300-plus pupils we saw were not, on balance, having a rounded learning experience. We might ask ourselves how typical this situation might be.

# Proper learning

If we think we are teaching fledgling artists, budding linguists, growing historians, emerging geographers, starter scientists and tentative technologists, should they not begin to use the tools of the trade? Would there not be more to write about if pupils had actually done something practical to take them forward? Would learning be more relevant and attractive if it focused on the real world, the big issues of subject disciplines and the world of work? The more learning becomes a treadmill through the course book or the plod to the examination, the more it loses vibrancy.

Good teaching in all subjects might in fact simply be a list of verbs and nouns that bring learning to life and provide the vehicle for relevant mathematics, relevant English and relevant theoretical understanding.

---

## THE NOUN AND VERB APPROACH TO LEARNING

Tent pitched, xylophone played, model tested, song sung,
play acted, fabric sewn, local community enhanced, fire lit,
flowers and vegetables grown, foreign language spoken,
poem appreciated, website constructed, meal cooked,
weather recording taken, armistice remembered, body exercised,
bearing set, artefact explored, film viewed, photograph snapped,
map interpreted, old people valued, dance composed,
money accumulated, long shore drift measured, pot thrown,
bouquet arranged, tickets ordered, bird spotted,
constellation observed, wall built, spirit lifted, book read, story written,
LESSONS LEARNT

---

If pupils took part in activities like these they would be covering the principles of most subject disciplines in a context that would bring alive big ideas and detailed understanding. Indeed, if we want pupils to be literate, then we need to offer, as much as possible, real literature in real situations. There is a massive difference between the use of the literature in the panel below for real reasons and the experience of many pupils of doing exercises with disembodied pieces of text.

## WHAT NEEDS TO BE READ BY THE CHILDREN

journals, diaries, novels, obituaries, almanacs, logs, inventories, ledgers, documents, plans, autobiographies, reports, agreements, plays, conveyances, summons, invitations, replies, summaries, critiques, reviews, eulogies, fixtures, indexes, bibliographies, parodies, comedies, tragedies, treaties, religious texts, menus, manifestos, promises, pledges, poems, comics, constitutions, screens, manuals, dictionaries, recipes, newspapers, timetables, books, words, books, words, books, words, books, worlds

Most teachers want to organise a more vibrant, embedded sort of learning for their pupils. Many get a long way towards it with a learning experience for pupils that oozes with activities. Animated films, camping expeditions, fieldwork, gardens, weather stations, international visits and performances are the sorts of experiences that draw young people towards learning. Basic principles, knowledge and concepts have be taught, practised and learned, and who better to transmit these things than the accomplished learner who is the teacher? It is balance that matters. Too much desk-based repetition will turn most pupils, except the teacher-pleasers and the swats, into those with learning sediment.

Over the last twenty years, the technology revolution has brought the possibility of many more innovative approaches. A few years ago all teachers were trained on the use of the interactive whiteboard, an investment that was set to revolutionise teaching techniques and classroom approaches. Somehow it didn't work in many classrooms; gradually many teachers have stopped using it to its full potential.

The profession seems to suck innovation into its current 'story'. Because schools are subject to a scrutiny that they see as demanding a formula that values 'traditional' approaches, there is a tendency to use new technology to achieve old expectations rather than do something very different. Hence many teachers and pupils now talk about the 'whiteboard' rather than the 'interactive whiteboard'. The whiteboard is used as an old-fashioned but electronic 'blackboard and chalk'.

Similarly, in spite of the millions spent on technology to create and offer 'interactive learning platforms', many classroom approaches remain stubbornly attached to a bygone era. Fear of getting it wrong, losing control, not being in charge, looking haphazard or being too open-ended – especially in the scrutiny of inspection – are all reasons offered for not using the potential of interactive learning. It is rather like not using windscreen wipers or declining to use the parking aids on modern cars.

## EFFECTIVE INTERACTIVE LEARNING PLATFORMS

• a piano keyboard • a nature table • a chess board
• an ordnance survey map • an artist's palette • a garden • a cooker hob
• a dance floor • a screen print frame • a gym mat • test tube
• a loaded book shelf • an e-tablet

Put a group of pupils around any of these with an informed and knowledgeable adult and the opportunity for profitable interaction is enormous. What if every adult in schools were trained to use at least four of these platforms well?

What stops teachers bringing the learning alive includes a range of factors. The pressure of accountability, with the ever-looming tests and examinations, is one and in turn this leads to practice and rehearsal of those very tests and examinations, which implies that these are the point of being at school. 'Past papers' is probably the most studied subject in Year 11 across the country. In Year 6 the practising of past papers becomes a given in the planning for most children's learning.

How much time it takes and how it is done make such a difference because poorly done past-paper practice simply reinforces failure or success; it's that labelling problem again.

Another inhibiting factor of good teaching is the prospect of inspection, although Ofsted has always supported practical application and memorable experiences. Similarly, Ofsted theme reports on subject disciplines, now called Survey Reports, have constantly highlighted the lack of dynamic, practical application of big ideas and bemoan the tedium of the exercising slog.

As discussed in the previous section, the root of the problem is game theory. Many teachers feel inhibited about being creative, practical and imaginative because they believe the schooling system values most the high performance lesson and the evidence of 'work'. The school has to run well, so the timetable must be sharp and time becomes the main arbiter of quality for outside viewers. Most of the activities listed in the panels above cannot be managed successfully, or have the necessary impact, in a 50-minute or even a 100-minute session. The secondary teacher who wants to take pupils on an education visit risks the wrath of at least three other colleagues who will miss their 50-minute chance to top up the exercising trudge. Timetables start from the time available and work outwards; couldn't they start from the learning we wish to achieve and work inwards?

In game theory, the work that pupils produce is seen as 'evidence'. For most schools it still seems easier to ask pupils to work in traditional exercise books as the main form of record. The course textbook is the primary vehicle for study. Add these two items to the timetabled slots and a dreary tone for learning is set. Recording risks being perfunctory and recall and practice dominate. Volume of work becomes important evidence of attention, understanding and effort.

One of the positive aspects of the new inspection framework is that inspectors now look at literacy across the curriculum and across the learning spectrum. This means that schools might ask themselves what the pupils are actually going to do and then plan the range of products they will work on during an academic year. As an example,

here is a planning list from a school in Doncaster where the work of
Year 7 was under consideration:

## SOME PRODUCTS FOR THE SCHOOL YEAR

- three pieces of extended writing of more than 1,000 words
- six pieces of writing of 500 words or more
- four letters – two imaginary, two real • three powerpoint presentations
- four stories • two reports • two humorous pieces of writing
- three posters (not the rules of the lab)
- three maps – of which two are real • four charts • five plans
- one individual presentation • two presentations as part of a group
- three annotated photo sheets • one quiz
- one partridge in a pear tree (just playing!)

## NOT FORGETTING NUMERACY

- two precise measuring tasks • two near-enough measurings
- two estimations – one big numbers, one small • two weigh-ins
- two shape activities • two speed measurements

## PRODUCTS LINKED TO OTHER SUBJECT DISCIPLINES

- two working models (with others) • two dances • two portraits
- two still lifes • one sculpture • one thing bigger than me
- one meal cooked with a group of five • five experiments
- three experiences of real artefacts or proper places

There is the underlying assumption that, to win the game, there is a silver bullet to be found, and that the high performance lesson is the key. Most new approaches are effective for a time; youngsters love novelty and will go along with anything for a change. Even the formulaic lesson works for a while and is certainly better than an unplanned shambles. But the three-part, five-part, diamond-shaped or spiral lesson will only have an impact for so long unless other things are in place, especially something interesting to learn about.

In the Black Country, a group of schools set out to explore what would make a difference in terms of attainment, attitude and achievement. They tried various techniques, evaluated impact and shared solutions. What they realised was that there is no one solution but more a whole blunderbuss of approaches that makes a difference. The list below summarises the approaches they used to effect better outcomes. These headlines summarise hundreds of hours of planning and work. Every strategy has been tried somewhere but the items listed indicate what made a collective difference. All of the schools involved had seen progress in terms of the 'raising standards' agenda. They also saw improvements in terms of pupil attitude and parent engagement.

## FEATURES OF IMPROVING SCHOOLS

- accept the testing/curriculum divide • improve feedback to learners
- consult the learners at every stage • pursue coherent themes in learning
- deploy teachers in teams • extend sessions – end five starts a day
- revamp homework • reconsider the use of exercise books
- enjoy articulacy and mathematicality
- focus on the real world and the news • vitalise assembly • exploit ICT
- use non-teaching staff better • resist ritual learning objectives
- coordinate products • provide audiences • keep assessment in its place
- talk about jobs/careers • use artefacts • visits and people
- talk about talent and vigour • encourage panache • enjoy childhood

Most of the list is self-explanatory. Reviewing the use of exercise books made a huge difference where the range of product was expected to be wide. The use of teaching assistants to ensure that pupils were being assisted to learn, rather than remaining a struggler, meant a change of practice for many. Using the news and the world of work as a regular source of stimulus for learning was vital. Accepting the curriculum and assessment divide – thereby helping pupils to see that testing was a specific experience and to be addressed almost as a separate project rather than it filling every waking moment of anticipation – was crucial.

The issue of lesson objectives, learning objectives, WILFs (What I'm Looking For) and WALTs (We Are Learning To) was fascinating. Because of the pressure of inspection and the perceived need to state objectives, some of the schools had set the expectation that objectives must be recorded for every session. The leadership team were insistent: it would provide evidence. In practice, the tendency is for pupils to routinely write down these objectives at the start of the lesson, but over time the sense of it can disappear and it all takes longer and longer. I have watched children take so long to write down their objectives that they have to stop to note down their homework tasks because the lesson is nearly over. Hence, the lesson consisted of them writing down what they would have learned, if they'd had time, followed by what to do at home to follow up what they would have done in the lesson if time allowed! I measured some objectives and calculated the average length of written lesson objectives in a primary school career: 2,300 metres. A mile and half of writing built on the myth that someone is going to downgrade your teaching if you don't do it!

The top item on the list in terms of importance is the one on articulacy and mathematicality (a made-up word). Each school had a real push on pupil-talk and this involved talking about mathematics – all day, every day, in every subject. There were four key focus areas: micro and macro numbers, estimation, measurement and bonds. With these under discussion everywhere, and in every subject discipline, mathematics became less clerical and more active, involved more conjecture and was more vital and interesting.

So, there is no silver bullet but there are still a few maxims for good teaching. Find an interesting way of teaching it. Make it practical. Create an audience as real as possible. Make it matter to the pupil. These are all things that typically bring learning alive. 'Watch this, write it down and mark it' do not typically turn on young people's learning. Good teaching has always contained an element of *'Je ne sais quoi'*!

At the root of the challenge is the concept of work. In the teaching profession, work is enacted through someone else's volition. The quality of teaching is also evidenced through the work of someone else. When a pupil is asked to 'get on with your work', the reality is that it is *our* work that is usually being produced. The class is working to produce twenty-five copies of a textbook answer as evidence of the teaching they have received. We differ greatly from the medical profession, where a patient receives some medicine or surgery and generally responds. Only in the case of mental illness does volition on the part of the patient require the doctor's efforts to succeed. In teaching, the best teacher can perform at a high level but we still need the learner to engage fully. The children who can suspend belief and play the game, usually but not always from the inside of the track, have a greater chance of success in the way we measure it. But we must do more to better measure success in learning. That, though, takes us back to examinations and tests, and all the portents there are bad.

## … on classroom talk

What children really need is very simple. They need someone to go places with, somebody to talk with, to open their eyes, to create some new environments and plan experiences. As very young children they are lucky if they have an adult who makes the difference – a parent or grandparent or one of those influential others.

Sadly, too many children lack this basic opportunity and therefore they turn to teachers as their most significant route to learning. In classrooms we have some fascinating things to talk about but they are also full of unreal conversations and bizarre questions. Being able to recall information generally dominates what children talk about; analysis, synthesis and conjecture are less prevalent. Classroom talk is frequently dominated by the ones who can talk the most; therefore the ones who can't talk very much and who need the practice get less chance to do it. And, of course, the one who can talk the most of all is the teacher. Teacher-talk is just amazing. It is completely unnatural and yet it has evolved over a century and a half to create a situation that is unbelievably odd. Nowhere is the bewildering game of teacher-talk demonstrated more clearly than in classrooms where some children 'get it' and a proportion, perhaps some 15%, can't work out what is going on and therefore can't play the game.

Classrooms must be the only places where the person with all the information asks questions of people who know very little about the topic. Furthermore, the person with the information also dominates the way in which the questions are asked in terms of order or perceived complexity. Those listening and trying to answer, without very much knowledge, are bemused and bewildered and become seen as knowledgeable based on their capacity to persist in engaging with the bewildering.

We will all recognise the scene in assembly where the teacher at the front holds up a common object like a drinking glass and asks the gathered throng, 'Who can tell me what I'm holding?' The straightforward answer is: 'You can tell us what you're holding because you know it is a glass.' Most children know this is purely a game that we play in school to try to keep the point of the assembly going. At the front the little ones stretch their arms upwards and strain to answer. Further back there is a resigned effort at answering. At the very back of the room there are the propped up arms of Year 6s who are muttering under their breath that they've 'seen this one many times before' and 'it'll be that assembly about whether you're a half-empty or half-full person'. Of course, what the teacher really wants is for somebody to talk about the fact that they are holding a glass with some water in it. They don't want an analysis of how the glass is made – its origin in sand or that it has been shaped by a machine or blown by a glassblower.

They simply want one word to keep the story going. So the question is not really a question. It is simply a device to keep attention.

What must children think when teachers ask questions like, 'What colour shirt are you wearing?' or 'What colour coat is that?' Most children know it is a game, a little checking-up practice, but others must just wonder why. Imagine the scene as a four-year-old runs into school and says to the teacher, 'I've got new shoes' and we look down and says, 'Aren't they beautiful? What colour are they?' Some must surely think, 'But you're forty-odd years old and you've been doing colours with us since last September. Are you saying you didn't know all along?' It isn't normal.

We also get the situation where teachers set children work to do and after fifteen minutes, because of the need to demonstrate progress, we gather them round for an instant plenary, the first question being, 'Who can tell me what we've been doing for the last fifteen minutes?' Again, most children get it but there must be a proportion thinking, 'This is odd. You planned it, you organised it, you told us what to do and now you're asking us what we've been doing. Do you have short-term memory loss?' When you think about it, they are the intelligent ones, but they can very quickly be considered difficult if they voice their perfectly rational thoughts.

Much of the work of Philosophy for Children has been about how to enable better classroom discourse to take place. The brilliant work of Jean Gross as the communications tsar began the process of encouraging adults in classrooms to reconsider the way in which children are involved in conversations and encouraged to speak. The methodology of 'mantle of the expert' – developed over many years by Dorothy Heathcote and carried forward by people who saw its potential and impact – relies on putting children, in role, into situations which rely on their ability to think, make decisions and take action. To do so, they must hold real conversations, exchange knowledge, find new information and write with purpose. Sadly, much of the emphasis on outstanding teaching involves 'challenging questions' and teachers end up forcing engagement with children through the questions they ask.

Furthermore, it misses the point that so much of what is discussed in classrooms is abnormal.

## ... on classroom environments

The classroom is where teaching happens. It might be called a lab or a gym, a studio or suite, a library or a workshop, but in the end it is the theatre of teaching and learning dreams inside the school.

We all know that classrooms should be organised and tidy because workshops work best when they are tidy. However, classrooms should also be full of work in progress. Classrooms should be places where demonstration and practice can take place. Classrooms should be places where individuals can work alone or in groups. Classrooms should be fit for purpose and speak to the learner about what matters in the learning process. Classrooms matter.

In classrooms, as in other areas of education, a few mentions in Ofsted inspection reports on so-called 'outstanding classrooms' will soon set a vogue in teachers' practice around the system. One of the trends of recent years has been the move towards 'working walls'. Clearly, it isn't a bad thing to put up on the wall a few things that might help us in our day-by-day needs. Once the technique has a name, though, there's no stopping it. Some classrooms are now inundated with the laminated world of the working wall. In fact, had Building Schools for the Future continued, some builders were thinking of producing a prefabricated version of the working wall ready for each year group to save the teachers the trouble.

Gradually, rooms are covered with words: the days of the week, the months of the year, 'common' words, sometimes subdivided into connectives, conjunctions and verbs or showing prefixes and suffixes. Mathematical words also appear along with random symbols. We see words that link with the latest focus of study: 'cycle' and 'water' appear, 'volcano' explodes onto the scene or phrases like 'turrets and tiaras' materialise (presumably for children who swear uncontrollably or like fine jewellery). A punctuation pyramid might show up, usually as a triangle; no wonder there is trouble in mathematics. Is the accepted wisdom that sitting near this pyramid will help children to use a semi-colon or that they will suddenly jump up and shout 'Goodness gracious!' after an hour by the exclamation mark? Then there are VCOP and wow words, anything as long as we can laminate it. I have recently seen classrooms where even the ceiling is filling up with words. Pity the children: they won't even know which way up they are. This is when learning gets really disorientating!

All of these strategies have value but they need to be used appropriately. The problem is that many teachers think that the working wall (or whatever) is one of the only ways they can demonstrate their efforts to the brief onlookers. However, unless they are used well, and used consistently, they serve little purpose except to fill the walls, and before long they are simply decoration. And with every bit of pub-lisher-produced and laminated wall-filling product, the space for pupils' own work reduces.

If we want children to feel that they are part of the learning process, that they are finding knowledge and have something to share and contrib-ute, the clever use of the wall and the rest of the learning environment is essential. A child's piece of work, carefully framed, even by the child herself, hung properly and used as an object of interest can enable oth-ers and build self-worth and achievement in the child; remember the importance of the child contributing to the school.

Over the years there has been much talk about classroom displays. We have moved on from the beauty parades of the primary classrooms in the 1960s with triple mounting and drapes. Ironically, secondary schools are now often better than primaries at using the environment to reinforce learning. The use and quality of pupil work displays around secondary schools is becoming a noticeable feature as teachers and students learn to appreciate each other's efforts.

All we need to do is refer to three principles for anything that is on display in a school classroom. Does the artefact answer one of these three questions well?

- What is it? (curiosity, interest, motivation)
- Whose is it? (valuing and self-esteem)
- Isn't it ...? (add beautiful, inspiring, clever, ingenious, odd, gruesome, neat, etc.)

Add good displays to a well-organised and well-disciplined physical environment and learning has a chance.

## What do good teachers do to make the classroom work?

- Make the environment talk of learning. Big ideas, constructs and concepts, examples of pupil work, what famous people have done, snapshots of knowledge, pupil work well used – all in a well-organised workshop environment that pupils should be able to manage themselves.

- Believe in quality. Good teachers talk about quality all the time. They get pupils to understand the processes involved in producing a great piece of writing, a good sculpture or tasty meal. They talk about when it has to be right first time, the importance of accuracy when it matters and near-enough when it is appropriate. They talk about delivering polish and panache at the right moment.

- Bring the world into range. The internet opens doors into the world beyond the classroom. A few minutes a day looking at something current, relevant, big in the news or just fascinating is worth talking about. The beauty of books that do the same should not be forgotten. The visit and the visitor to the school can make learning make sense because children see it in context. These sorts of things make the abstract seem worth persevering with.

- Know that assembly, form time and tutor time matter. These are occasions that can be lost or frittered away, yet well used they become pivotal moments in the routine of teaching. They offer chances to share together, enjoy success, work on challenging problems, be fascinated and celebrate.

■ Create limelight for every child. There are children in the school system who seem never to get noticed. Go back to the grids that show whether children are making a contribution in school. Some are never in a team, a choir, a band or a debate. They never get asked to sort out the cupboard, feed the fish or water the plants. They never collect money for Poppy Day and they never meet the mayor. Some get so fed up with this that they do bad things just to be seen. Surely every child should at some point be acknowledged, applauded, celebrated, praised or recognised by their fellows. Every child should experience the limelight on themselves.

■ Laugh. Schools are funny places and funny things happen. We shouldn't be afraid to enjoy them.

■ See the best in their pupils and believe in unconditional learning. It matters that a child has never successfully read a page, sung a song, painted a picture, written a report, built a model, read a map, sewn a costume or completed an experiment. It matters that maths is the biggest conundrum of all. It matters that a child is uncoordinated, can't be quiet, is too quiet, sings all the time or can't be bothered. It matters; but it doesn't matter so much that the teacher gives up on the child.

## … on teachers

Teachers are amazing people. The vast majority are extremely committed to the pupils they teach and believe they are part of the development of society. They enjoy being with young people and seeing them grow. They grapple with the challenge of making the world make sense to youngsters, whatever their background. However, many of them are worn out and many more are caught in a game they don't fully understand.

Most teachers believe they trained to help pupils learn and to teach interesting things, but instead they find they are slaves to targets, results and the data that goes with it. Their working life is spent getting ready for, or getting over, the latest observation by someone who was inspecting or performance managing. They hear endless criticism of the schooling system in the media. Somehow the joy of being an educator is evaporating. Yet a day in school with the children is often everything they would want.

Over time, teachers have become pawns in a bigger game, to the extent that they are less clear about their role.

The subtle undermining of professionalism referred to at the beginning of this section can lead to teachers seeing themselves as technicians. What used to be a profession with real integrity is now often regarded as a technical job. We use phrases like 'delivering' or 'covering' the curriculum rather than planning the learning adventure. The rules change so often and the frequent demands of government mean constant readjustment and coping with something new. The constant observation leads to the reassurance of positive feedback, but also to the unwelcome feeling of needing to be told about our own competence. The endless training subtly leads teachers to believe that they are never quite up to speed.

Teach First is different. Just ten years ago, Teach First began with the intention of encouraging those leaving top universities to 'teach first' in a school in a deprived community for a couple of years, before heading off to a lucrative and challenging career elsewhere. As the next ten years begins, the programme has expanded into many depressed areas of the country and is intent on achieving impact goals that help to close the gap. Many individuals have stayed the course beyond the first two years and some are now school leaders.

Meeting Teach First teachers can be illuminating. Typically they believe they make a positive difference. They bring a confidence from their background and success (see the section on unleashing aspiration below) and many have had a major impact in their schools, some of which have employed several Teach First teachers as catalysts for progress. They have given the pupils self-esteem by the very fact that they are prepared to spend time with them. They are naturally committed to social equity. They work hard and economically. They often claim that they are struggling – which implies that they are also humble and better than they assert. They always state that they are going to get stronger as a teacher. They have such an affirmative image that most start two notches up the observation pole. It is a genuine phenomenon.

Might this be linked to the way Teach First teachers are recruited? They are *sold* teaching; they are told that teaching needs them and that they are of vital importance. They start with the belief that they are doing good for the system and will be valued and rewarded for doing so. They are informed that they are superior and so need less formal training than other teachers. They are almost guaranteed promotion if they stay the course. In speeches, politicians single out Teach First graduates as being a success story in the face of general failure from other teachers. This is a significant difference. It could be that building confidence in Teach First candidates has created more capable teachers. We should be trying some of the same techniques with all teachers.

So how can we get this same buzz around teachers recruited from other routes? Most have aspiration for their pupils, their schools and themselves. How do we build their belief in themselves as they enter schools so often fearful of their future?

Teaching School alliances offer one route to the provision of high quality learning opportunities for pupils. Typically, these teaching schools are developing new techniques to help fledgling teachers to fly. They match trainees to settings, ensuring highly effective mentoring and coaching and making rigorous self-analysis part of the routine of training. An alliance in the north of Birmingham is being truly innovative in, among other things, exploiting technology and helping trainee teachers to experience the entire age range, thereby gaining insight into progression. Trainees are imbued with what it is to be a professional teacher and they rise to the challenge of supporting their schools in the broadest sense from the beginning of their careers. There is a drive in teaching schools about professional endeavour. The money is slight but the sense of vocation in the head of the Teaching Alliance is powerful. The goal is long term – a generation from now.

However, the vast majority of trainee teachers will continue to travel through the traditional routes. We must ensure that this training takes would-be teachers deep and wide and encourages a professional outlook and behaviour. Some of that will be related to how time is spent during training. Training institutions are Ofsted inspected and, as elsewhere, they employ game theory. Emphasis on literacy and numeracy requirements can overshadow breadth and wider understandings of how children learn in the primary phase. A focus on model lessons can narrow the range of teaching strategies employed by teachers.

We are told that teachers today are better than ever. How do we know? Inspection. They are also better trained. How do we know? Inspection. Schools are better led. How do we know? Inspection. When we set up criteria to measure effectiveness, and then begin to believe in our own data, we might be missing something. Teachers in primary schools may well be better trained than ever to teach literacy and numeracy. But are they better trained than ever in teaching art, PE, drama, dance, music or cooking? Are they better trained than ever to teach history, geography, design technology and so on? If they are, why the constant complaints from HMI themed subject discipline inspections that teaching is narrow and formulaic? In many teacher training institutions, the time dedicated to foundation subject training has been more than halved, with the extra time handed to core subjects and, in particular, the teaching of phonics. The result is that many primary teachers are less confident than ever before when teaching subjects outside of maths, English and, to a lesser degree, science.

Are the children who rarely use equipment because the pace of the lesson doesn't allow enough time really getting the best teaching ever?

When the numeracy strategy began there was a massive growth in the use of apparatus within the new numeracy hours and SATs results rose dramatically. Unifix and multilink cubes, Diene's blocks, metre rules and counting sticks all had their heyday. We see much less use of these tools now. In schools with a specific risk of low SAT scores, the equipment stays away while we practise more of the written examples likely to be tested.

Teachers seem to know that when young people do creative, engaging, imaginative activities for real purposes they grow as people and apply themselves to other, more abstract learning. Yet teachers feel inhibited about the creative, cultural and expressive world of learning and schooling because it doesn't seem to be valued. The contradiction between the HMI National Subject survey and their individual school inspection matters little. What matters is the outcome in school.

Sadly, many teachers have little argument for better practice other than gut feeling and are offered scant justification beyond the fact that they will be judged on certain outcomes. There is seldom reference to our hopes for our young people – the reason most teachers are in the profession in the first place. There is little reason to teach things just because children like them or their parents enjoyed them when they were at school. Children's likes and needs are different. They tend to like chocolate but need teeth.

We must address subject knowledge and confidence in teachers. Many primary children must think that only literacy and numeracy really matter. Geography, history and science are interesting but they tend to come back to another version of literacy teaching in a different sort of book for a lot of the time. For art, music and PE the school often arranges a 'specialist' to take the class, which can give the impression that art, music and PE must be very complex because you have to go to an expert, and therefore it isn't for me. If there are fifteen teachers in a school but only one can manage music, and I'm in a class of 30 (and good at numeracy), I might deduce that only two people in my class will be any good at music. And if I am good at numeracy, the chances are I won't be any good at music. It can be strange how children think.

At the secondary stage many skilled and knowledgeable teachers despair that they can't enjoy their subject discipline with pupils because of the pressure to 'get on'. They have a syllabus to cover and examinations to prepare for, so they must keep the wolf at bay. They know as they say farewell to pupils at the end of the year that they might have been able to excite a passion in their subject as well as providing them with the means to pass the exam. At the same time, they want to explore new ways of bringing their subject alive, becoming yet more proficient teachers and making learning matter in their school.

Being a professional is more than being an expert: it is being part of a fraternity with the same intent. Professionalism involves reading and questioning deeply and being involved in debate with others on important matters. Being a professional implies a contribution to the group's effort and a willingness to experiment in a structured way to improve outcomes. Being professional involves being recognised and accepted by one's community and having a status built on respect.

## What should we do?

■ My proposed National Council for Schooling would designate approved subject associations and communities of interest that would receive a £100 tariff from government for teachers registered with them. An inflow of funding on this scale would provide for courses, training, publications and updates (many of them online).

■ Every teacher would be required to be part of at least one approved subject association. 'Subject association' is a broad term to include such things as Early Years professional communities or organisations concerned with, for example, using outdoor education effectively.

■ Each teacher would spend at least two days per year taking part in continuous professional development with their association. These days would come from the current five days allocated in each school for training each year. Professional expertise will spread more effectively if teachers feel part of a profession as well as part of their school community.

- Each teacher would be allocated £100 per year initially to fund such involvement in their approved association.

- Teachers should be licensed and registered. Their licence and registration should last for five years and it should be assumed that during this period they are acceptable, approved teachers. They should not need further observation. Their licence would remain in place unless they are reported by another professional, a complaint is upheld from pupils or parents, or unprofessional conduct is proven.

- A teacher would be re-licensed after five years. The relicensing process would include evidence of further development, professional contribution to teaching and five observations in teaching situations.

- School closure for training should reduce to three days per year. The amount of money saved on this would easily pay for the £100 tariff for the subject associations.

- Each teacher should spend the equivalent of two days per year in another school observing practice. This could lead to partnerships in which teachers teach in each other's schools, co-plan and team-teach and build evidence across different contexts. Of course, an initial reaction is to argue that these suggestions would incur cost, especially in terms of supply cover. If two days per year are designated as teacher professional days nationally, the subject associations could plan around this and so there would be no need for cover. For the other two days, the school closure would release all staff to visit and spend time in another school. This leaves one day from the current five for the school's in-house development work.

- Each teacher should produce a research paper every two years for use within their own school and by their approved subject association.

■ These research papers should lead to structured trials to demonstrate effective practice and should be taken to scale with approval from the National Council for Schooling.

■ Teachers need initial and continuing training. Their initial training should include immersion in child development, the psychology of learning, the history of education in the UK and an understanding of social issues. Most importantly, the preliminary training should begin a lifelong study of the psychology of learning; after all, the focus of a teacher's work is the brain. This training should be accessible, relevant and up-to-date and must be a central component of the methodology of the professional teacher.

■ While we know teachers will learn from those they respect and that their colleagues and they will adopt and modify ideas that are close to their practice, there has to be a more calculated approach to innovation. Just as the literacy and numeracy strategies set out a model of good practice, it should be possible for there to be a model for all aspects of teaching at all ages. These might become approved good practice, which would then be recommended to others through the acceptance of properly conducted and disciplined innovation.

■ The emerging approaches could be set before an educational version of the National Institute for Health and Clinical Excellence with evidence of impact and recommendations for approval. Teachers could still experiment, but the requirement to produce a research paper regularly would ensure a more thorough approach which might evolve into a structured trial with a resultant recommendation for approval.

■ We need to cut down on some of the futile chasing of spurious data, the constant checking on pupils' progress and the extensive detailed planning of every lesson; much of which is done to provide evidence for onlookers, and instead encourage a little more warmth and human spirit.

# … on unleashing aspiration

Aspiration has become one of the terms used in education to describe lifting performance. As a means of explaining why pupils who are well taught fail to engage and succeed, a lack of aspiration is a good rationale. 'Lacking aspiration' can sound so much better than 'deprived' or 'disadvantaged'. When everything else seems to have been addressed, there is some logic in believing that the underlying problem lies with the individual. There is no doubt that some children aspire and some do not; because they tell us. They say things like, 'When I grow up …', 'When I'm at university …', 'When I'm famous …' or 'I don't care about …', 'I'll never be any use at …', 'People around here never …' Each of these statements, and others like them, reveals the extent to which the child thinks he or she can take on the world. Often it is linked to whether they are aware of their place on the track or which lane they think they occupy. It follows, then, that *raising* aspiration is important but more vital is *unleashing* aspiration.

Unleashing aspiration is more than simply encouraging young people to believe that they can achieve good test results or higher examination grades, important as these are. It is about more than emphasising levels attained, progress made or qualifications achieved. It is about more than widening career outlook and prospects. Unleashing aspiration involves children seeing their own worth, aspiring to contribute and being inspired to succeed rather than just try. It is about developing a will to keep going, to do the best we can, to beat challenge, to overcome failure, to aim for something special. Unleashing aspiration is about sending the human spirit soaring.

Try viewing the world through the lens of a young person in the current economic gloom. Listen with their ears to the messages from politicians and the media and imagine the impact in their lives: vocational courses don't count and exams are too easy. What questions might they ask when they are told such things? Is the system weighted against me? What is the point of trying? Where are the jobs? Do I want a long-term debt from university? Everywhere they look they seem to see that teenagers are disliked and, in the UK, are deemed to be the worst in the world by the media. Where do they look for hope? Television and celebrity magazines. And so they come to think that fame brings fortune. Then they despair. Nobody in my family has ever achieved anything. All the things I enjoy – creative and sporting activities – have been cut back. Away from school, the support to my family has changed. Our local library closed. Why try?

Clearly this gloomy outlook is not likely to motivate children to want to learn, especially when the things we ask them to learn seem so abstract compared to their everyday life. Children near the inside lanes of the track are much more likely to suspend belief and go along with it when a teacher is explaining, for example, some obscure aspect of geometry, because they know it will lead them somewhere. They know this because it led their parents somewhere and most of the other adults they have met in their lives. Rehearsing yet another example question for an examination is more likely to be tolerated by those on the inside of the track who know that the ticket of qualifications will open doors and they have seen what lies beyond those doors. The interiors are not a foreign land; they are familiar environments.

Those in the outside lanes do not know what doors might open and, in any case, they are frightened of what might lie behind. Urging youngsters on with exhortations such as 'We can do it,' 'Let's show 'em' or 'Who says we can't get high scores?' will work for a while, but in the end we have to see aspiration as more than simply upbeat slogans. Aspiration and motivation go hand in hand.

# Priority approaches

## Me and my self ... a healthy outlook

I sometimes ask teenagers the following question: 'Imagine there was something that you possessed that was the only one of its type in the world. How would you treat it?' They chat in small groups and come up with lists: treasure it, protect it, hide it away, clean it, get it out and be nice to it, only show it trusted people, make sure it was warm, feed it carefully, exercise it.

My point is that if they think about their own body they do have the only one in the world. Love it , loathe it, hate it or like it, their body is the one they've got and what they choose to do with it is an important set of decisions for which they have the ultimate responsibility. What they feed it, what they put into it, who they let see it or touch it and how they treat it are important and life-changing decisions. The first thing they must learn is how incredible their body is, but also how dependent their lives are on how they look after it.

Most children acquire this knowledge through their home and, while other influences might challenge this, those towards the inside track have a better opportunity of understanding their own health needs. Those on the outside have much less chance. Some will be in a world where food is rarely fresh, where the wrong types of food are available, where sufficient food might not be available at all, where drink and drugs are present and where cleanliness doesn't seem to matter. They may be vulnerable to abuse.

Most schools accept that they are an important part of the health provision for children but they need more support to help their efforts. General appreciation of the importance of the school's role in healthy living and learning is often slight. The renowned independent school's introduction of sessions for pupils on 'happiness' attracted unfair sarcastic comment in the media. Such assistance reaps benefits because the healthy child is most likely to learn and achieve. Health includes 'contentment' and where might youngsters find contentment other than in the natural world. One of the hopes outlined in the first section of the book referred to our young being fascinated by the natural world. The dawn of the day, the opening of a flower, the power of the weather and the bird on the wing bring solace, joy, appreciation and delight. They are basic experiences for some children; for others not so. It could be argued that such simple areas of experience lie outside the province of the school yet, for many the residential visit brings an awakening of spirit that affects human potential and well-being.

## The real world

If we want children to aspire there are some priority approaches that will enable better outcomes. The first thing children require is real-world examples of what they are learning about. At the youngest age children need to see their learning fit in with their play. As they grow there is a need to see the magical world that is unfolding around them as something to learn about, through and from. They require the constant example and articulation of the real world.

Every day there are news stories that fascinate, amuse, intrigue, inspire, appal, offend and puzzle. These stories could form the basis for months of learning but so often schooling goes on in isolation from the world outside. We take schoolchildren inside very tall fences to help them prepare for the world that goes on outside those fences. A world that is constantly changing, while they are inside learning things that often seem have little relevance to them.

How many physics teachers will have felt able or had time to mention the ongoing Hadron Collider experiment, ash dieback or the death in 2011 of Norman Foster Ramsey who was awarded a Nobel Prize in Physics in 1989 (he had an incredible career as one of the 'makers' of the bomb that landed on Hiroshima, the developer of the atomic clock and was one of the pioneers of MRI scanning).

Did mathematics and geography teachers take advantage of Samoa changing the International Date Line as a chance to discuss an abstract concept and its link to the economic world? Did English teachers single out the anniversary of Dickens's birth as a focus for discussion about his legacy and celebrity?

In primary schools, the excitement of a Golden Jubilee might be met with a party, but how do we extend the learning opportunity to uncover historical issues by seizing the moment? Is a frosty morning a chance to discuss temperature? Or condensation on the windows an opportunity to learn about scientific principles?

Teachers know these things matter but too often they feel under pressure from the need to 'get on'. They feel so bound to plough on through turgid texts and worksheets to achieve their planned goals and demonstrate progress that they have little time for the real world.

It is salutary to talk with children about their own school. So often they don't know why their school has the name it does, even when it is named after a prominent local person. They don't understand the school motto or the relevance of the badge or why houses are named as they are, even when the badge was designed by pupils and the houses named by pupil vote. The story usually is that these decisions were made a few years ago and the younger children weren't here then. What this demonstrates is the need to let children dwell on the world they are in, their school, its purpose, history and its place in the world. We cannot just keep getting on and hope to secure aspiration.

## The world of work

From real-world examples it is a small step to the world of work. What openings might each subject discipline offer in terms of occupations? Too often careers guidance is a peripheral aspect of schooling. It needs to happen all the way through. The children on the inside lanes of the track know what opportunities are out there and how to get to them. They also know the ones that they would not countenance and from which they will steer clear. Those towards the outside lanes of the track see only the prospects within their own compass unless others, mainly schools, point them out.

does someone become an archivist, a market gardener or a Where might the arts take us? From garden design to sculpture to cake decoration to hair styling to poster design to photography and journalism, the arts opens doors. In fact, every subject has a route into journalism if only we could excite pupils about it by working out how to deliver literacy across the curriculum.

From primary age through to secondary school, meaningful work experience, observing people at work, studying work places and following the career paths of ex-pupils can all add to a growing aspiration for young people.

There are more and more primary schools giving pupils an insight into the working world. From the school in Milton Keynes that enlists the local bank manager to sign off the business plans of budding 'companies', to the school in Morecambe where the children run businesses such as nail bars for 'profit', there is real purpose and audience in the authentic application of literacy and numeracy in a context that pupils can understand and enjoy. Elsewhere, in Basildon, children research a range of jobs to explain at their school careers' fair – and some parents find it informative too.

In the secondary sector, ironically, it gets harder as pupils need to 'get on' so that they earn the qualifications to gain employment, while having little time to explore the possibilities that might motivate them. There are dramatic examples, such as the school in Hampshire where a helicopter landed on the playing field to deliver engineering interest from the air. The Jaguar Cars Maths in Motion Challenge has for years shown the link between mathematics and car design procedures.

Some schools build formal links with sponsors, such as the school in Sandwell where a global communications giant has a structured involvement in a range of departments. In some areas where economic decline has dominated for years there is a genuine effort to address the aspirations of pupils. In the Pendle area of Lancashire, a group of primary and secondary schools is working with employers and other agencies to make learning resonate with young people and their parents so that the long-term purpose of learning, rather than just the measurable outcome, is articulated and understood. One of the real benefits of the academies programme is that sponsors from business can see more clearly where their contribution can fit and work to help the school make it happen.

Robert Peston, the BBC business editor, recently established Speakers for Schools. As a comprehensively schooled youngster, he had come to realise the need for young people to see the possibilities in the world ahead and has enlisted individuals from the world of business, industry, commerce, journalism and beyond to join a register of speakers that state schools can turn to in order to inspire their pupils. Many of the speakers report that they have been asked many times to speak at schools in the independent sector but have rarely been invited by those in the state sector. There are a lot of messages in that.

## Applications, processes and contexts

If we develop real-world awareness and demonstrate constantly the world of work, we start naturally to show application and process for abstractions in learning within the curriculum. Geometry comes to life much more when it uses genuine examples; computer science makes more sense when put against events in the news. This awareness of application, process and context becomes more important the further we travel in the learning race. While the elite learner can somehow cope with, and often enjoy, the abstractions of subject disciplines (knowing that they are in a fraternity of linguists, mathematicians or artists) the nearer we get to the throng of learners, the more there has to be a point. Further back, with the trailing learners, we have the challenge of encouraging students not to drop out, while helping them to achieve as much as possible. Recently, there have been proposals for a new suite of post-sixteen examinations known as the Advanced Baccalaureate, which would contain a 'new approach to mathematics' to encourage more pupils with good GCSEs to continue the subject. The main thrust of this new examination would be teaching through real-life examples as a way to encourage numeracy. Why wait until the age of sixteen?

## Essential experiences

Aptitude, attitude and personal confidence.

**... NEEDS FOR THE TWENTY-FIRST CENTURY**

The etiquette and tactics for success

Rules of life game

Who we think we are

What we do, where we go

A guarantee of experiences

Assessment to build self-image

What we know

Who we know and meet

Learn to use contacts

Qualifications

Earlier in the book, this diagram gave a snapshot of what young people need to do well in the twenty-first century. Aspiration is highly influenced by the way that we develop the confidence in young people to face new situations. Qualifications are vital as a ticket to the next arena, but without personal confidence many dare not cross the threshold. This is where life experiences – understanding etiquette and protocol – become important, and it is why children from more limited backgrounds are prone to doing less well than those on the inside track. Virtually anyone who attended public school carries a certain presence and a belief that they have a right to be heard. They are comfortable in a wide range of social settings and when they feel uncomfortable they have the necessary techniques to extract themselves without feeling they are losing face.

At the other extreme are those families where parents have not had rich experiences and feel nervous about their own children going into new territories. A primary school head teacher in Wythenshawe, organising a residential visit for pupils in Year 6, overheard parents discussing how they wished they could visit the Lake District. Within no time, she had organised a residential experience for the parents themselves, many of whom had never been away from home, had never had to work together or had an educational adventure of a positive kind before. The results were dramatic for the parents and their children.

Similarly, imploring young people to try hard for examination success so that they can have the opportunity to attend university only works if university is an attraction – and it can't be an attraction if it is mysterious and daunting. Disappointingly, less than a third of secondary schools took advantage of the coalition government's initiative to enable their students to visit a top university to see for themselves how welcoming and exciting such places could be and tempt them to apply.

Some work I have done with young people on personal confidence has had some fascinating results. The teenagers are given a series of pictures and asked how comfortable they would feel on a scale of 0–5 in each scenario. 'It is not for me' would rate a 0 and 'I would be at ease here' would rate a score of 5. The pictures are settings such as a fast food outlet, record store, sports venue, high-class restaurant, the London underground, a pop concert, theatre and so on. Basically, the more affluent the area and the wider experience of the youngsters, the greater their ease with new surroundings. If we want children to learn to cope in the wider world, they surely have to experience it to know that it is worth learning about. So many youngsters reject the fancy restaurant saying, 'I wouldn't know how to order', 'I wouldn't be able to manage the menu' and 'I wouldn't understand the cutlery'. The London underground is frightening for those who have never used it for fear of getting lost, going the wrong way or looking stupid.

Convincing youngsters to believe they can cross thresholds, and helping them to do so, is one of the major tasks of the teacher. It is how we help young people make progress towards the inner lanes of the track; the lanes that many think are not for them, with different social codes, protocols and niceties. Children need to understand that we all feel nervous about new experiences. We all worry at times about feeling foolish. We all dread something embarrassing happening. We all need help in knowing what to do and we all feel a little bit more confident when we have some tactics for coping and surviving in new settings.

The excitement of experiencing new environments felt by the primary-aged child seems to evaporate for many in adolescence. Intense peer pressure makes it easier to reject the unfamiliar. Opportunities familiar on the inside tracks might be described as 'soft', 'stupid', 'weird' or 'snobbish'. It is hard to be consumed by the joy of ballet, the sound of classical music or the beauty of a garden if you feel you don't fit in with the people there, don't understand the rules or have little conversation to offer because you are the first one from your family or community to take part. And what if your family and friends find out you have been to the inside tracks? How will you explain?

We used to think like this about doing well in examinations. We would say that some communities thought it wasn't cool to try to do well or that some social groups believe that university is not for their type. We have done much in these regards, but there is much more to do about widening childhood opportunities generally. We need young people to be asking, 'Who says this isn't for me?' They need to be thinking about what they might be missing. They should be asking themselves how they will know if they don't take the first steps. They require teachers who open doors and push them through the threshold, and they need a welcoming adult society on the other side who will initiate, encourage and enrich opportunity so they want to stay and persuade others to join them.

To succeed in the twenty-first century, young people need more than examination success and qualifications; these are the tickets that open some doors. They also require experiences that will take them to new places and they need to know what to do when they get there. They need to know the etiquette, the rules and the tactics for success. This awareness is almost as profound as the knowledge they can acquire from any subject discipline.

## Essential learning experiences

So what might the essential learning experiences be for, say, pupils in the Key Stage 3 phase? We might think about the activities that young-sters should take part in as aspects of the context for learning about subject disciplines. Most schools organise some of the activities shown below and we could add many more to the list. These are not add-ons to the curriculum, treats or extra-curricular activities; they are contexts within which learning takes place, the things that we know bring learn-ing alive for children. Some of the contexts are day-by-day routines such as assembly; others are events such as visits or inter-school mock trial competitions. They offer meaningful opportunities to create con-texts for learning from subject disciplines and give children that guarantee of experience that builds aspiration through confidence in the wider world.

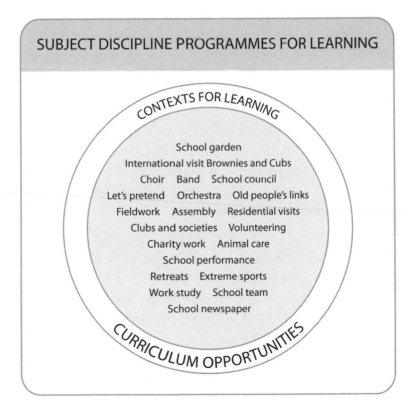

**SUBJECT DISCIPLINE PROGRAMMES FOR LEARNING**

CONTEXTS FOR LEARNING

School garden
International visit Brownies and Cubs
Choir   Band   School council
Let's pretend   Orchestra   Old people's links
Fieldwork   Assembly   Residential visits
Clubs and societies   Volunteering
Charity work   Animal care
School performance
Retreats   Extreme sports
Work study   School team
School newspaper

CURRICULUM OPPORTUNITIES

The Henley Review recommendations, coupled with the pupil premium might come to the fore in terms of unleashing aspiration. Cultural awareness and education should be embedded in our learning offer to pupils. The opportunity to visit an art gallery or museum ought to be a regular experience; if young people could be persuaded that this is a valuable way of spending a little time then we might have a very different society. It is reasonable to assume that youngsters should go to the theatre. Often schools take whole classes at once and in some areas the auditorium is taken over for the day by an audience of teenagers. While this can be beneficial, one of the problems is that it doesn't necessarily induct young people into the real experience. It is just as important that the child realises what it is like to go to the theatre and to sort out their own logistics, rather than being shepherded through by adults who are managing large numbers.

If every child during Key Stage 3 was expected to study and report on someone at work over an extended period, a whole group of children would come up with a repertoire of knowledge about how work operates. The experience of children who have shadowed someone – whether they are working outside in all weathers at a manual task or inside at executive meetings making so-called big decisions – need to be conducted and the implications explored. The amount of information generated would be enormous within a group of twenty pupils. But so too would be the understanding that work is in the main tedious and any enjoyment is to be gleaned from such things as doing a job as well as possible, customer satisfaction, working as part of a team and feeling the camaraderie of being with other people – as well as the pay.

The experience of creating something that could contribute to a bigger community endeavour might be an experience that would endure in the lives of young people for a considerable time. The chance to organise an event or construct a permanent facility can give a sense of purpose as well as achievement.

Every subject discipline ought to be able to demonstrate its application within the real world and hence fieldwork matters – it should be a natural part of school study. And the more that subject disciplines link together over fieldwork, the more coherence youngsters see in their learning.

If we want young people to understand the importance of healthy eating, then they surely need the opportunity to prepare fresh ingredients and cook nourishing meals. One vehicle for this that might give added purpose is to invite an audience of diners from the local community. Not only does this emphasise the importance of healthy food but it gives students the experience of many of the 'soft skills', such as adaptability, teamwork, persistence and customer awareness, that employers say are important in the world today.

Observing at local council meetings or a court in session, and attachments to police, fire stations or hospitals, might awaken young people's understanding of the civil society in which they live. Seeing behind the scenes might lead to more respect for our emergency services and more understanding of the way democracy operates.

In a society that asserts that we need an international outlook, it would seem relatively obvious for adolescents to have contact with young people from countries beyond the UK. This might include the traditional, but now declining, opportunity to take part in a foreign exchange and learning the language and culture of another country, but also the opportunity to link with less developed countries in an effort to develop understanding and make an active contribution to global sustainability. While an understanding of other faiths is part of the expectation for most religious education syllabuses, the opportunity to visit places of worship from different faith groups ought to be included in the child's experience.

Travelling alone is an important aspect of growing up and many young people have still not had this experience by the time they leave home and head off into their version of the wider world. Surely an unaccompanied journey of fifty miles with one change of transport is not an unreasonable expectation for a teenager. It could be that they travel in twos and are shadowed along the way. It has got to happen sometime and, on successfully completing a journey of some significance, many youngsters feel an enormous sense of pride and confidence.

We should surely have as an aim for our children the opportunity to visit and spend time in London. London is acknowledged as one of the greatest cities in the world and the children who grow up there have access to arts, culture, sport and experiences in every subject discipline. Equally, many children from elsewhere in the country have never, even by the time they reach adulthood, visited the capital. Likewise, every child, by the time they reach their teenage years, should have climbed a mountain, visited the sea and spent time on a farm. Seemingly very few children do these basic things any more.

Representing their school in some capacity is an honour that should fall upon all youngsters. So many young people leave school never having been trusted to represent the school in the world beyond. How can they feel they have anything to contribute?

The pupil premium has been much heralded. While no one would deny that the resource is welcome, the manner in which it has found its way into the system does not match the much-vaunted promises the Liberal Democrats made in opposition. The pupil premium was intended to enable young people who were unwelcome in schools, because of a history of problems, to be accepted and acclimatised into the system. The coalition trumpets the assertion that politicians should not tell schools how to use this prized extra money because they do not want to tell head teachers what to do. However, the findings of the 2012 report published by the Sutton Trust on the pupil premium and the cost-effectiveness of a range of common approaches to raising attainment will be the focus for inspection under the new framework. The one area where government could insist on certain required aspects of schooling is in the use of the pupil premium, with an expectation that every child in the country would experience some of the things listed above. It is surely the child's right to have doors opened.

## Learning about education in England

I've never quite understood why, in all the consideration, discussion, argument and suggestion about what should be included within a national curriculum for children in England, we never seem to conclude that children should be taught about education itself. There seems to be no structured way of helping children to understand how schooling fits into their wider life, but there is an assumption that they will understand the point of it, presumably by taking part and through their parents. Given that there has always been criticism about the extent to which some groups of parents help some children in education, it would seem that there is more work to be done.

First of all, maybe we should make sure that every child in the early teenage years has a clear understanding of why education matters. What has happened in education to bring schooling to the position it is? How did schooling come about? Why do people in developing countries campaign for the right to schooling? Why was fifteen-year-old Malala Yousafzai shot by the Taliban for campaigning for education for girls in Pakistan? Why, when incarcerated in prison in Robben Island, did Nelson Mandela and other learned prisoners spend time out of sight of guards teaching other inmates the basics of reading, writing and maths? Can we help our young people to appreciate that education is a pathway to emancipation? If we only worked a little bit more on trying to teach them about education, we might convince them of the view that learning is worth it because society values education so much.

What might we want to teach children about English education? It seems fairly simple really. We might start with how the school system works. We could explain that the schooling framework has been set up by the nation to ensure that all children have an opportunity to learn. We could teach them about the history of the school system and how, at first, it was for only the privileged few and later was offered to the masses in order that they might contribute to the country's prosperity.

Also, more recently, how we have recognised the need to use schooling as a way of enhancing childhood and preparing for adult life.

We could teach them about different sorts of schooling. Indeed, any work on sets and subsets with overlapping Venn diagrams would be enhanced by a study of the schooling possibilities in the country – everything from primary and secondary to a range of church schools, combined schools, middle schools, first schools, infant schools, junior schools, upper schools, lower schools, high schools, academies, free schools, technical schools, specialist schools, comprehensive schools, grammar schools, trust schools, independent schools, preparatory schools, nursery schools, co-educational schools and any more you may wish to add. What's in a name? All of these various subsets all have a history.

It might be beneficial for young people to realise how much it costs to educate them individually per year, per lifetime, per hour, as a way of helping them to understand the investment made in them – and why they should be committed to the task. This could start from working with the really big numbers concerned with national expenditure. Or the cost of the pen and piece of paper that the child is using to take notes, then gradually increasing this to take account of other equipment used, the cost of non-teaching and teaching staff, and the expenditure on resources and facilities and buildings. It could go further to look at the infrastructure costs around school. If we want something to investigate in maths, youngsters might be amazed at the cost of their own education.

Our young people might be taught why the country invests in education; as a study of historical and sociological development this is a fascinating story. A look at how other countries compare, organise and achieve might also help our pupils to understand something of the bigger world. They might be helped to realise the way in which other nations are developing their schooling system at a greater rate than we seem to be in Britain.

We could teach our youngsters about the pathway from Early Years through to university and even further into continuing adult education and training. There is so much to teach, yet so often we fail to realise the impact of educating them about the very thing they are experiencing.

## Being confident in new surroundings

There are some very simple customs and protocols that children need to learn. The problem is that etiquette often touches on that nerve that many people call social engineering. The reality is that if young people cannot understand the way in which the world operates then they have very little chance of making progress within it, to the betterment of their lives. At the heart of what youngsters need to recognise is the meaning of the word 'register' – what behaviour is appropriate and in what circumstances?

Let's start with speech. Most children at some time in their lives swear. They use language which they know will have maximum effect and they use expletives as a natural part of their everyday conversations. They are not very nice words but we all know that many people use them. The fact is that children from all walks of life, at some point, will probably use swear words. Most of them work out that these words are only acceptable in certain circumstances. But some children grow up in families where four-letter words are just a natural part of conversation; these families occur right across the social spectrum.

The interesting thing is that some families know that when there are visitors around they should remove swearing from their conversation and manage without; the swear words are in fact a substitute for other adjectives, nouns and verbs. They understand that vulgar language is not acceptable in certain circumstances and hence a modification of register occurs. For children on the outside of the tracks it may be hard to realise that swearing is frequently unacceptable. Television close-ups showing football players at moments of tension uttering expletives are common and, increasingly, TV programmes and films include examples of people who swear as a matter of course.

Children who are educated at public schools use bad language just as much, and often more so, than children in other settings. The difference is that they know that swearing is inappropriate in some circumstances and they modify their language accordingly. Their big advantage, of course, is that they have a repertoire of vocabulary upon which to draw in order to continue conversations with their elders, betters and those they want to impress. We need to teach all pupils about appropriate language and how inappropriate language can serve them badly.

The richness and beauty of regional accents is there to enjoy. The lilt of the Norfolk accent with its rising pitch towards the end of a sentence, the burr of the south-west and the lyrical tone of the north-east are all delights among the wide range of British dialects. Some accents are widely enjoyed: the north-eastern accent is reportedly popular with call centre employers because it is seen as warm and friendly. Others are less well appreciated. Whatever our individual preferences for, and opinions of, accents, children need to learn that a regional accent is a pleasure but it might need to be slowed down and made clearer in order for others to be able to communicate with us. The accent itself is not the issue but clarity is. That might have more to do with pronunciation, speed or being clear about the fact that a local dialect might contain vocabulary that others would not understand.

When competitors were interviewed after their events at the Olympic Games, it was striking how absent were phrases such as 'you know', 'like' and 'innit'. Young people need to appreciate how speaking in certain circumstances demands different models and registers and that this can be as vital as qualifications in taking forward opportunity. Children should be informed that some of the mannerisms of their speech are traits of the time and not habits for life; that there are places and times when it is inappropriate to use the current lingo and jargon. Young people need to learn about the scale of formality, register, vocabulary and dialect.

## Table technique

This applies to organising your office table as well as your dining table. One of the things that puts off many youngsters from making progress in new circumstances is fear of the way in which table manners are expected to operate. Table manners are one of the stock-in-trade jokes to show how individuals are not fitting into their new surroundings. The challenges of grappling with various items of cutlery and crockery, as well as the intricacies of service technique, are the substance of many film and stage productions. For young people in particular the step into a new social class is very difficult in terms of the dining experience. This is even more so since our eating habits have changed so significantly in the last twenty years. Eating from cartons and wrappers while walking along the street has become part of everyday life. For youngsters the routine of eating at a table, in company, and using the appropriate cutlery is a less natural affair. For those towards the outside of the track it is an even bigger challenge, even a threat. Hence, when they know they are going to be in a position where they are being judged, particularly when one of the aspects of the occasion is a meal, we can see why tension builds up. Add to this the fact that school dining in its traditional sense disappeared in the twentieth century – youngsters often now experience a rushed canteen meal – and we can see why this has become an important issue for them.

When I was chief education officer, my deputy and I used to take small groups of children to relatively posh restaurants to enjoy an evening meal. I'm not sure the groups got that much pleasure from it at the time, but it was a small experience that helped them on a stairway to success. They were taught dining etiquette: how to understand the menu, which plate mattered, which knife and fork was for what. Critics would often gripe that we had little chance of making an impact, given there were only eight children present per session and therefore just twenty-four children per year having the experience. My reply was that if every senior leader in every school did the same with eight children, a lot of youngsters would know a lot more about how to manage themselves in such circumstances in the future.

## Dress

In our society, dress has become a much more casual affair and a much less predictable element of our lives. However, first impressions are still drawn on the basis of what we are wearing and it is not unusual to hear people comment on an inadvertently wrong choice of clothing for a particular occasion. This has become a difficult area for teenagers who see celebrities they admire and are encouraged to emulate wearing all manner of clothing at various events. On special occasions in the film and pop music award calendar, our television screens are full of celebrities wearing everything from full evening dress through to highly individual fashion statements. No wonder youngsters become confused. When they dress for an interview, teenagers need to understand the importance of suitable clothing, taking care to wear decent, clean and conservative clothes, rather than attire that might give the impression that they don't care or have an inappropriate attitude.

## Conversation

Making the next step into a new community means being able to talk well. This often means being able to speak without saying very much at all – small talk. Youngsters need to be able to practise making small talk: conversing with people they have never met before, having brief conversations, talking about themselves without saying too much and presenting themselves as interesting and interested individuals. They need to be enthusiastic, knowledgeable and able to talk about pretty well anything. How are they going to learn these skills? One problem in schools is that we meet our pupils so frequently that it can be difficult to create an unfamiliar situation. Would it not be possible to invite people in from the governing body or from local businesses to give youngsters the experience of holding conversations with individuals that they are meeting for the first time?

I was fortunate to join in with the efforts of a school in Barnsley which ran a superb event involving local employers in providing mock interviews for Year 10 pupils in formal surroundings outside school. Pupils were interviewed by a panel and given feedback from employers as well as from their fellow pupils and parents who had been invited to sit in on the sessions. For many parents, as well as their children, this was a very important occasion for which they presented themselves formally. Many schools run similar activities, which can build upon the clever use of role-play situations in form times so that pupils can practise on each other. Some schools use pupils in rotation on their reception desk so that they can learn to meet and greet and develop conventional conversational skills.

### Poise, posture and personal presentation

It is difficult to be poised when you are nervous. It is hard to be natural when you are tense. We need children to understand how we can all feel awkward in these sorts of circumstances and help them to be prepared to cope in new situations. Our brains are amazing machines and they help us revert to flight-or-fight when we are nervous. For many children and adults, saying something silly in moments of tension that we later regret is a natural occurrence. But standing or sitting in a sloppy way is something that we can avoid as long as we know we are prone to doing it. We all need help; young people need it more.

## So what can we do to help children improve their chances?

It is simple really, but it does require endless perseverance to enable our young people to understand that these activities will have massive benefits in the future. Here are some things that could be done in form time, at an after-school club or as part of the general timetable. It might be that a timetabled slot would be a better mechanism for learning if just one hour a week were devoted to some of the suggestions below.

- Read a newspaper daily. This could be an actual newspaper or a skim through an online version. Young people should understand that they need to see the way the world is unfolding from the point of view of the national press and to understand about bias.

■ Compare a tabloid and a broadsheet editorial twice per week. If youngsters read the editorials they will start to see how the media is influenced by various political persuasions. The same events will be commented on in tabloids and broadsheets in different ways. Many children live in homes without newspapers but even those whose parents read the red-tops have a very different picture of the world from the people we might want them to be mixing with and influencing. Roy Hodgson, upon appointment as England football manager, was referred to as 'a broadsheet man in a tabloid world'.

The youngsters whose view of the world is informed only by the trivial tabloids will form very limited understandings and opinions. They will see celebrity as vital, soaps as real and gossip as worth it. Unless we offer them something else many children will remain limited in their outlook. Their work in subject disciplines will be all the more distant and irrelevant unless we make links to the real world as it happens.

■ Select two documentaries to view per week. Television viewing in these digital days can be a very haphazard affair, but if youngsters want to build their capacity for conversation, documentaries are a good place to start. This means discipline and self-management. Looking at the television schedules and selecting two documentaries is a starting point (they may need to be recorded) but after viewing they also need to be discussed. Teachers can help youngsters to practise small talk by setting up opportunities for them to do it.

■ Visit a gallery, museum or exhibition on a fortnightly basis. Suggest to teenagers that they study three portraits or three landscapes. They don't have to be there for long but they do need to get into the habit of going. Once they have been to a gallery or museum they will have something to talk about with people they are meeting for the first time and will be able to make links in conversation that help them to feel confident and competent. Schools can help youngsters by alerting them to exhibitions or productions in the local area, whether it is an internationally acclaimed art exhibition, an amateur photography show or the opportunity to see a visiting Shakespeare production.

- Take part in debating groups. It is rare these days for schools to have debating groups as part of the natural offer, yet these are brilliant opportunities for teenagers to both explore serious issues for society and develop the vital skill of public speaking. They can work in groups, with some teenagers preparing points to make in the debate, others developing the skill of asking questions and others perfecting the put-down and coming up with a riposte. After nervous beginnings confidence will grow.

- Start a conversation circle. One step down from a debating society, this is a less-structured but useful way of helping teenagers to develop the art of conversation in a confident and natural way. Interestingly, book clubs have grown in popularity over the last ten years as adults discover that there is something enjoyable about reading a book and then talking about it with others. It is simple and doesn't take a lot of organising, but youngsters will find it enormously beneficial once they get into it.

- Research references on the internet linked to studies. When a particular topic has been discussed in the classroom as part of subject discipline studies, it is well worth youngsters exploring some aspects of this on the internet to find out about further developments, small sub-shoots of interest or controversial issues within the subject. A short time each week spent debating these findings would help to build teenagers' confidence in taking forward some of these ideas.

- Look at university websites linked to their favourite topics. If we want them to do well in a more rounded course of study then, as they enjoy aspects of their subject discipline, they could be pointed towards university websites where debate about these matters is underway. The confidence that we build in youngsters as a result of this can be immeasurable. They begin to see discourse as a natural part of learning and understand that learning is a bigger thing altogether.

- Join an association. It doesn't really matter what the association is, as long as they are a part of one and receiving the journals, updates and email newsletters and feeling part of a bigger community. There are associations for everything – some of them linked with subject disciplines and others simply areas of interest that people enjoy. If each pair of youngsters in every class were part of an association there would be a non-stop source of conversational opportunities.

- Be part of a club. Gardening, astronomy, gastronomy, sailing, singing, wartime memorabilia, bhangra drumming, square dancing, cricket, cycling, climbing, philately, amateur dramatics or canal restoration – it doesn't matter what, but we have to get young people working with their interests and spending time with adults. In this way they will learn essential skills, build knowledge, understand campaigning, develop patience and commitment and play their small part in society. They will start to see that the adult world is caring and kind and sometimes odd. They can try out the jokes their friends laugh at and realise that many adults find them less funny. They can find people to talk with and listen to their experiences and who might, in turn, help them over thresholds.

- Read a periodical. These don't need to be read in depth but can be skimmed through and enjoyed. School libraries should be full of periodicals, whatever the budget constraints, so youngsters can enjoy articles and comment on them as they catch their interest.

- Take an active part in charity work. Being part of a charity helps youngsters because it takes them towards people of different generations and backgrounds who are committed to a purpose, and it gives them the feeling that they are benefiting society. When they have done something good for their community, they can talk about their positive contribution when they find themselves in conversation with people they are meeting for the first time.

■ Learn to play an instrument. It doesn't matter how little progress is being made; when someone says, 'Do you play an instrument?' we say, 'I can play the clarinet just a little' or 'I'm learning to play the piano', and confidence grows. This is a much better opening to a conversation than, 'I'm sorry, no'.

■ Eat olives … metaphorically. Teenagers need to understand that there are certain aspects of life for which they may not yet have developed the palate, but they must persevere in order to get into circles that will open doors for them. Eating olives might not be important but it is an example of how people meet aspects of life before their palate is fully developed. Olives, gorgonzola and red wine might be perceived as wasted on the young, along with Shakespeare and ballet, unless they can persevere and understand the joy to be had when the acquired taste has been developed. We need to make clear to our children that the first samplings of new experiences may not always be exciting – indeed, at times they can be embarrassing or awkward – but how we do it and how we get them through is a vital aspect of learning in order to cope in adult society. We need to develop the learning palate of youngsters whose lives have been devoid of rich experiences. For all sorts of reasons, many of them are put off sampling things that seem beyond their realm. We need to draw young people into the sophisticated, the complicated and the complex.

■ How to work the room. I have a colleague who does coaching with senior executives and now and again he organises a one-day experience for them, during which they get the opportunity to work on the many aspects of their executive life that they worry about. Basically my colleague takes twelve executives for the morning and works around the following agenda:

---

### WORKING THE ROOM

• meeting • greeting and being welcomed • announcing oneself
• holding drink and food • talking and eating • shaking hands
• remembering names and who's who • coats and bags
• getting stuck in one place in the room

---

These are things that make senior executives anxious. Can you believe it? My coaching colleague describes various ploys to manage these sorts of incidents and then at lunchtime the twelve executives are joined by twelve jobbing actors who play various roles within the group. The actors pretend to be senior executives who exhibit certain traits. After lunch, the actors feed back to the executives on their experience and how it felt for them. The results are often revealing. The actor who was partially deaf (or pretended to be) explains how virtually nobody realised or noticed. The actor who came carrying a coat explains how nobody offered to take it from her and make her feel comfortable. The actor who was nervous explains how he couldn't get away from being trapped in the corner and so on. The point is that if senior executives of big companies find these things challenging, then surely we need to give our young people a chance to develop tactics to succeed in any set of circumstances.

## Giving your teacher a hard time

When I am working with teenagers I sometimes put up a slide with the title 'Giving your teacher a hard time'. Then I say, 'There are six bullet points on this slide, can you guess what they are before I reveal them?' They always enjoy playing this game and spend some time coming up with various suggestions like 'Forget to do your homework', 'Pretend that you haven't done your homework', 'Rock on your chair', 'Don't do your tie up properly', 'Have your shirt hanging out' and 'Talk across the teacher'.

These are all things that will give the teacher a hard time, but I then talk with the students about how trivial these issues are and how we spend our life doing absolutely bizarre things to each other in classrooms (and outside them). I then reveal the six real bullet points:

- Demand an explanation of the application of knowledge, skills, processes and procedures. So if, in a physics lesson, we have just carried out an experiment to calculate aspects of density, you should turn to the teacher and say, 'This has been interesting and worthwhile, can you tell us how this fits into everyday life and how we might use it in the world of work?'

- Ask searching questions. Typically searching questions are not closed questions. They are questions that invite the teacher to explain further and develop things more fully.

- Ask the teacher to take you deeper. What happens in most schools is that teaching sessions become a chance for the teacher to deliver the next bit of information or understanding and most of us seem to wait until the bell rings to stop having to swallow it. Could we turn that into something that was far more enriching for the students and the teacher? By asking the teacher to take us deeper and further into the subject, we develop a natural enthusiasm, both within the taught and learnt.

- Expect a response to submitted work within a three-day period. Say to teachers, 'Please can I have that work back, I've put a lot into it and I would love to see your response.' At the same time, you could negotiate with the teacher to get more extended and demanding pieces of work and less small-scale, spoon-fed exercises. Instead of the 'produce and mark' routine, we could develop a system like the tutorial process at university where a group reads each other's work and considers a topic together to offer guidance for the future.

▪ Ask for text and websites to study. Not all the time, but now and again ask the teacher, 'How can I follow this up in my own time and pursue this in a way that would take me deeper?'

▪ Ask for places to visit so that topics or ideas can be seen in action. 'I've enjoyed seeing the way in which this food technology has been developed. Is there somewhere I could visit to see this being fully exploited?' Children should be given information about exhibitions as a natural part of their learning calendar and should be encouraged to visit places which would take their learning much further.

Overall, the message to the children is that they need to build their teachers' enthusiasm for helping them, as opposed to the teacher seeing a successful lesson as one that finishes without too much low-level trivial disruption. Typically I have found that teenagers, once helped to see how this works, are able to see their learning experience in a much more mature way and pursue learning in a manner which benefits them and their teachers.

## In the primary phase

The importance of relating learning to the wider world is well recognised by many primary schools. In the leadership section of this book I write about the way schools seek to embed learning or create one-off special occasions to try to make learning matter. Naturally, it is best if the school can get to the truly embedded state where children come to class each day partly to carry on with a long-term project, partly to see what is new today, partly to 'carry out their jobs' – the routines of responsibility for small aspects of school that they cheerfully do, and partly to have a go at something exciting. Some of the day, of course, is when they settle down to be instructed, to 'do their work', to practise or to meet something new, as part of the purposeful embedding of learning.

There are primary schools everywhere that ooze authenticity. From the school in Bradford with its splendid garden to the school in Cornwall with its farm (where the children say farewell to the pig they have nurtured fully aware that next time they see it it will be as sausages), to the school in Stockport that has produced a full-scale film depicting local history, to the schools that produce newspapers, websites and exhibitions for their communities to enjoy. They all know that authentic learning strikes a chord.

The forest school movement has been gathering pace since the 1990s, giving credibility to those who appreciate that the classroom is artificial and the outdoors is a natural learning environment. The number of organisations that welcome children – from the National Trust and the Royal Society for the Protection of Birds to the Forestry Commission – all point to the growing awareness that if we make learning real and give children the right early experiences, then we might see the benefits later.

Children engaged in enterprise activities, such as Go4it or the Children's University, are shown to make better progress than those who do not (though sadly such progress is often articulated in the limited measures of mediocre schooling for which successive governments seem to strive: better SAT scores). As an aside, I was asked to speak recently at an event at the House of Lords to celebrate five years of the Cabinet Office funded Go-Givers programme, a flagship initiative for the Citizenship Foundation to develop caring and concerned citizens. Children from several primary schools spoke about work within their local communities. They talked of campaigns associated with knife crime, cleaning up a local play area, looking after older people in their locality and trying to get guardsmen to wear something other than fur busbies to save bears! The political speakers praised the children and the Cabinet Office and stated that such work was vital for children's education. This was echoed beautifully by the Children's Laureate, Julia Donaldson. In my few minutes I tried to show how the children's work had been invigorated by, and also supported, work in subject disciplines and at the same time developed skills that employers say are vital. It was a pity that the lords who were so effusive could not make the link between the Cabinet Office and the Department for Education where the tide seems to be running in the opposite direction. Afterwards people were complimentary, but many referred to me as 'being brave' to speak as I had. Worse still, the lords who had spoken asked me what I thought we should do about it all! This is parliament!

Many secondary colleagues talk with admiration and envy of the way their feeder primaries seem to be able to make learning come alive with flexibility and spontaneity – learning as it should be. This doesn't happen only after the SATs are out of the way. It many schools it happens all the time and, if we believe that authentic learning has integrity, then we should exploit it all the more. It is difficult though when the only measure is testing.

One way of addressing the aspiration issue is through the '101 things to do before you're 11' approach. I have used this for several years to show how the curriculum can be implemented in a dynamic way and, at the same time, childhood can be cherished and everyone is involved in learning. My thunder was stolen a little in 2012 with the publication of a National Trust book called *50 Things to do Before You're 11¾* (I'm sure the author Jane Eastoe must have been to one of my talks to governors! But no matter; if it makes an impact, does it matter where it came from?).

The basic principle I have worked with in schools is to identify a set of essential experiences for children under the age of eleven that will sustain, support and develop them as learners as they meet the more formal and structured world of the classroom. For instance, children need adventure. This might include wearing helmets and hanging from ropes but it can include much more. Basically, an adventure is an occasion when we step outside of our comfort zone and engage in something that we makes us ask why on earth we started this in the first place and, when it ends, we reflect on with pride and satisfaction.

When we see a four-year-old dressed as a dragon running around and roaring at everyone, the chances are that the child in the dragon costume is one of the most frightened people present because there is uncertainty about how others will react. A while ago, I was in an infant classroom so spacious (falling rolls can sometimes help) that there was room to create an authentic play area garden centre. The children had little stalls selling real plants, proper garden tools and a decent patch of garden through the big doors in which to dig and plant, sow and harvest. In the room the teaching staff had created a pretend water feature and the site manager had made a wooden bridge. As the teacher and I crossed the bridge, three little tots sprang up and chanted, 'Trip, trap, trip, trap, who is crossing our bridge?'

Pulling myself to full height and in my loudest voice, I answered, 'I'm crossing your bridge!' At that point three little tots disappeared outside at great speed. They told their teacher later that they were so surprised because they had never done their chant to a real person before. Adventures come in different forms.

Similarly, children of all ages should be involved in building a collection. Collectors have an interest that is sparked by the opportunity to take their collection forward. Collections come in three main sorts. First there is trying to collect a complete set. Many of us have experiences of collecting cards or stickers from companies that were really trying to sell their products and develop customer loyalty. The second sort of collection is mementoes, whether it is toy cars, rabbit ornaments, bells or simply pebbles from beaches we have visited; often these are random collections. Third is the never-ending collection, where we might collect stamps knowing that we will never get to the end of our collecting. There are stamps from different countries, stamps with animals on, stamps of different colours, stamps of different denominations; the subsets that build are enormous. Generations ago boys used to collect engine numbers from trains. There was no inherent purpose in this, except to discuss numbers with train-spotting friends. Over the years people have collected music and music recordings, football programmes, works of art, *Star Wars* memorabilia and objects of nature. Whatever it is, collectors always have something to talk about and people always have something to ask them about.

Children of all ages should care for plants and creatures. If we want them to grow up to be responsible then they need things to be responsible for; over time they are usually rewarded for their efforts. They should also make things and mend things and take things to bits. They should experience the weather in all its forms rather than find themselves cosseted indoors.

There are a 101 things that children should try by the time they are eleven. What do you think they should be? It doesn't take long for a group of teachers to make a list of way beyond 101. These are the essence and essentials of childhood: making a cake, building a sandcastle, sleeping in a tent, counting the stars, singing on a stage, blowing bubbles, rowing a boat – the list soon emerges and people usually have to narrow it down to get to 101.

Then comes the good bit. Of the 101 things a child should do by the time they are eleven, which should be done at home with the family, which with the local community and which with school? How do we talk with the community and families about the role they can play? The best way is to get them to help in putting the list together.

I remember being in a County Durham primary school in a large village on the coast. The families typically came from the lanes towards the outside of the track. We were discussing with parents the importance of talking with children and enjoying experiences together. There was mention of a beach which was a stone's throw away and several young mums said they didn't take their children to the beach because they went when they were children themselves and didn't find it exciting any more. This kind of outlook defines the failure of society and schooling and we need to work hard to redress the balance. Undaunted, the school worked on the 101 things, gave the parents each a passport to fill in (like the one below) and before long the children were collecting experiences and their parents were filling their time more productively rather than watching daytime TV.

| Activity | Completed when and where | Signed and dated |
|---|---|---|
| Climb a tree | | |
| Go on a train | | |
| Skim stones | | |
| Build a snowman | | |
| Sleep in a tent | | |
| Have a picnic | | |
| Bake a cake | | |
| Care for an animal | | |
| Care for a plant | | |
| Pick fruit | | |
| Fly a kite | | |
| Get soaking wet | | |
| Play a musical instrument | | |
| Know and sing ten nursery rhymes | | |
| Go shopping with your own money | | |
| Go on a boat | | |
| Make a book | | |
| Make and toss a pancake | | |
| Play hopscotch | | |
| Go on a hike | | |
| Go across stepping stones | | |
| Go through a tunnel | | |
| Make and fly a paper aeroplane | | |
| Watch a sunrise and a sunset | | |

The 101 things idea is simple and really catches on. There is a school in Smethwick with their 101 things on a Perspex sign in the entrance hall, a school in Redcar has produced a booklet of theirs, a school in Sheffield has put theirs on their website and there are endless other examples. It builds relationships, provides a means and purpose to do things for busy families, widens experience for children, improves vocabulary and articulacy and opens doors on the world. It is worth a try and is a lovely way to unleash aspiration in communities.

In order to succeed youngsters need aspiration and that aspiration is about more than simply being urged onwards and upwards. Without seeing aspiration in its broadest sense we risk selling children short of our hopes for them. There is much more to aspiration than passing exams and doing well in tests. We want them to achieve, gain qualifications and be prepared for the world beyond in further and higher education, training and employment. We also want them to fulfil our hopes for our young people, as discussed in the opening section of this book. There is more to aspiration than believing that career paths are available that they never knew existed. There is more to aspiration than believing that work or university or further training beckon. It is about recognising the awkwardness of growing up in society, both within school and beyond, understanding why some keep going and others slow down, and finding ways to stop young people giving up. Aspiration is about contribution, belief and spirit. Teachers everywhere try to build the spirit of the pupils they teach. Schools should be working to promote the belief in young people that the world is their oyster – and that they have the tools open it.

## Unleashing aspiration … so what might we do?

- We need to build a sense of purpose in our young people and include them more fully in society, with schooling as an integral part of, rather than parallel to, their growing experience.

- We have to recognise the trepidation that many young people feel about worlds that are unfamiliar to them and their tendency to avoid new situations in which they might be outfaced.

- We must open doors to the unfamiliar and support young people as they cross thresholds. We need to recognise that qualifications provide a ticket to new arenas but that young people need help in order to make use of the invitation the ticket offers them. The school has a role in helping young people to cross thresholds.

- We should be confident enough to talk with young people about etiquette and protocol as a way of making all aspects of society more accessible.

- The school experience must bring children and young people into contact with the widest world through authentic learning activities which build real-world relevance into what they do.

- The pupil premium should be properly targeted at the children in the outside lanes of the track and focused upon essential experiences as a route to literacy and numeracy.

- Employers should be more fully engaged in schooling with children at the youngest ages and they should receive tax allowances for doing so.

- Every club, association or recreational organisation that receives any form of funding from national or local government should only qualify if its membership comprises at least 20% of people below the age of fifteen.

- School inspection should include an analysis of the each pupil's participation in wider activities at school and their engagement in interests beyond the school. The school ought to be expected to work with children and their families to ensure engagement. The school's success in this regard should be a measure of the quality of the school and the school should be credited without recourse to the impact upon data for examinations or test scores.

# ... on assessment, international comparison and research

How can assessment, international comparison and research be grouped together as a section in a book on schooling? Surely they merit more than a short, almost 'by the way', treatment. The reality is that these three elements cast a shadow over the schooling system by being abused while their potential to put education onto a different plane is largely ignored. As they stand, assessment, international comparison and research have significant impact on practice and structures in schooling, often with too little logic for action to be taken. Properly exploited, they could be stepping stones to a better school system.

Let's take one simple example: phonics. This small aspect of learning to read has had a high profile over the last few years. Understanding phonics is a vital aspect of reading. The findings of Johnson and Watson's seven-year longitudinal research study of 300 children in Clackmannanshire published in 2005 concluded that 'the synthetic phonics approach, as part of the reading curriculum, is more effective than the analytic phonics approach'.

The coalition government has decided that synthetic phonics is the silver bullet in teaching young children how to read. Of course phonics matter but so do many other aspects of learning to read: understanding context cues, enjoying the story, interpreting rhyme, perceiving shape, recognising whole words and repetition. Use one to the exclusion of the rest and we risk children not learning to become readers. But the government has made its decision: it has issued guidance and set up a screening process for all children aged six to identify those who may be falling behind. The test contains words that are not words – nonsense such as 'stin', 'proom' and 'sarps' – so that children can be properly tested on their phonic capacity.

The government is not wrong to insist that phonics teaching takes place. Where it is mistaken is in the implementation – that is, using research evidence as a basis for unconnected actions. The government is not wrong to suggest or even insist that children should be screened to check on their development in phonics. The principle of finding the children who are not making expected progress early on and trying to help is a sensible one. It is mistaken in leaping from stressing the importance of teaching phonics as *part* of a reading approach to assuming that competence in this one aspect is enough to measure a school's success in producing a reader. It is wrong in recording the results of screening tests for every six-year-old in the same week of the year and then using this as a yardstick to measure the progress of schools.

Why does the test need to be such a high profile event? Does it need to be drafted from scratch every year? What of the cost? Wouldn't one test used for screening each year be better than spending enormous amounts of money annually to devise a fresh test, think up new nonsense and invent new imaginary characters? The fact that tests are sent to schools and shouldn't be opened until the big day seems to imply that there might be cheating. Surely there would be no deception in a screening test designed to help children to get the support they need. Those requiring the no-cheating approach must either have some motive for insisting upon exam conditions for six-year-olds, distrust teachers or simply lack any understanding of how children learn.

Why does the process have to be national in every aspect? The age range of children taking the tests is considerable: a 17% difference in age between the youngest and oldest. Why can't the test be available to schools to be administered with a child the week before their sixth birthday, allowing for school holidays? Why not do the test with the parent and child sitting together? If the test is about individual progress, at what point does collating the results make the process a data-gathering and school comparison exercise? How do we stop a laudable process becoming part of the market-driven school accountability regime?

If phonics becomes part of the market-rules approach, then schools will begin drilling children for next year's tests. Some would argue that it doesn't matter because, if the children get to the point where they know their phonics, all well and good. But childhood is not about phonics. If the test is used for anything other than screening individual children's acquisition of phonic recognition, it will become yet another useless statistic.

And what of the nonsense words that make up part of the screening test? Apparently there is a worry that some children will know their phonics too well and deceive the screening by 'just seeing and saying them'. Nonsense words are included alongside drawings of imaginary creatures, presumably to make it a fun experience. In the trials it was found that six-year-olds who were good readers sometimes stumbled over the nonsense words and an assumption was made that they weren't reading properly and just knew some words. When faced with nonsense words the children said things like, 'I can't read that, it's nonsense.' It is a bizarre type of screening that shows the best readers to be not the best readers. The danger is that, to ensure children can pass the test, teachers will spend whole lessons getting their classes to read non sense words. Some do this imaginatively: 'Hmmm, I wonder what the alien is trying to tell us?' Others less so: sitting children in front of endless flash cards of made-up words. Surely this time would be better spent expanding their real vocabulary.

Another way to learn phonics is to enjoy sounding out incredibly complex words such as *triceratops, ichthyosaurus, pterodactyl* and *diplodocus*; words which used to be the life blood of every child's riveting study of dinosaurs. There are nursery rhymes in virtually every culture that would acquaint children with words and nonsense. There seems no time to play with long words and riddles these days as teachers have to comply with demands to work with nonsense.

Some will remember the Schonell test of reading. Children were offered a card to read containing disembodied words set in rows of five. They simply had to get as far as they could and, after eight consecutive errors, the teacher would stop the process. From that would be calculated the 'reading age'. 'Tree, little, milk, egg, book' the children would chant and some would get as far as 'terrestrial' or 'idiosyncrasy'. Many schools used this as a simple method of acquiring a yardstick on reading performance and looking at progress. There might be a natural tendency to compare progress between parallel classes but it was a rule-of-thumb method of assessment. It was quick, low stress and gave a picture. It showed where a child was in comparison with its peer group.

It fell from favour because of questions about relevance, the reliability of results in a context-free test and the problem of the potential labelling of children – as well as teaching to the test. Is what we have now any better?

# From assessment to testing

The example of phonics serves to illustrate how the terms 'assessment' and 'research' can be abused by the system. They sound like good, professional, official acts when in fact they are suspect when used for political ends. We have become used to educators talking about evidence-based decisions, being data rich, using data effectively and making international comparisons. The reality is that we find little of this happening in the school system. Politicians, like most people, are selective in their use of data as a reference point, but they are also economic in the ways in which they justify policy as a result of research.

The school system is so data-heavy nowadays that is hard to believe there was a time when it was not so. Until the appearance of the national curriculum, with the exception of the Eleven plus, the form of assessment used, if any, was left up to schools and teachers. Some did weekly tests, some marked every piece of work, some did termly exams. Marks were awarded in different ways: a number out of twenty, a letter A to E or simply a comment written by the teacher on the work. What then happened to the results varied: some schools ranked the children in order, others simply told the parents or the pupils their marks, some produced reports. The school or the teacher decided and the decisions were based on principles and philosophies about learning or the acceptable burden to the teacher.

The shift to central control through the national curriculum brought with it the move to assessment to ensure progress for individual children. Some will remember the late 1980s, when time was allocated in political broadcasts for the Secretary of State for Education, Kenneth Baker, to explain the national curriculum and assessment to parents. Because of concerns at that time about lack of progress and sloppy teaching, levels of attainment were to be specified for the end of each key stage indicating what would be expected of a child making average progress. Kenneth Baker showed on screen how mathematical calculations would get more complex as the children progressed through the primary years.

In order to check progress and give parents information, the government was to introduce assessment of each child in the core subjects at the end of each key stage. This assessment would be carefully constructed to find out what pupils knew, understood and were able to do. It was to be a new form of testing that took place in the classroom in normal everyday conditions so the children could show themselves in their best light, almost without realising they were being tested.

As the national curriculum was introduced, the first assessments took place in Key Stage 1. Teachers were sent Standard Assessment Tasks (notice what the 'T' in SAT used to stand for!) to be carried out with small groups of pupils over a period of a few weeks in science, mathematics and English. The tasks included, for example, a science session around the water tray where children were asked whether a number of objects would float or sink and why this might be the case. There were jokes about children being asked whether the pineapple would float and, when the child was asked why he had given his answer, he replied, 'Because it has floated every time someone else has done it.'

The normally acquiescent teachers of young children were less than impressed. While they were 'assessing' four children for twenty minutes, what was the rest of the class supposed to do? With classes of thirty-plus children, this was at least eight sessions with each of three subjects in a very short time period. How were they supposed to teach anything while this was monopolising their attention? No matter that, at the time, so-called 'small group' approaches were the favoured method of teachers of young children where four children might be the focus of a twenty-minute exposition while the others got on separately. If that was how they worked as a matter of course, why would the SATs be a problem?

The problem was that the SATs all had to take place in a short time frame. All children were to be assessed in June, regardless of the fact that some were 15% older than others. The pressure on teachers to get it done was significant and, following union criticism, the system was tempered in the next few years. The tasks were modified and pencil-and-paper assessments were introduced so that whole classes could be tested at once.

## It could have been different

The Standard Assessment *Tasks* could have remained and been spread over time. Children could have been assessed a week before their seventh birthday, give or take a week or so if they fell in the holidays, and that would not only have spread the assessment burden but also given a good marker for parents, as opposed to what quickly emerged, which was a comparison of children in a year group.

Instead, the pencil-and-paper assessments made their way through the system into Key Stage 2. At the time, little was done with the assessments. The results were communicated to parents and used to inform planning or grouping of children in Key Stage 2. In some cases, local authorities asked for the results to see if there were ways to help schools with particular concerns. In the main it was all low key, except for the burden of the assessment season.

That all changed when the national curriculum and assessment reached Key Stage 3. Some unions responded to the complaints of their membership in the secondary sector about the additional workload associated with the marking of assessment tasks and organised boycotts. The government gave in and agreed to external marking. Unions celebrated a victory, the results of which would come back to haunt the system for decades.

For now the system would be managed centrally. The 'T' in SAT shifted subtly, but importantly, from 'Tasks' to 'Tests' with the results collected and collated nationally and communicated to schools. As the growth of computer technology coincided with this development, there was suddenly the capacity to use the results as 'data'. If data was available it could be deployed to demonstrate which schools achieved more with their pupils and which less. The publication of the first set of test results for Key Stages 1 and 2 came in 1996 and appeared to show that over half of eleven-year-olds were not reaching the expected norm. Without considering whether the tests, the marking or the expected norms might not be correct, the search was on to find the reasons. Variable teaching and issues such as commitment to equal opportunity were cited. Within no time we had performance tables for local authorities and for schools within local authorities. SATs were now about school comparison more than they were about assessing individual pupil progress.

Fischer Family Trust started to make the data work and gradually produced 'evidence' for the now burgeoning Ofsted inspection teams that were sweeping all before them. Schools subscribed to Fischer Family Trust; the more widespread the use of data the more credence it gained. The Department for Education's own RAISEonline became the starting point for inspections. There seemed to be few questions about FFTD being used to make some shocking assumptions about fixing a pupil's learning trajectory. I would argue that this data has led to complacency, labelling and fixed mindsets. It is part of the game theory problem: once the data becomes a measure we work out how to improve the picture of the data without questioning the integrity of the learning experience for pupils. Success brings renewed vigour to respond. We talk the language of FFTD because it is there rather than because it is valid.

The department realised it could support ministers' pet projects if it had evidence to justify the focus of the next challenge. Little stick men entered schools green and came out red to show a lack of progress; here was the next would-be target group. So sophisticated is the database that it is virtually possible to find a child in Widnes who leaves out an apostrophe and get one to him by first-class post. But that would take time and why provide the apostrophe when you can just beat his teacher with a stick (or a red stick man)?

Pressure on schools through data and league tables became pressure on children through test results. Pupils became the currency in the system. How many were labelled as 'potential Level 4s' or were considered to be a 'guaranteed Level 7'? Concerns about labelling, the inappropriateness of testing young children and the game theory reality that testing had become led to more teaching to the test. Complaints from a wide sector, consisting not just of teachers but also academics and parents, built into pressure groups and these, working on the media and politicians, gradually made an impact. In 2004, Charles Clarke announced the end of external testing at Key Stage 1 and a return to teacher assessment in order to reduce stress on children and to encourage more creativity in teaching and learning. It was an opportunity but, since teacher assessments form the basis for Ofsted inspection, many teachers simply turned to old SATs papers to form their judgements. There has been very little training put in place to allow teachers to develop credible alternatives and so the testing continues.

After a national marking fiasco in 2008, the Secretary of State for Children, Schools and Families, Ed Balls, decided that Key Stage 3 tests weren't needed. Nobody seemed to complain but some schools continued testing anyway – they couldn't see how progress might be shown in the absence of a test. To gather a more balanced base of evidence for their judgements more imaginative schools turned to portfolio-based evidence. They seized on initiatives such as Assessing Pupils' Progress (APP) which had been developed by QCA to support periodic assessment of progress. However, as inspection for a while had focused on 'progress', APP soon became used as 'evidence', and in a very short time it too fell victim to game theory with teachers spending endless time completing their records rather than using APP as formative assessment.

Having seen the Key Stage 1 and Key Stage 3 tests go, and having serious concerns about the validity of results at Key Stage 2, some of the teaching unions decided to boycott the SAT tests in 2009. For all sorts of understandable reasons, many head teachers, who for years had collectively despised the tests, decided that they could not support the boycott in their own schools. There were various reasons for this: they were due an Ofsted inspection and needed evidence of progress; parents wanted the tests; the children had spent years preparing for them and now wanted the opportunity to sit them; they needed them as a lever to make staff work hard; they believed in the tests and wanted to prove the upward trajectory. A by-product of the patchiness of the boycott was that any future government was now aware of the extent of compliance in the primary sector and that, while their policies might upset, alarm or cause affront, the policies would happen.

The level of compliance in many schools is such that many senior leaders and teachers simply ask the question 'What do Ofsted want?' in order to plan their strategy for teaching and learning. In higher education, pressure from Ofsted and the TDA has led providers to simply trot out training in synthetic phonics and any other government priority with no exploration of alternatives and without engaging students in critical analysis of the wisdom of the approach. After all, their funding depends on compliance. From teacher training to senior management, pleasing the inspectors is key to survival. Any action that might upset them is akin to institutional suicide. No wonder the profession is feeling lost. How can professional and intellectual autonomy be maintained in such a system? Worse, when given freedom, what is the likelihood of a teacher choosing a new path when all they have known is the old one?

The Bew Review, set up by the coalition government to respond to the boycott, moved testing into a new realm with its questioning of the validity of the writing test. This had been exposed by QCA in 2008 but had never been picked up by the media, unions or schools. A child's chance of being placed in the wrong level in the writing test was as high as 30%. On a national scale (600,000 pupils), the data evens out and statistical significance is a minor issue. The implications for the secondary career of individuals, however, were significant. Here was a clear statement that the SATs were about school performance rather than individual progress. The tests have been modified but their impact still determines the starting point for inspection and the school's credibility within its local area.

The situation is that national assessment in England is central to an accountability-led, market-driven approach to schooling. It has little to do with individual children's education and it significantly dominates the agenda of schools under pressure by Ofsted and league table position. It is called 'assessment' but really it is 'testing'.

## The grip of testing

Since the early 1990s, we have tried to use our testing regime for too many purposes. In theory, one national test is used to check on the progress of the individual, to inform teaching, school comparison, national year-on-year progress and to give information to parents. There are numerous other purposes but already these are too many for one test.

QCA did an analysis of each year's test on a question-by-question basis to inform schools how their pupils had performed. The effect was that schools would focus next year's cohort on areas that were lacking in this year's in order to improve results for the school. The children who had their results analysed were by now in the secondary school, untroubled by any effort to address their own highlighted shortfalls.

The four-year-long Key Stage 2 was felt to leave too much time between assessments so something needed to be done to demonstrate progress. We saw the development of sub-levels, designed to show whether pupils were making progress in sufficient numbers in order to justify government policy. It was never intended that national curriculum levels of attainment should be subdivided in this way but the sub-levels gained credence as a lever in the system on schools, teachers and children.

Then there are the 'optional tests'. These help schools to check their own perceptions of children's progress through each key stage. Sadly, the other great cloud hanging over schools, Ofsted, creates so much pressure for evidence that the most valid evidence schools can think of is collected via the nationally produced option. So optional tests take children and their teachers through a testing experience in Year 4 which tells good teachers little and risks reinforcing self-fulfilling prophecies of children and teachers alike.

The 'testing when ready' concept nearly broke through. Aware that the end of key stage testing was losing credibility, the Labour government allowed a trial of testing designed to bring forward children when they were ready, based on teachers' assessments. Sadly, it was so poorly explained that the pilots went badly wrong. The results were fascinating however. Children generally performed poorly and much worse than anticipated. The analysis of the reasons for this showed a poor understanding of the assessment process by teachers. The DfES (as it was then) gave three reasons for the failure of the pilots: children were entered for inappropriate levels, the children were not 'up for it' because there was no hype around the testing and the tests were held too near to Christmas so schools had other priorities.

These reasons say much about the futility of testing in the way we do it. Some schools were entering all of their Year 7 children for Level 7 tests, Year 5s for Level 5 and so on. How aimless, and what an indictment of the way that the nationalisation of testing has led teachers to walk unquestioningly to national demand. The idea that children were not 'up for it' raises all sorts of questions about the reliability of results in the end of key stage tests taken in summer and the claims that children are hot-housed to achieve results for their schools which, after a twelve-week break between testing and entry to secondary school, often seem to bear little relation to their real performance. The Christmas distraction adds fuel to the hot-housing argument.

The reality is that, as schools and their verifiers pore over their RAISEonline data, FFTD spreadsheets, mid-year reviews and Cognitive Abilities Test (CAT) forecasts, they are only partially into assessment and very much into test analysis. When children do their umpteenth SATs practice test, it might be that the only assessment that is happening is the child's own assessment of their capabilities. The setting of targets for individuals to work to at the next national curriculum level might feel like part of the assessment process, but might also be having the effect of diminishing the learning outlook if not done well.

Of course, there is an argument that, whether we like it or not, testing has raised attainment and produced better qualified pupils, so it serves its purpose. There is no doubt that children need to read, write and manage numbers but the doubts about the validity and reliability of the testing regime and its impact on the learning diet of young people make it an extremely questionable practice. How far does the emphasis on testing, and the resultant manipulation of the work of schools, take us away from the wider hopes for our young people?

## From testing to assessment

The assessment approach that has most impact is talked of least. This is ipsative assessment – the assessment of ourselves by ourselves, often called self-assessment. Basically we all do it all the time. We rate ourselves internally in response to what others tell us. It is what keeps some of us going when all other indications are bad. It is how we keep in proportion the accolades heaped upon us because we know the truth. A beginner's width certificate can be a major achievement or a mere trifle depending on how well we can swim. We all know whether we truly earned our degree or A levels or whether we 'played the game' to perfection. Ipsative assessment is affected by the way we are assessed by our teachers.

The effective teacher uses formative assessment well through insightful observation, sometimes structured, which sheds light on aspects of development so that the next step of teaching becomes clear to the teacher and pupil. Formative assessment is much more subtle than the analysis of summative assessment data or the construction of a series of minor and incremental summative assessments.

A really good reference point on assessment is Carol Dweck, who has written two major books on the theory of 'mindset'. Her extensive research concludes that people with a 'growth mindset' will approach learning in a different way from those with a 'fixed mindset'. Those who have a fixed mindset tend to limit their aspirations and wilt when the work gets difficult or when assessments reveal that things aren't going well, whereas those with a growth mindset are not afraid of failure and are much more resilient when faced with tough problems and the need to work better and harder.

If we want to really unleash aspiration there is surely something valuable about encouraging an outlook in pupils to see problems as obstacles to be overcome rather than challenges that are insurmountable. Carol Dweck has researched many of the positive strategies that schools – some schools – are using to encourage a growth mindset outlook in classrooms. However, governments are slow to adopt practice resulting from this type of research in ways that can take it to scale. There are various reasons but there is often a long time lag between the input and the measure which is hard to value in a world of accountability based on test results.

Other examples, such as the small-scale but detailed longitudinal Sandercock Study, pass largely unnoticed. Dr Gavin Sandercock, a children's fitness expert at Essex University, studied how a group of 315 Essex ten-year-olds in 2008 compared with 309 children of the same age in 1998. Among many measures, he found that the number of sit-ups ten-year-olds can do declined by 27.1%, arm strength fell by 26% and grip strength by 7%. He concluded that this was due to changes in activity patterns among ten-year-olds, such as taking part in fewer activities like rope climbing in PE and tree climbing for fun. Many children refused to try some of the tests and some worried about 'being out of breath'. However, in the same time, the body mass index (BMI) of the children had not changed significantly. Sandercock suggested that the government should review their use of the BMI test in the National Childhood Measurement Programme and institute a fitness-testing regime for children. The government brushed this aside – who would want yet more tests? The focus of these tests might, however, have a bigger effect on the health and well-being of our children in the future than the introduction of phonics tests. The point is that our assessment of children has become limited to a small, if important, aspect of their development. Alternatively, we could look at other elements which would serve them well in later life as well as give us indications about the changing state of childhood and what we might need to do about it.

## Research

There has always been a lot of research about but examples that have made an actual difference to what goes on in schools, to the very practice of the place, are few and far between. Why is this? One reason is that research is often seen as shedding light on an issue that a government can use for headline-grabbing gain rather than trialling a new approach to achieving better outcomes. Another explanation is that the research community tends to validate itself through scrutiny of the study rather than the testing of outcomes. A new drug or surgical technique would be tested in field trials, with the result that only after proven success would it become accepted and expected practice for the profession.

A further cause is the lack of engagement of teachers in the research process. Educational research and teaching are essentially separate activities. There is rarely an advertisement inviting teachers to put themselves forward as participants in a pilot study or field testing process. Free access to Master's programmes had the potential to address this to some extent, encouraging teachers to take on action research projects, which might, if utilised properly, have fed into university-led research. Unfortunately the re-introduction of fees and the abolition of the MTL has seen a sharp fall in teacher engagement with higher education, and the constant attacks by Michael Gove on what he perceives as a left-wing higher education establishment has further distanced research from classroom practice.

In addition, many studies have little impact. They are small scale and serve to ensure an individual's or group's profile within a research community, which largely debates its own research activity, usually without any groundbreaking findings which could influence practice on a large scale. The survival of a research unit depends on its standing in the annual Research Assessment Exercise (RAE) tables which collate the number of publications in academic journals and grade them according to significance. Only academic periodicals count and publication in an international journal carries more points than a national one, for example. If an academic writes a book aimed at enlightening teachers or students there is no credit in the RAE, so what's the point in writing it? Teachers don't tend to read academic journals. There they sit, on the shelf, read only by other academics. So there is no incentive to create a body of evidence that aims to improve teaching and learning as a whole.

Some institutions buck this trend. Much has been done at the universities of Cambridge, York, Bristol, Exeter, the Open University and the Institute of Education in London to extend our understanding of creativity, assessment and dialogue in the classroom, but these findings are rarely accessed directly by teachers. They are sometimes used selectively by governments and these watered-down, policy-infused versions find their way into our classrooms without expanding the theoretical underpinnings of the findings. How many teachers are using the 'traffic lights' approach in their classrooms to limited effect? If so why? What research led to the three-part lesson and back again? Where have mini-plenaries come from?

Incomplete and piecemeal understanding of research can be cata-strophic for teaching because the mouthpiece through which it is presented is too often Ofsted. Teachers need to go back to the source. Higher education institutions need to be thinking about impact that is wider than their own league table standings. Everyone needs to start looking at the children instead of each other, and governments need to recognise that there is too much diversity in the schooling system to be able to say that results can be replicated at scale, especially when there is no coordination. The only statement that fits all schools is that one size does not fit all.

In addition, there are problems with scale and funding. Too often, the research does not 'prove' anything. It does not find the solution to problems for learning but simply sheds light on the issues. There is usually insufficient financial support to allow the trial to go to scale. There is no chance to set up double-blind trials. Very little research in classrooms has led to a system-wide change of practice or methodology.

Funding for research is haphazard and often comes from charities or philanthropists with their own agendas. As a result, the findings are often viewed with suspicion by governments that suspect an ulterior motive. Studies funded by government are often limited by its hypoth-esis or question which in turn is framed to support an existing viewpoint. When the research does not support that position it is fre-quently ignored. This is perhaps not as obvious as Michael Gove ignoring his own expert panel on curriculum reform, but certainly many 'off message' research projects have been swept under the carpet by ministers, even while capturing the imagination of teachers. The shameful dismissal of the Cambridge Primary Review is only one example of this.

# Research that made a difference

Now and again, a piece of research grabs the attention of the media and politicians seize upon it as evidence to support their policy. The development of phonics has been reinforced by the small-scale Clackmannanshire research that I mentioned above and which fell into the Tories' lap while in opposition.

At a time of growing concern about primary schooling in the 1970s, Professor Neville Bennett of Lancaster University poured fuel on the fire. He knew how to make an impact. The release of his book, *Teaching Styles and Pupil Progress* in 1976 coincided with a BBC *Panorama* programme that questioned modern 'progressive' methods. The programme attracted widespread attention for its major conclusion that formal teaching styles foster greater pupil progress than more informal ones. That Bennett had used a small sample of only thirty-two schools and only one met his criteria of being 'informal' in approach to learning, was constantly questioned by the research community. The impact of the Eleven plus, which still operated in the schools where the research took place, was also challenged. Indeed, fellow researchers gave the study short shrift but Bennett's cooperation with the media had made a big impact on the public and the profession.

I attended several presentations by Professor Bennett at the time and almost every question from the floor began with something like 'I haven't actually read the book, but ...' Bennett, to his credit, always stated that the TV programme had told only part of the story. The die had been cast though, and as an example of influence on the national scene, it was significant. Callaghan's Ruskin speech, the William Tyndale School and Professor Bennett all raised questions that have repercussions today in forming the basis of the sort of thinking, supported by Michael Gove, that traditional forms of teaching are best. This view persists in spite of the fact that it flies in the face of all that cognitive psychologists and neuroscientists are discovering about memory and emotion in the learning process.

Over the years there have been some significant pieces of research which were good in their own right and have had a positive effect, even if they were short-lived. In 1979, Michael Rutter and colleagues published *Fifteen Thousand Hours: Secondary Schools and Their Effects on Children*, which looked into patterns of life within the walls of a school and how these patterns affect pupil achievement. This was one of the first studies to draw attention to the variable performance not only between schools but also within schools. The researchers concluded that each school, had its own 'ethos' or ambiance which was largely responsible for its success or failure. The results emphasised that schools can do much to foster good behaviour and attainment and that, even in a disadvantaged area, schools can be a force for the good.

This was groundbreaking stuff but a look at the actual findings of the complex and detailed studies would mirror many of the mantras of the current time as espoused by the recognised school improvers. In Rutter's study, it was found that schools with a good ethos had several things in common. Teachers got along well with students and their expectations of the students were high. They assigned homework regularly, marked it rapidly and returned it with helpful comments. They came to classes well prepared, managed classroom time effectively, moved smoothly from one activity to the next and maintained appropriate discipline. Children were seen to be very receptive towards teachers who had high expectations about pupil achievement and behaviour within their classrooms. Good behaviour was also associated with the system of discipline that the school had adopted. Rutter's list has proven to be accurate over time. If his findings had been implemented, the time taken might have been shortened and the benefits been greater if each subset of the research had been part of detailed improvement practice, with the trialling of techniques brought to scale.

The research team did not deny that family background was important. However, they demonstrated that schools play a crucial role in educating children, and that some schools do a far better job than others. Children are very quick to pick up other people's expectations of their academic competence and their behaviour. They tend to live up (or down) to what is expected of them. If this is what Rutter found in

1979, let's not decry research or academic study. Let's instead work out how to get the research and the practice communities working together to make progress based on the findings of valid research. Since Rutter there have been umpteen government reviews into pupil expectations in one form or other. We have re-ploughed the ground several times, planted many seeds of experiment but not had the combined resource to harvest the crop.

In 1997, Peter Mortimore, one of Rutter's team of et als, replicated the findings in a study of fifty primary schools and produced a book called *School Matters,* in which 2,000 pupils were monitored closely over a four-year period. The factors influencing school success were spelt out and vary little from those emphasised today. The schools that have made such dramatic progress over the last few years have often done so because, knowingly or unknowingly, they have heeded research findings and put them to good use. What we need is a systematic approach to research that engages the profession more fully and more coherently.

In the late 1970s, Maurice Galton led a team of researchers in a series of classroom studies (Observational and Classroom Learning Evaluation – ORACLE) and continued with a 'replication study' twenty years later to investigate the effects of transition from primary to secondary schooling. In the intervening two decades a great deal had changed. Transition as well as transfer is now on the agenda for most schools, with transfer better organised from the point of view of teachers, pupils and parents. Much, though, still remained to be done to overcome the more intractable problems to do with curriculum continuity and teaching and learning at points of transition. The study looked at the attitudes of pupils and revealed that secondary schools frequently see the years between national key stage tests and public examinations as somehow less important and do not appreciate that working hard during these periods can have pay-offs later. Pupils can become pre-occupied with friendships and gain a reputation for 'messing around'; pupils who want to change from being a 'dosser' to a 'worker' find it extremely difficult to shake off their old image. Consequently, they may decide to 'give up' rather than to 'catch up'.

Galton's was an example of classroom-focused research that struck a chord with teachers in both sectors and where a national approach could have been developed with structured trials to establish and refine best practice from the point of view of pupil learning. Sadly, the move to parental preference in admission to secondary schools, the gradual shift to competition between schools and the increasing diversity of transfer arrangements have meant that the preconditions for the search for best practice at transfer become less of a professional teaching matter and more of a public relations exercise.

Robin Alexander is a researcher of note and integrity. His controversial and widely read report on primary education in Leeds (1991), examined an ambitious programme of local reform aimed at improving teaching and learning in the primary schools of one of Britain's largest cities. It addressed important questions about children's needs, the curriculum, classroom practice and school management and was recognised for its thoroughness and detail. It was also quoted – and misquoted – in support of widely opposing political and media agendas. The report called into sharp question the role of local authority advisers and the tendency for them to be drawn to schools showing the practice they espoused and away from those that differed. Indirectly, it led to the establishment of the nationwide inspection system which was initially a good thing in terms of developing consistency of focus within the schooling system. In the same report, Alexander highlighted the dangers of trying to ensure all teachers adopted consistent practices without proper awareness of the research background. His call for a more research-orientated teaching profession was largely unheeded. Politicians are selective and, sadly, the profession often oblivious when it comes to research.

By 2006, Alexander had become more savvy when he took the lead in the Cambridge Primary Review, the most exhaustive and thorough review of primary education since Plowden forty years before. Supported from 2006–2012 by generous grants from the Esmée Fairbairn Foundation, the scope of the Cambridge Primary Review and the depth of its evidence allowed it to go beyond being simply a report and permitted it to give attention to dissemination, policy engagement, setting up a professional network and building professional capacity.

With a strong team of researchers and his customary attention to secure methodology, Alexander set out to build awareness of the system, its successes and shortcomings, and to help those in schools do something about it while recommending policy considerations. It was a profound piece of research and analysis and Alexander had developed the idea of publishing sections at intervals which had the effect of building awareness and attention. His work on children's lives, their parenting and caring, paved the way for interim reports on learning and teaching. The periodic release of these staged reports caught media attention and anticipation of future interim reports grew as the spread of the survey touched more people. In 2008, the Labour government, stung by the Cambridge Primary Review's criticism of their strategy for testing as well as literacy and numeracy, tried to head off Alexander's work on the curriculum by instituting a separate review of the primary national curriculum under the guidance of one of his 'Three Wise Men' colleagues from the early 1990s, Jim Rose. What followed was two years of parallel reviewing which was confusing to schools who thought Jim and Robin were doing the same thing, or one was working for the other, or worse, that they were in opposition.

The much-anticipated final Cambridge Primary Review was published in 2009. It never got to first base politically, let alone past it. One of the report's areas of concern had been the extent to which 'formal' approaches to children's learning were being seen with increasingly younger pupils. Alexander and colleagues recommended that early learning should build on the natural state of childhood and that structured and formal approaches should start later than they currently do. His mistake was to put a time limit on the proposal and, once the report had recommended that formal structures should begin for children at the age of six, there was a target for politicians to exploit through the media. The recommendation was interpreted as 'children would not start school until they were six'. The media loved it and the Labour government was made to issue a one-line response saying that it had no plans to raise the starting age for schooling. The Tories gave the review short shrift and, within days, it was off the radar for most of the general public.

It was all very sad. The section reviewing international evidence was more thorough, insightful and rational than most others and, written from a UK perspective, gave clear indications on how the system might improve – not simply to beat the rest but to achieve our own cultural aims for schooling. Apart from that, the developmental work done by the review on curriculum was strong and could have dovetailed easily with Rose's recommendations, but the Labour government's hesitancy meant that nothing was finalised before their election defeat and we were left with the current mess.

The coalition has taken scant regard of Alexander's recommendations. Some lip service to incorporating aims in the interim review have been ignored or forgotten as the government dictates what the chair of the National Curriculum Review Panel, Tim Oates, writes. The recommendations of the interim review on encouraging oracy are well borne out by Robin Alexander's previous research in his work on talk in classrooms but with the interim review out of the way, the programmes of study lack much reference to the vital importance of oracy. No wonder Andrew Pollard, another researcher with integrity, decided to step away from the national curriculum development work. And so the nation squandered one of the most large-scale and comprehensive reviews of primary education ever. It lost the chance to build that into action research through dissemination and collaborative follow-up. Instead, it is acquiring an outdated national curriculum based on the prejudices and personal ideologies of transient individual ministers.

# A current example ... and an opportunity

In 2012, Durham University published the findings of a piece of research, funded by the Sutton Trust, into the use by schools of the pupil premium. The research team focused on what the evidence indicates is effective in improving teaching and learning and then working out what additional costs are associated with these approaches. What emerged is an indication of the comparative impact of a range of 'school improvement solutions' on a bang-for-the-buck basis. There is no claim that necessarily this will be the impact when schools try them out. Some of the approaches that are less effective on average might be more effective in a new setting or if developed in a novel way. The intention is to give schools the evidence they need when it comes to making a good bet on what might be valuable, or help them to proceed with caution when trying out something that has not worked so well in the past. The study points out that it will still be necessary for each school to evaluate the actual benefits of any changes in their own context to ensure the investment really does help pupils from low-income families achieve their educational potential as intended. The intention of the second stage of the process is to follow through with case studies to evaluate impact locally.

A solid national step would be to build on such analysis through a research-engaged professional teacher community so that effective practice becomes recommendation and then approved practice as per the world of medicine. As it is, some schools will be oblivious to the detail of the research, though no doubt Ofsted will alert them to it, and it will make its way into the school system in a patchy way, its true benefits missed on a large scale.

# International comparisons

Until a few years ago, few people in English schools had heard or taken notice of PISA (Programme for International Student Assessment) or TIMMS (Trends in International Mathematics and Science), two sets of initials that have gradually exerted greater influence on practice in our schools. These international comparison statistics went largely unnoticed in the early days; indeed the UK (not England alone) rarely provided a big enough sample of pupil data to be included. All this changed in 2008, when the release of test data from the previous year's round showed that UK pupils' results had fallen in comparison with other jurisdictions. Since then, any policy change seems to be based on the need to arrest the decline in performance of English schools as compared to the rest of the world. No matter what the tests actually show, no matter what the Organisation for Economic Co-operation and Development (OECD) analysis actually indicates, the PISA tests are ideal as a baseline for the sort of sound-bite politics that the media enjoys.

The data itself, and the testing process that provides the data, are now subject to methodological critique by defenders of our own system but it is a bit too late to criticise when the country's performance is sliding downwards; it is not exactly working from a position of strength. The rationalisation for the downward trajectory feels equally hollow. It may be that China is doing well because poor families send their children to live rurally with grandparents and the only pupils left in towns to be tested are the more affluent. It may be that in Scandinavia there are government PISA offices and teenagers compete to be in the national PISA entry. Does it matter? Equally, the questioning of whether our society is the same as Korea or Singapore or Finland, and whether we would want to have the same social structures, are really side issues. What matters more is whether we are being honest about communicating the outcomes and findings. If we are just going to use headlines and sound-bites, let's at least use accurate ones.

So what are the headlines? The PISA tests actually show that the highest achieving pupils in the UK perform just as well as any across the world. Our nation's problem is with the long tail of low achievement. This begs the question of how implementing accountability in the form of an EBacc type suite of qualifications for the pupils at the top of the achievement scale in England would make a difference to the pupils at the back of the learning race – the ones who are walking or giving up, which the OECD, through PISA tests, highlights as our biggest issue. Questions have been raised about the nature of the test used in the PISA analysis. There is an assumption in the media that the test focuses on knowledge, when in fact a closer reading of the OECD analysis points more to application. Many UK youngsters struggle to interpret visual data and make connections in their thinking. No amount of rote learning is going to address this issue. Instead pupils need a diet of learning that is authentic in approach and enables real application of knowledge and skills in worthwhile contexts.

The OECD then looks at what it calls 'high performing systems' and tries to tease out what enables them to succeed. A very significant factor in all the highest performing systems is the prestige with which the teaching sector is viewed. This includes salaries compared with average for the country and the narrow gap between the highest and lowest paid earners. The autonomy of schools is also cited as a factor in high performing systems and this is one of the sound-bites used in England to show how we are learning from abroad. The problem is that the word 'autonomy' seems to have several interpretations. In Scandinavia, autonomy is a respect for the profession of teaching which recommends the way forward in schools collectively and individually. In England it seems that autonomy describes what you are allowed to do within the confines of your shackles.

What of highly regarded Finland? How might we learn from their approaches? Well, children in Finland begin schooling at the age of six, there are no homework requirements and uniform rules are minimal. All pupils receive free education, including meals, transport, support services and resource materials. Pupils experience less 'class hours' per week and experience informal relationships with teachers compared to most systems. There are no national examinations until the age of seventeen. The OECD observes: 'There is significant autonomy for schools over curriculum and examination usage. Teacher based assessments are used by schools to monitor progress and these are not graded, scored or compared; but instead are descriptive and utilised in a formative manner to inform feedback and assessment of learning.' It adds: 'A combination of alternative pedagogic approaches rather than mere instructional methods are utilised by teachers' and this leads to 'greater creativity, productivity and innovation'.

The OECD analysis, though, points to one factor above all others that defines and correlates with each jurisdiction's relative success: the gap in wealth between the highest earners and lowest earners in any country relates directly to performance on PISA tests. The UK has one of the highest 'equity gaps' in the world but, in terms of test performance, our pupils do relatively well. We don't hear much about these aspects of the analysis because they don't play easily in the press and are critical of government social policy over time. So, instead, we are fed lazy, unscrupulous and disingenuous headlines to give an air of authority to support controversial proposals based on personal ideology.

## What should we do?

- The schooling system needs to invest in the continuing learning of every teacher.

- Every teacher should be part of an approved subject association or wider community around learning, such as an Early Years organisation, health education or careers, which would in turn see them as part of a teaching and learning network.

- Every teacher should see it as their professional role to be part of the research community. They should produce papers on their work every three years as a condition of their licensing as a teacher. Time needs to be directed to research and scholarly activity as part of their allocated annual commitment.

- A National Council for Schooling could establish trials and pilots to further research recommendations and could support projects as they go to scale. There could be a coherent plan for research into new approaches and recommendations for approval.

- We need to articulate clearly the difference between assessment and testing, and then work to increase the former and reduce the latter.

- We need a media that strongly questions ministerial and opposition assertions about 'evidence'.

- We need a research community that works in partnership with the profession to manage and articulate key approved practice trials that are focused on making a difference rather than creating a splash.

- The new Teaching Schools and partner Higher Education Institutions should work together to develop practice from research approaches as an integral part of their long-term endeavour.

- We should select and train a specialised team of pupils to represent the UK at the next round of PISA tests in order to improve our standing. I am joking – but it is possibly being done as I write ...

# … on qualifications and examinations, academic and vocational

If ever there was an aspect of the schooling system that needed sorting out, it is qualifications. The relatively simple challenge of asking the individual to prove that they are qualified for the next stage of their lives, for a particular role or an avenue they want to pursue, has become so complicated over time that it is virtually unworkable. Worse, the impact of the importance that qualifications have now acquired means that their influence is impinging on the learning of increasingly younger pupils – and not for the better.

This section of the book is largely about GCSEs and their equivalent. If you are involved with older or younger periods of schooling, you might be tempted to think it isn't for you. It is. If your concern is primary education you will see the backwash of pressure on secondary schools coming towards you. If you teach beyond GCSE you will see how your students are affected. When I went to QCA as director of curriculum, I had visions of affecting the curriculum in schools for the better experience of pupils and I began to formulate a grand plan. Some of my senior colleagues in the curriculum division counselled that we would need to influence the qualifications division. I had thought this was an area beyond our scope; each to his own. I came to learn how the pressure on schools from high-stakes accountability meant that the design of qualifications probably had more impact than anything else on the learning life of the pupil. We always tried – but against the odds.

There are fundamental and overlapping problems with the examinations regime and it comes down to the polarised arguments:

■ Whether we are examining children to find the best performers or to recognise what pupils can achieve now or in the future.

- Whether examinations remain as demanding as they were in previous times.

- Whether so-called academic qualifications are more valid or harder to achieve than so-called vocational ones.

- Whether the individual should have a rounded set of qualifications or specialise.

## Whether we are examining to find the best performers or to recognise what pupils can achieve now or in the future

The English Baccalaureate was proposed in order to ensure that the examination identified the best performers and future prospects. Or was it? The EBacc was proposed and instigated as a new classification, designed not for the benefit of the pupil but as a measure of the school. It was introduced by Michael Gove, in 2010, as part of league table analysis in order to encourage schools to enter pupils for examinations at GCSE in five key areas: English, mathematics, geography or history, sciences, a language, ancient or modern. Computer science was then added to the list. Instead of explaining why these subjects had been selected, the secretary of state simply insisted these were 'harder' subjects – an assertion that was actually contrary to the 2009 research findings by QCA, the then regulator. His argument was that these subjects were more demanding because fewer pupils took these examinations at A level. From there on, the other subject communities sought to argue that their discipline should be included in the EBacc, with relatively little question about whether the fundamental idea was a good one.

As a result, many young people who had recently received their GCSE results would feel that their good grades in music, design technology or art counted for little. The government fell into the same trap as previous ones by linking individual achievement with school performance.

The arbitrary decision to include the chosen subjects in their retrospective EBacc was beautifully arrogant.

There was initially little debate over whether the EBacc was a good idea or not and even less debate over what subjects should be in it. The Taunton Report of 1868 seemed to form the basis of much of it and the rest seemed to be the result of those who screamed most loudly. If an EBacc was a good idea to encourage a rounded education, then maybe the model of its International Baccalaureate forerunner would have been worth considering, including as it does elements of contribution and growth beyond examination success. If the focus was on what is needed for our society, then where might ICT fit and how might we explain Latin or Classical Greek in preference to Mandarin or Punjabi? And what about economics, which ought to be an important requirement at a time when we are told that our society faces its biggest financial challenge ever.

And how about study of an applied nature, such as a BTEC? If a vocational element were to be included as a compulsory element then independent schools would see their league positions dramatically changed. Perhaps the EBacc Certificate might have included a balanced proportion of qualifications achieved through final examination and continuous assessment. Maybe all children would have been expected to provide portfolio evidence of progress and participation in an arts subject.

Forty years ago, just 15% of sixteen-year-olds were entered for an O level qualification. Gove's version of the EBacc would have returned us to a position where just 15% were seen as successful. There seemed little attempt to determine whether this would count as an achievement, even by comparison with the so-called 'best in the world'. There is a moral duty on the part of governors, heads and teachers to expose the wrong that was being wrought on learners. The trouble was that many understandably worked to ensure that their pupils were not disadvantaged or that their schools would not be unfavourably compared, and involuntarily complied with the new direction.

It was not the fundamental principle of the EBacc that was questionable, but there was something quite distasteful about the way it was being implemented. Maybe the five subjects were not the most challenging at all. Possibly they were easier to achieve for some of the people who take them. A bit like being elected to parliament in a safe seat; not much is required but once you are through, you can do as you wish. Maybe some of those with high academic achievements might have benefited from a little vocational knowledge and skill. Having an EBacc would not have been much use for DIY moat cleaning, chandelier bulb changing or duck house installation.

## Whether examinations remain as demanding as they were in previous times

The reliability and validity of the system is always in question. Are the examinations easier than in an indeterminate golden age? Why are more youngsters passing them? How do more young people achieve higher grades? Have modular courses made it easier to pass by offering bite-sized learning? How many re-sits are acceptable? How can practical applications in a vocational subject be equal to academic rigour in a scholarly subject? Is there grade inflation?

Sixty years ago, the Advanced level examination was established to test whether an individual was fit for a course of further study or employment; success would produce a qualification to demonstrate that to universities and employers. The Ordinary level examination served to indicate the best pathways for individuals in terms of A level study or employment. It is important to recognise that the A level was originally a norm-referenced test. When grading was introduced in 1963, only a certain percentage of the cohort would be allowed to achieve an A grade and results gave an indication of the relative standing of an individual compared with others who took the examination. Indeed, the entrant was called a 'candidate', someone who was putting themselves forward for 'selection' for a grade based on the evidence of the examination. It meant that even if teaching improved and the performance of one cohort exceeded that of the previous year, there would be no significant impact on the proportion of pupils achieving a certain grade. All that universities or employers knew was that the A grade pupils represented the best 8% of that year's intake. Whether the B graders were better than the previous year's A graders was irrelevant. In fact, if university entrance is the focus then it doesn't matter if the test is norm referenced because there are a limited number of places and the entrance is an annual event. However, as the qualification began to be used as a means of judging entry into employment, sometimes years in the future, the unfairness of this system began to become more apparent. In 1987, specific criteria were fixed for grades B and E, with the other grades divided out according to fixed percentages.

The onset of the GCSE in the late 1980s was intended to recognise the achievement of a wider range of young people and to use the spur of a qualification as a motivational pull through secondary schooling. It was heralded as the 'Qualification for All'. The new GCSE examination was a criteria-referenced test. The numbers at each grade were entirely dependent upon the performance of each pupil. Anyone who could demonstrate their ability as an A grade would receive an A grade. Everyone's efforts would be acknowledged, with a G grade being available to those who met the criteria.

With better trained teachers, now needing both a degree and higher professional qualification to teach, and with the development of a clear syllabus and freely available criteria, the number of pupils passing and achieving grew exponentially. Seeing the impact on motivation in the latter years of secondary life, efforts grew to establish a wider range of more accessible courses that would and should be recognised for qualification and to make the examinations more suited for pupils of varying aptitudes; hence the move away from the 'one sitting of a pen and paper test'.

At the heart of the Tomlinson Report in 2004, was an effort to ensure that pupils would receive qualifications that were fit for purpose, understandable and represented the individual pupil's performance in a balance of practically applied and scholarly work. Tomlinson's recommendations for a diploma qualification sought to bring coherence and continuity to schooling for pupils, while bringing some logic to qualifications for employers and higher education institutions. The diplomas introduced in the pilot phases were generally well regarded, but the twin pressures of the complex local organisation of provision for the fourteen-to-nineteen age group and resistance from the traditional qualifications lobby meant that progress was slow; slow enough to halt entirely with the change of government.

Now that every child was being entered for GCSE qualifications, the examinations had become the equivalent of a school-leaving examination and, since virtually every pupil was entered, comparisons in performance could be made year on year and between schools. The examination of pupils shifted to accountability of schooling and, once again, game theory came into play.

League tables achieved prominence in the mid 1990s. The Labour government questioned why every pupil was not achieving at least one GCSE and set 'floor targets' for five decent (i.e. grade C and above) GCSE passes. Schools, playing the game, embarked on finding the courses that offered the best access to qualifications and market-driven awarding bodies set out to provide them. The awarding bodies then had to find the augmented product to attract more schools to them: the course text produced by the chief examiner, handy guides for students, analyses of the previous year's papers to give advice on approach and courses for teachers led by examiners. As results rose, so did congratulations, criticism and future floor targets. With every year-on-year rise there were questions about why so many were succeeding – along with complaints about grade inflation and easier examinations – and condemnation of the fact that a large proportion of pupils were leaving school without five GCSEs. The newspapers would find a 'warm-up' question in a lower tier examination paper that they said showed how trivial and easy all exams had become (interestingly, they invariably offered the answers at the foot of the page!).

But the game was on and ministers realised how swiftly schools would respond to the pressure of league tables, especially as Ofsted inspection was now in full flow and the data from GCSEs was a key indicator of school quality. From 'five GCSEs' to 'five GCSE equivalents' was only a small step. The fact that we then saw dramatic rises in individual schools' results proved that some head teachers were 'getting it right'. What they were getting right was that they were using every trick in the book to lift results. And why wouldn't they? All heads and teachers have the future well-being of their pupils at heart and they know that exam success gives a better opportunity in life. But many had the nagging feeling that pupils were now little more than a currency. The average point score was as vital as the future outlook for the pupil; if a pupil was capable of passing thirteen GCSEs, why shouldn't they? Spreading the net and finding the courses that would offer the best 'equivalents', where simple accessibility had now been reduced to spoon-feeding, would be more tactically astute for the school than securing more demanding success for the pupil.

In the face of criticism of questionable rising standards, the Labour government upped the ante on floor targets to five good GCSEs 'including English and mathematics'. Again schools tried to respond and again results rose. The fact that this meant in some schools that arts subjects were removed in favour of more maths and English (a classic game theory move) didn't even make headlines; extra maths, extra English, more and more intervention and coaching to the exam, repeated re-sits. All this without consideration of whether or not it was reducing pleasure or engagement with the subject disciplines or creating less well-rounded pupils.

As the system changed so did the game, and the twin pressure of Ofsted and league table position ensured the game continued. All the time, the Labour government had a heart, maybe a wooden one, but a heart all the same. It made allowance for the disadvantage of background. Since the publication of the first league tables, parents were attracted to schools which were doing well or making most progress in year-on-year performance. Labour allowed the inclusion of contextual value-added measures to validate the efforts of schools in challenging circumstances when comparing their results against others in more affluent areas.

In the face of questions about the credibility and roundedness of examinations, Labour sanctioned the International Baccalaureate (IB) as a qualification to be available through one school in each authority, but only in the sixth form. The IB is attractive to many and it is an approach to learning and an ethos as much as it is a qualification. It begins in primary school with the Primary Years Programme and continues through the Middle Years Programme, which incidentally isn't externally assessed, leading to the summation of the IB. To introduce it simply as a sixth-form level qualification flew in the face of its very purpose. The IB has served a small internationally mobile community who needed an education system that might be transferable from country to country, allowing children to stay with parents who had to move for work. To go to scale as a national qualification would be virtually impossible for the IB as it now stands. It was a populist move by Labour and was largely forgotten politically by the time the next set of league tables appeared. However, there are a growing number of schools in the UK that are passionate about the impact of the IB.

Year-on-year results rose through the 2000s, but there was always a problem over their perceived validity. As schools sought to find the qualification that would meet the needs of every pupil, even the most disaffected, they were clear that they were offering the best bet for the children they served. Seeking to kick downhill with the wind, as it were, on behalf of their pupils meant that they pushed on every allowable tolerance in the system. Powerful awarding bodies, driven to find new ways to support the government's achievement agenda, constantly developed new courses and examination techniques. The regulator, QCA, was in the invidious position of being both the validator of the exam and its regulator. Whenever questions were raised, awarding bodies would go straight to ministers to complain, leaving the regulator hamstrung, much as the Financial Services Agency was unable to regulate the actions of the big boy banks.

In December 2011, the *Daily Telegraph* exposed some examiners who were secretly filmed giving teachers clues about what aspects of subjects might feature in exams the following summer. The furore that, for a few days, led to enquiries and investigation also added to the claims of Michael Gove that the examination system needed an overhaul. Much excitement then followed as the wolves howled around another story about how much money was being wasted and whether we can trust our 'gold standard' exams.

Most teachers want to impart the joy of their subject discipline. However, most admit that 'getting at least a C grade' has to be the aim and so the curriculum narrows down to the practice of finding 'bankers' on the syllabus – which poems or plays to focus on. How we can say children 'know Shakespeare', when they meet one text, study three significant speeches and answer a few questions about key events, is always a puzzle. And how many pupils feel inspired to take their interest further? The exam system undoes so much of the good work teachers and others do in exciting in children a passion for the subject. Pupils find themselves studying the tedium rather than the beauty of the subject discipline and tend to get hooked on cynicism and cannot break out of the mindset that tells them it is not worth learning. Many 'successful' youngsters say they find their schooling less than inspiring. They understand the pressure and put up with it to get the results. Others find it fruitless but work because of loyalty to their school or the belief that their teacher is right when they tell them about the value of qualifications. Others give up altogether.

## An end to all this

Along came the coalition government in 2010 with specific and stated ideologies. The prime minister called for an end to an 'all-must-have-prizes' culture in his conference speech of 2009. Michael Gove and Nick Gibb expressed their intention to clearly differentiate between academic and vocational qualifications in the RSA speech in June 2009. Gradually these ideologies have been turned into policy, often well intentioned, sometimes with long-term ulterior motives and often through confusion and an arrogant assumption that nothing the previous government might have left in place could be worth keeping.

For decades, UK party politics has seriously undermined the ability of the teaching profession to move forward in the interests of children. As Gove outlined his plans in September 2012 for the future of examinations for sixteen-year-olds, the implication was that this is all about pupils: harder papers, no re-sits and plenty of reassurance that this will be a 'Qualification for All' – which is where GCSEs started. The reality is that his proposed EBacc was rooted in political ideology and had little to do with what any child or, indeed, wider society, needs from its education system.

Within a month of Gove's announcement of the EBacc, Ed Miliband announced his party's commitment to a 'Tech Bacc' for 'the forgotten 50%'. Instead of challenging the secretary of state's fundamental premise, the statement revealed an acceptance of the EBacc principle. In February 2013, when Gove announced his 'one reform too far' decision, Labour called it 'a humiliating climb down' yet only weeks before they had been talking about an alternative. Lost in opposition and frightened of the vocal middle class media, Labour seem devoid of principles these days and seem satisfied instead with building upon Tory ideals. So where do they stand now? And do they stand for educational principle or jockeying into the best position in the polls? This is the political version of game theory when the votes of a few floating voters are sought for office while the integrity of young people's education is compromised. So now we risk a new polarity in the academic versus vocational debate: Accabacca vs. Techabacca ... sheep and goats. Why not a CultureBacc, PhysiBacc, HealthBacc or CreativeBacc? We might even end up with a MediaBacc and then we would really know which Bacc was worth the least. It is all so hollow; politicians out sound-biting the previous sound-biter in search of votes is hardly good education policy in the making.

The proposed introduction of the EBacc was game theory at its extreme. This was not a qualification but a measure of schools and one which would shape the way many secondary schools offered provision to their pupils. Indeed, many primaries would have to revise their learning offer, or at least repackage and remarket it, in order to satisfy parent concerns that their children were being prepared for baccalau-reate-renowned secondaries.

## Are we heading Bacc to grammars?

Many schools were caught out by the announcement of the emphasis on the EBacc in the publication of examination results in 2010. Some called the lack of notice unfair while others welcomed the emphasis on traditional subjects. As a result, some schools were quickly reviewing course options to ensure their pupils are not disadvantaged with regard to higher education. Awarding bodies were arranging the hoops to be jumped through by future candidates. The lack of any vocational ele-ments led to questions around the claim that the EBacc would represent the product and evidence of a rounded education. Indeed, league tables would look markedly different if a vocational element were included. The difference between the proposed EBacc's collec-tion of subjects and the International Baccalaureate (or baccalaureates in other countries) raised concerns about the combination and emphasis that had emerged. Above all, the perceived devaluing of the efforts of pupils and their teachers was cited as a negative outcome of the step to publish results in this way. Many parents would be feeling a little less proud of their children's previous achievements.

There could be another, unspoken reason for the effort to introduce the EBacc and its inclusion in league tables. It might herald the return to selective education. Parents have grown used to being informed of the importance and value of league tables. They have been told for years that these tables give an indication of the best schools and where they might seek admission for their children. The proposed new sys-tem refined the results to the extent that, with a bit of persuasion, parents would be helped to understand which were the most demand-ing schools and which achieved most in terms of access to higher education. Cut away many courses in universities by reducing funding for arts and culture, limit sport and mock media studies, then parents would see yet more clearly where the path to ambition lies: the EBacc schools. Soon there would be a clamour to get children into these schools to go alongside the critical uproar from those who say that, for many youngsters, a study of history is not appropriate, another language is too great a challenge and other subjects offer a brighter prospect.

Heads, under pressure to dance to the right tune, would identify those pupils who might just scrape the EBacc list and persuade some youngsters away from BTECs that might show better relevance and application for the student. Those students studying design technology would come to realise that, somehow, Ancient Greek or Latin hold more currency for the future they face. Awarding bodies would work out how to put the spoons in the right place to feed the new appetite. Underneath, most would complain that there is little logic.

Consider how a government that seeks to look sensitive might respond:

> Well, let's not denigrate schools that are achieving great things where the aptitude of the pupils is not right for the EBacc. There are many excellent schools doing remarkable things for youngsters with less academic outlooks or less innate ability. Let's recognise this and take the pressure off such schools by producing separate but demanding performance indicators for them. Perhaps a TechBacc.

> We might have EBacc school league tables and general school league tables. We could call the EBacc schools 'grammars' and the general schools could be called 'secondary moderns', but might be more wise to use new terminology. We would need other descriptors but in the emerging mass of school types it might not matter.

> What will matter is that the EBacc schools are there for the elite and provide the best chance of a ticket to a brighter future. There will be clamour for entry and they will be oversubscribed. Then we will need a selection system, say at the age of eleven, where we try to identify those with the potential to succeed in the limited

and rigorous learning that the EBacc demands. Of course, the pupils in them will mostly succeed, so we were right.

But what of the rest? Few would doubt the secretary of state's commitment to a better future for our young people, but many would find it difficult to balance espoused freedoms and autonomy for professionals with the devaluing of so many aspects of study open to young people.

Michael Gove is often accused of muddled thinking. Building Schools for the Future, School Sport Partnerships, the Education Maintenance Allowance, arts and culture are all used as examples of how he lacks a clear strategy and diminishes aspiration and endeavour for our young people. How did his proposed EBacc fit with his opening exchange to the Education Select Committee in July 2010?

> One of the problems that this country has had historically is that we've been very good at educating a minority – the gifted and talented – quite well, but the majority of children have not been educated as well as they should have been. The days have gone, if they ever existed, when a society could survive by having an elite who were well educated according to a particular set of narrow academic criteria, and others who were simply allowed to become hewers of wood and drawers of water.

Maybe underneath the secretary of state's approach there was something more calculated. No doubt he would be prepared to state clearly that the proposed EBacc was not an under-the-radar move to reinstate the selective system. It might be worth having the debate but at least let's have it out in the open. Now, after Gove's decision to abandon the proposed EBC, the debate will shift again. The EBacc category could remain as a measure of school performance, so how will the opposition respond?

The danger is that as game theory takes hold and others enter the game, even unwittingly, the purpose and intent become forgotten. A possible TechBacc set alongside the EBacc immediately sets in people's minds the selection of the sheep and the goats referred to above. Does Labour really want a selective system?

## Whether so-called academic qualifications are more valid or harder to achieve than so-called vocational ones

The argument about the merits of academic versus vocational qualifications is largely an academic argument. After all, when we say 'It's all academic' we usually mean that we are talking about something that makes little difference.

The concept of vocation is at the heart some of the most highly valued professions. Medicine, the law, even teaching are seen as vocational careers and few would argue that one doesn't need to be scholarly, even academic, to enter them. Why is it that people who are engineers, research chemists, fire fighters or plumbers are deemed less worthy than those who manipulate words or abstract concepts for a living? The fact is that those who have proposed baccalaureate-sourced subject qualifications are given high status whereas those who can lay bricks, join wood or manage farms are somehow seen by some as of a lesser status.

In early 2012, Michael Gove was right to order the recalibration of vocational qualifications following the very sound Wolf Report but once again the government attacked the symptom rather than the disease in the system. While this action had considerable merit in terms of bringing order to the system (where the urgency of league tables had been poorly met with the use of GCSE equivalents), the manner of the recalibration was ill advised. The ridicule heaped on vocational qualifications was terrible and an insult to the efforts of thousands of young people and their teachers. Surely an employer recruiting for an apprentice in a motor workshop would prefer a youngster with a basic qualification in mechanics and the owner of a hairdressing salon would value a qualification in hair and beauty. Some evidence of experience and training in practical subjects is beneficial for youngsters as they come forward to secure a modern apprenticeship. It is not the qualification that is the problem.

Instead of making a song and dance (performance arts) about qualifications there could have been better consideration about how the situation arose. The market-driven school system, built upon accountability through high-stakes examinations, puts enormous pressure on schools to improve their results. This led to a call from schools for more accessible examinations and 'equivalents' were developed. Indeed, some schools began the process by designing courses and applying to the regulator for validation. A key criterion in validation was the amount of 'guided learning hours' and it was here that the smoke and mirrors began. The market-driven awarding bodies claimed that a qualification needed the equivalent of four GCSEs worth of time when in reality it was all pretty swift. Hence the growth in long thin courses and short fat courses; anything to get the qualifications banked ready for the annual league table.

Just for once, though, the perverse incentive worked in favour of the youngsters. Many teenagers found themselves doing something at school that engaged them, applied knowledge and skills from elsewhere into something practical and seemed to have some link to the world of work beyond school. Some were so proud of their qualification that it spurred them on to do well in other less mouth-watering courses.

Behind all this, of course, was a bigger agenda. The secretary of state wants to drive a wedge between academic and vocational learning as part of an ongoing need to polarise debate. However, it is possible to learn skills *and* knowledge, to engage in practical *and* scholarly learning, to learn about contemporary issues affecting our world *and* enjoy facts about the development of the world. It does not have to be one or the other. However, playing with polarity and working on extremes helps to develop the notion of sorting people out. This need to sort the sheep from the goats (animal husbandry) is fundamental to the ideology of the government. Indeed, the term 'practical' would be better than 'vocational' and the term 'scholarly' better than 'academic', though the division between subjects is still false. Geography, for instance, is an intensely practical subject but also exhilarating in its application and theory.

The diplomas developed following the Tomlinson Report of 2004 sought to bring together the academic and practical aspects of learning in realistic contexts. Those schools involved in offering the early diplomas (and which, in some cases, continue to do so), reported increased pupil engagement, parental interest and employer involvement in relevant and pertinent activities, tailored to the aptitude and capability of the youngster.

The diplomas are pickled, of course (food preservation), because Michael Gove was wedded to the EBacc subjects, despite pulling back from the proposed EBC. He believes that by kicking out the clutter of these equivalent qualifications we will be able to see yet more clearly where the 'good' schools are. Fischer Family Trust, another question mark in the system, was already sending schools their estimated EBacc results for 2013 with comparisons to previous year's and their local and national performance. Because it is in charts and in colours it must be accurate.

What all this emphasis on so-called academic learning does is to drive youngsters away from the much-needed skills in design, technology, culture, arts, enterprise and engineering. It would not be so bad if the subjects included in Gove's EBacc encouraged students to delve into deep study and scholarship, but the spectre of the league tables means that many teachers and their pupils will frustrate each other with the need to swallow gobbets of learning to satisfy the next examination rather than explore the big ideas. Eventually, pupils coming forward for A level will have a narrower range of experience and, as they feed through to higher education, there will be less call for degree courses in performing arts, mechanical engineering, health and construction. Recent statements regarding transferring the oversight of A levels to universities are code for the Russell Group to maintain a mutual self-interest in perpetuating the 'gold standard' of A levels, while other universities will pick up the crumbs with their alternative offerings, thus ensuring that the two-tier positioning is sustained.

The outcry over the results of GCSE English in 2012 was about a Libor-type level setting process where Ofqual had told awarding bodies that results should be 'roughly comparable to last year' – a return to a norm-referencing process in a criteria-referenced context. The secretary of state may not have spoken to awarding bodies but, in game theory, it is not hard for them to pick up that the trend should be away from the upward momentum of the last few years. Playing with young people's futures in an attempt to make a point about the education system seems to sum up the mess in which qualifications and examinations have found themselves.

## Whether the individual should have a rounded set of qualifications or specialise

Yet somehow, the school system keeps trying. In response to the imposition of the EBacc performance measure, several attempts at designing something better had begun in the belief that the secretary of state might be persuaded to think again. Of course, he did think again and in February 2013 he announced that the reforms were going too far. The newly listening Michael Gove is determined to make examinations harder and at the same time ensure that the subjects that might have been vulnerable have a chance.

He could try to really listen and maybe even work with educationalists who would like to try to help. There are positive alternatives to Gove's EBC – Whole Education has begun the process of consultation on its Better Bac scheme.

The Build a Better Bacc campaign is built around some key principles, including establishing coherent pathways, recognising knowledge and skills and securing pupil engagement. It aims to offer flexibility and challenge with multiple accreditation routes and balanced assessment. Credibility with the general public, employers and higher education institutions would grow if the government could work with all sectors to build a system of recognition for young people that was truly worthwhile. John Cridland, director-general of the CBI, noted at the organisation's 2012 annual conference that 'if we're all committed to raising the education leaving age to 18 over the next few years, then the tests at 16 are hugely important but they're not the end point. They're a staging post. Sometimes the entire debate seems to be about our exams at 16.' Further, he noted, 'The best teachers we've talked to are rebels against the system. They have had to break out of the straitjacket of the curriculum which has stopped them delivering the sort of education our young people need.'

An academy in Hull has been instrumental in bringing interest groups, including business, employers and parents, together around the ModBac (as in modern). The ModBac is designed to be:

- *Highly aspirational* as it is not a 'single threshold' award, so the achievements of the highest achieving children are fully recognised. In this way, the ModBac can help raise aspiration and attainment in all subjects, including those specifically included in the EBacc.

- *Inclusive* because even the lowest attaining students can aim for the award at entry or foundation level.

- *Personalised* as it caters for the interests and passions of all students, building character and resilience both in and beyond the classroom.

- *Motivating* through recognition and reward. Motivation is probably the most significant factor in the level of attainment outcome.

- *Driven by students* through their own online portfolio and interface.

- *A much broader profile of achievement* than simply a qualification transcript, including a 'skills passport' (which encourages children to develop and apply life skills) and to become 'learning ready' for Key Stage 5 and 'work-ready' for life.

■ *Acceptable across Europe* and the rest of the world, taking into account the fact that qualifications are becoming increasingly globalised as communication technologies and worker mobility advance.

These things are happening. The ModBac is gaining pace to the extent that the early adopters, buoyed by a successful trial and first phase, now want to introduce a MidBac for younger pupils. The purpose is in the approach – perhaps *the* place where a consideration of the link between curriculum, qualifications and examinations should begin. This is an example of autonomy making a difference. As with all brilliant developments in the English system, though, it will be difficult to develop to scale without funding and, even if government money were forthcoming for further trials, a change of government could see yet another change of direction. For those involved in the ModBac, the impetus comes from their widely held belief in education as more than schooling and success as more than a few limited examination passes. Do look it up (www.modernbaccalaureate.com).

Like everything else in schooling, examinations and qualifications are full of contradictions in purpose and the pupils suffer eventually, not least in the perception, merit and value of their achievement. On the very last day of the 2012 examinations, Michael Gove announced that GCSEs lacked credibility and he proposed to replace them with a version of traditional O levels. What effect might this have had on the pupils catching sight of the media reports during what they had been told is one of the most significant events in their lives to date? Surely, after years of formal schooling, we should want as many of our children as possible to succeed and be grateful to the system when they do. Now the same GCSE system, discredited by the secretary of state, is going to be the core of the examination system in England. Do we have a problem?

Schools often open up to the local press on 'results day' to have the whooping and hugging celebrated as students find out their grades. The results could be sent by email but this now traditional ceremony has become vital as a way for teachers and pupils to join together 'after the game'. Pupils rightly recognise that their hard work at trying to pass exams has paid off. Teachers rightly recognise that they have done their best at helping their pupils pass the exams. Both parties rightly recognise that they were in it together and are indebted to each other in different ways, often in spite of the pressure each put on the other at times during the past couple of years. Sadly, though, numerous young people rejoice in never again having to 'do' certain subjects and many teachers acknowledge that they did not fill the pupil with the joy of the subject discipline but succeeded in simply taking them through a course of study with the right outcome. There is no disgrace in that, but many are left wondering whether they came into teaching simply to boost league table scores. Lots of pupils later question why they did multiple GCSEs when they only seem to be asked if they got five. Indeed, did game theory not always apply? Has 'past-paper practice' not been the most timetabled activity in Year 11 for most secondary schools for generations? Many adults laugh about their exam strategy of revising four key areas or practising three model answers and hoping that at least two appeared on the final paper. We cheerfully wonder how we passed particular subjects given our lack of ability. These adults realised that qualifications were the ticket to a part of an arena and the exam represented the entry price. It was an example of game theory, but the difference was that it was fairly low level rather than the career-creating, image-building, future-defining experience it is now for teachers and for pupils.

## What can we do?

- We probably need to rethink the whole system properly. Endless ministerial tinkering simply complicates the game with its perverse incentives and competing vicious circles, so that eventually the entire process becomes self-defeating.

- We could begin by considering the need for school examinations at the age of sixteen in the first place. This could be a job for a National Council for Schooling. Now that pupils are required to participate until the age of eighteen, is the GCSE outdated? Numerous international jurisdictions have no examination for pupils at aged sixteen. Many, including head teachers, would argue that some sort of external check is needed for pupils at sixteen to maintain confidence in the system. This is hard to substantiate since there is such doubt about the exams anyway. Perhaps an examination suite at the age of fifteen would help young people both prove their application and progress as well as decide on their future pathways. We should, however, strive to ensure all pupils do well, rather than use examinations to put people in rank order of potential.

■ We could ask whether we need to persist with the 'rite of passage' experience for young people, one that is archaic in nature, a sort of trial by ordeal. When else in life would we enter a room, sit a metre away from everyone and work in silence for two hours? In real life, presented with a problem at work, most people immediately contact others, ask for opinions, test solutions, seek information, pool knowledge and construct solutions that others critique. How could we organise an examination that mirrors real situations so that we can more properly claim that we are checking that the pupil is 'fit for their future'? Do we assess the past or predict the future when we set an examination?

■ We need to do something about logistics. The sheer scale of the examination set-up is out of proportion. Schools create exam facilities in places such as gyms, dance and drama studios so the curriculum narrows for all year groups. This is not just for the month or so of the examinations but also for the mocks held earlier in the year. Do we really want twelve-year olds to have no organised physical activity for two months per year because exams are taking place?

■ The examination industry is big business. With schools spending up to £500 per pupil and half a million pupils per year coming forward for exams, awarding bodies are in a big market place. Could we place the money with the pupil via the parents and allow a total spend of, for example, £200 to use on their child's examinations? At the same time, we would take the excitement out of the annual August bash and stop the league table jostling. Most importantly, the game would be played around the principles that we say are important: the right choices for the pupil.

- We could cap the number of GCSE-type examinations to be taken at, say, eight. This would enable time to be spent on in-depth study on a specialism or the challenge of learning something that is less comfortable than the often formulaic approach to examinations.

- We could look at the qualifications that would be needed to demonstrate a well-rounded achievement at school and beyond. Would it not be beneficial for a youngster to approach an employer with a rounded record of achievement? For example, ten formal qualifications with no more than seven GCSE types and no more than seven vocational qualifications, plus a set of evidence of civic participation from validated sources and confirmation of effort to maintain personal health and fitness.

- We could consider offering GCSE examinations in composite subject disciplines rather than the tired old subjects. Why not a GCSE called 'Rebellion' or 'Risk' or 'Reaction'. A course on Risk, for example, could bring together the history of exploration, the geographical analysis of siting for habitation, health awareness and statistics. These areas could be used to inspire enjoyment of the subject disciplines as a precursor to further study rather than seeing success in GCSEs as permission to give up.

- We could look at developing an alternative such as the ModBac and take it to scale.

- We could consider whether a suite of baccalaureates is a good principle to explore. Now Michael Gove has established the EBacc principle to lots of criticism, we might look at whether a worthwhile and valuable EBacc could be developed. Perhaps there could be a core EBacc of rounded achievement with additional elements to cover specific aspects of study and proven achievement; technical, sporting, creative, experimental, global, innovative and scientific are the sort of aspects that could be recognised without recourse to saying that some are superior to others or for the ones who 'can't achieve'.

■ If we have to have exams, could the syllabus for a subject be made available just fifty days before the exam so that the big ideas of a subject discipline would have to be already understood in order to be revised at that point? We might enable teachers to enjoy their subject disciplines as they want to do rather than teach for the tests.

■ Alternatively, we could publish the 150 possible exam questions two years ahead of the exams and generate the actual paper on the day. For many pupils and teachers, so much of their final year is spent studying past papers and practising the 'bankers' needed for the final exam that the subject can lose its energy and attraction. An approach such as this would ensure breadth and depth in study rather than continuous exam practice. We might end up with real scientists, historians, geographers, designers and linguists, rather than people who pass exams so that they can drop the subject immediately.

# … on curriculum

Before we do anything further with the exam system we need to decide what exactly constitutes the school curriculum. Too often we make it overly complicated. Here is a simple way of looking at it.

The school curriculum comprises the elements that young people need:

- to nurture them as individuals and meet the hopes we have for them
- and help them to appreciate their community
- so that they learn about their county, country, the world and the universe
- and it includes the national curriculum.

Basically the school curriculum is what the children need to learn. The *national* curriculum is simply a part of that overall programme for learning. Many of us will remember being children ourselves and writing our address. First of all we wrote our name and then the number and the street. Then came the town and maybe the county and then we got on to the really big bits, England, the United Kingdom, Europe, the Northern Hemisphere, the World, the Universe. As headlines, this is not a bad curriculum. We could learn about all these things, including ourselves, and we would certainly cover the national curriculum.

The important thing to remember is that, in an English school, teachers can teach their children anything at all as long as it is legal and safe. The nation also has a curriculum that tries to specify the elements that children should learn to ensure entitlement and quality. One of our problems, however, is the extent to which the national curriculum is used to exert pressure.

I have always believed that the curriculum should be the entire planned learning experience that children encounter. Naturally it includes lessons, but the child's learning experience in school also includes the events and routines that the school offers and the advantage the school takes of activities the child engages in beyond school. These might be clubs, hobbies and pastimes or work experience and would include charity work, part-time jobs and being part of local community activities as a rounded whole. The events of a school are often the memories that, in later life, people most vividly recall, along with school visits, dramatic performances and sporting occasions. To these we could add many activities that youngsters undertake when they feel in charge and where they feel something special is happening.

We know that enjoying a school performance gives an opportunity to learn about the subject disciplines of dance, drama, art, music, English and probably design and technology, but it extends to include many of the skills that employers say are vital in the working world today. In a performance we work as a team. Someone is in the starring role. There is the chorus line, the backstage and the front of house. If we work together then we've got a chance of a successful show. In a perform- ance we learn about strategic management. Typically we start in a mess, we gradually evolve some sort of order, we practise, we rehearse, we perform and, in a good performance, we evaluate. In a really good performance youngsters learn about the way in which various aspects of organisation fit a timeline, so the costumes, lighting, scenery and props have to be managed in a way that supports the performance and makes it work. The youngsters learn how to manage an audience, about ticket sales, profit and loss.

Similarly, during a competitive sports event youngsters understand how to extend themselves in the subject disciplines of PE and sport. They learn to win with grace and lose with dignity. Equally, when it is well managed, they learn to be congenial hosts or good visitors. Schools that make the most of the opportunity to let their youngsters see the event as a sporting occasion, rather than simply a competition, are opening up the chance for them to talk with people they have not met before in a contrived occasion. Here we see the very beginnings of aspects of networking which become vital in the working world of adulthood.

The school visit will take subject disciplines outside of the classroom and give opportunities for youngsters to experience real-life field sketching in geography, the exploration of artefacts in history and active engagement in scientific discovery in the real world.

Most schools recognise that the routines of school are vital for inculcating aspects of learning in young people. The way in which we conduct assembly will either bring learning to life or create tedium for a short period of every day. While it is only perhaps twenty minutes in any day, if we add up the time spent in assembly over a week, a term, a year or a key stage it reveals how, when put together, the volume of time needs to be very effectively used. A good assembly can bring the school together, help children to feel part of a bigger community and celebrate, applaud, recognise and emulate each other's efforts. Similarly, the routine of the library or ICT suite or the use of outdoor facilities can become simply habitual, but for those children who can manage them well they are all opportunities for learning.

Events and routines should be part of the planned curriculum of the school in the way they contribute to the learning experience of the child. They are not add-ons or extras or extra-curricular activities. They are not just quirky ways of doing things to make school life enjoyable. They are learning opportunities where the curriculum is taught. Some things cannot be taught in passing or through events; for these, we need lessons.

In its 2012 Generic Grade Descriptors, Ofsted simply says that an outstanding curriculum is one that 'provides highly positive, memorable experiences and rich opportunities for high quality learning, has a positive impact on pupils' behaviour and safety and contributes well to pupils' achievements in their social, moral, spiritual and cultural development'. Many people in schools cite Ofsted as a constraint upon their practice but, in fact, the frameworks have always encouraged width and breadth in learning.

## Uncertain curriculum agendas

The problem with the curriculum is that it can get too complicated. Over time we have added too much to what children *need* to learn and therefore we have an uncertain agenda of what children *should be learning* in the twenty-first century.

The curriculum that young people meet in school has also evolved over time. Since the early days of state schooling there has been debate about the appropriateness of content that pupils should address. On top of a full learning experience for pupils in 1870, schools have had to consider whether to add emerging content so that their pupils might be fit for a changing future.

When state schools began in the 1870s, it was natural that we would teach children some of the things that the public schools had been teaching. So children learnt about the classical traditions. The Romans and Greeks featured highly in the syllabus, as did the Age of Enlightenment and astronomy, with a shortcut to Archimedes' principle and Pythagoras' theorem, all of which were seen as vital aspects of learning. The beauty of poetry, as depicted by classical authors of the time, was also seen as vital for children's edification.

As state schooling began, it did so on the back of a period of global success for Britain as a country. We had set up an empire across the world and were on the crest of an industrial revolution which was bringing prosperity to many like never before. Indeed, this success had helped to fund the very beginnings of the state school system and the need for continued national success was one of the key drivers for its establishment. It was natural, therefore, that children should be taught how Britain was a key player in the world, how as a country we had triumphed over others and how our industrial strengths, including the building of the railway and canal infrastructures, were of vital importance.

Through the twentieth century there emerged a series of efforts to secure emancipation, first for women, then for racial groups and, more recently, for people of different sexual orientations. In each of these campaigns, education was seen as crucial and protagonists endeavoured to ensure that what children were taught in school reflected their ideological concerns. Equally, others felt that these issues should not be encouraged as part of the formal learning experience of young people.

From the 1950s onwards, the development of the media has led to what many have described as a creative upsurge. There was plenty of creativity before this period but creativity is now very much associated with the arts, particularly the performing arts and the media.

At the latter end of the twentieth century, and moving into the current millennium, we have seen an era of connectivity like never before. The explosion of technology linked to satellite communications has meant that people can be in touch with each other across the world at the press of a button. Many people in less economically developed countries have access to communication while they still lack what for the developed world are the basics: clean water, food and electricity.

The gradually emerging array of emphases on possible content to teach children leads to all sorts of arguments about what should be in the curriculum. The classical tradition, the Age of Enlightenment, Britain's place in the world, emancipation, the creative upsurge and the era of connectivity provide too much to learn about in the time available. The modernists believe that we should start from where children are – the world in which they live – and then work backwards to how we got here. The traditionalists believe we should tell the story from the beginning and eventually young people will learn to see how we have emerged into the lives we live today. Whenever there is a campaign to ensure that learning for young people is more 'modern', more creative or more technologically driven, there is a panic by the traditionalists who seek to roll back the tide and get back to where we were a century ago. Whenever those who want to start at the top of the list begin to gain stock, they are mocked as being out of touch and irrelevant and the arguments go on.

The fact is that our children today are growing up in a more complex society than ever before. The arguments are well understood. We live in a socially diverse community on a more accessible planet with changing employment patterns, with more people moving around the world than ever before, with the population of developed countries living longer and all in a technologically vibrant atmosphere. There are plenty of books, and short videos on YouTube, that demonstrate these things. The fact is our children are growing up in a world that is complex and exciting. Our challenge is to make our children's learning fit them for their future.

The ongoing debate about the content of the national curriculum has skewed understanding and distorted consideration of children's wider needs. It leads to petty squabbles and point scoring, jockeying for position and territorial behaviours. The bigger picture gets lost.

## A big picture of the curriculum

When I worked at QCA, one of the best things we did was to encourage a conversation about a bigger picture of the curriculum into which debate about the detail of a national curriculum could take place. We created an A3-sized chart to depict the various elements that come together to create the curriculum decisions within an individual school. This simple device seemed to strike a chord with pretty well everyone who met it: teachers, heads, school governors, parents, employers, even civil servants in the Department of Education and other governmental departments, such as Health and the Home Office. Young people always got it. They could see the big picture and were acutely aware of the parts they were and were not able to access. International education communities loved it and there are versions of this 'big picture' in national educational policies in all manner of places from the Maldives to Australia. It has been translated into different languages and forms the basis of some countries' curriculum legislation.

The big picture was always deemed to be in draft, with detail amended every three months to take account of recent debates. Not everyone got it. I remember a session at the Prince of Wales' Education Summer School where one of the leaders was concerned at the excitement of the subject-discipline specialists and exclaimed 'the box for English is such a small part of the picture'. (The size of the boxes was determined by the number of words that needed to fit in, not by any relative weighting of merit!) Some years later, I still see copies of the big picture chart in schools and senior leaders tell me it has led to some of the best discussions about the overall work of their school. It seems to make sense, then, to include a version of the big picture in this book concerned with thinking about schooling. Available at http://www.crownhouse.co.uk/featured/Mick_Waters).

Along with the chart, a consideration of its construction provides an insight into the complementary aspects of the elements of the big picture. If we want the curriculum to make sense and do its job in a school, we might begin with three key questions:

1   What are we trying to achieve?

2   How do we organise learning?

3   How well are we achieving our aims?

These questions form the bedrock of thinking about the learning offer for pupils in our schools. Interestingly, as the big picture builds up, we might begin to consider the end results – the accountability of schools.

How well are we achieving our aims? We're trying to secure, of course, five fundamental aspects of a rounded education for children. These were the Every Child Matters outcomes where children were expected to be safe, healthy, enjoy and achieve, participate and be economically capable. Naturally we want high attainment and good performance for young people, meeting the standards expected nationally but also within the school at an individual level. Most would agree that we want good behaviour and attendance. We want to see youngsters making sensible healthy lifestyle choices. We want to see them engaged in aspects of their community through civic participation and, at the end of it all, to be ready to take further involvement in education, employ-ment or training. Although Every Child Matters is not something with which the coalition accords, these five areas become accountability measures for a system that attempts to realise the hopes for our young people as outlined in the first section of this book. These five areas become accountability measures for the system. They are the baseline for the big picture, the bedrock for everything that we try to do in our schools.

So, back to the aims. What are we trying to achieve for children? In essence we want our children to be successful learners, confident indi-viduals and responsible citizens. Nearly every country in the developed world has aims similar to these. In some countries they are extended. For instance, in Scotland there is a reference to 'effective contributors'. These aims came about through dialogue and conversation with stakeholders in the education process and are almost universally agreed. The previous government's Every Child Matters agenda had the five key outcomes listed above that were expected for all children. This had been a popular agenda for many, since it brought together the physical, intellectual, social and emotional aspects of growing up and seemed to make sense in the complex world of the twenty-first cen-tury. The current coalition government has abandoned the focus on Every Child Matters and seeks instead to construct a different outlook.

On top of our hopes for the children and the Every Child Matters agenda comes the focus on learning. That balance between the atti-tudes and attributes children need, the skills we want them to acquire and the knowledge and understanding we seek to develop needs to be kept in sync, so there is a sensible blend in the learning experience. Again, the coalition government seeks a different balance, with a stated smaller emphasis on skills.

The theory is that the things we are trying to achieve, our aims and hopes, are met in the accountability measures and we do that by look-ing at the way the second question on the big picture can be answered: How do we organise learning? First of all, we need to understand that the curriculum is the entire planned learning experience that children encounter. As it is underpinned by a broad set of common values and purposes, the curriculum encompasses not only the lessons that children experience but also the events, the routines of school life and what children do outside and beyond school. The entire planned learning experience takes children to a range of locations and gives them experience of different environments. It is through this composite learning experience that they will achieve the aims we have for them.

Next, we need to look at learning approaches. We need to ensure that children engage with their learning so that they become active, practical and constructive, and in order that they develop skills from enquiry and scholarship. We need to make sure that there are opportunities for youngsters to build on their learning in school by doing things beyond it. A good curriculum includes every learner and provides opportunities for learner choice and personalisation, a word that has virtually dropped out of the schooling vocabulary in the past three years. An emphasis on learning approaches will make sure that the experiences children have are in tune with their own stage of human development and maturation, and that there are links to their community and aspects of business and employment. Above all, the curriculum needs to meet children's experience in the way we match time to their need, so that they get deep and immersive as well as regular frequent learning, where they revisit concepts in authentic ways.

A really important aspect of the organisation of learning is the extent to which different dimensions of real life in the twenty-first century can be incorporated within curriculum planning. Fundamentally, these are overarching themes that hold significance for individuals in society. They deal with things such as enterprise and entrepreneurship. They focus on cultural diversity, identity and belonging. They encourage young people to be active citizens, committed to taking action at a local, national and global level. The important issues of global sustainability are addressed within the context of the unfolding technological and media agenda. Central to it all is the importance of young people developing a personal health and well-being dimension that makes sense in their own lives.

It is within this construct of the school curriculum that national expectations should be set. In the Early Years Foundation Stage, these expectations appear within the Early Years Profile and from the age of five children experience the national curriculum. While both of these are currently under review, the fact is that national programmes of study need to be incorporated within the school curriculum to make sure that they bring about the expected aims for pupils. Each subject study programme or aspect of the Early Years Framework can exist on its own account, but it is likely to have more impact if we organise it in a flexible way to take account of the aims and accountability measures before us.

So, having outlined the aspects of the way in which we might organise learning to achieve our aims, we move to the third key question: How well are we achieving our aims, the accountabilities we set ourselves at the beginning … the bottom line? This is where assessment fits in. Fundamental to this aspect of curriculum design is the notion of creating assessment that is fit for purpose. This means making sure that assessment draws on a wide range of evidence of pupils' learning and that it actually promotes a broad and engaging curriculum, rather than becoming an end in itself. In essence, assessment is integral to effective teaching and learning. Assessment ought to maximise pupil progress and embrace a whole range of assessment techniques, including peer-to-peer and self-assessment. This means that tests and tasks designed to assess young people's progress are used appropriately, so that we can identify clear targets for improvement through helpful feedback for the learner and, of course, other stakeholders such as parents or employers. This is where the national standards are addressed, in that any assessment should be consistently linked to their interpretation.

So there we have it, three key questions considered; a big picture for curriculum. The premise is that nothing exists on its own in curriculum design and every aspect is interrelated. How do we encourage the teacher of history to see that they are helping young people to become successful learners and responsible citizens? What does the teacher of PE do to make sure that they are able to enhance a child's developing contribution to society? Does the business studies teacher or the teacher responsible for design and technology see the important role they play in helping to form an overall assessment of the young person's general progress? Does the Year 4 teacher realise that they are helping children to take a step along a pathway that will help them towards their goal of becoming responsible citizens who will make a difference to global issues? All of these come down to accountability measures in terms of the school and its ability to meet a range of national targets and expectations.

A broad view of curriculum design at the school level is absolutely essential if we are to achieve the sort of learning diet that will make young people fit for the twenty-first century. This broad view is something that successive governments have squashed and confused over the four decades since the introduction of the national curriculum. Ironically, their collective ineptitude – fuelled by a media that loves to keep stories going – has helped to keep alive discussion about the true work of schools within the context of the needs of childhood and society. Successive secretaries of state have talked about the curriculum children need and what society requires and, in doing so, they usually imply that the national curriculum needs to change, thereby demonstrating their own influence.

Before they meddle with the national curriculum, however, it would help to put some basic principles in place, but few do so, which is why they bend with the wind without putting two and two together. Hence, in 2011 we had riots which were described as 'criminality pure and simple' and which would require, as an antidote, character-building in schools through better codes of behaviour. One year later, we needed competitive sports in primary schools to build on Olympic success. (We already have a competitive sport in primary schools: it is called SATs.) We also have calls for learning about global sustainability, drug awareness and careers, coupled with phonics, long division and the poetry of Dryden.

*Singing Together* was a radio programme that many remember from the 1960s and 1970s, either as a primary school teacher or as a pupil. Schools would buy a class set of song books each term and every Tuesday morning the equivalent of Years 5 and 6 would prepare for the programme that came through over the loudspeaker. Many will recall the plywood radio on the wall with the gauze over the circle in the middle and, somewhere on the wall below, a black knob that controlled the volume. On cue, a voice would tell children to turn to the appropriate page, wait while they did so and then teach them the song. The children would read it through, practice particular segments and eventually sing the whole song so that, by the end of the term, their repertoire had increased.

Although this wasn't very long ago, it was a time before tape recordings and the national curriculum. Schools had absolute freedom to teach whatever they thought met the needs of their pupils. Yet the vast majority elected to buy the books and take part in a massive national community lesson led by the presenters in London. Now, twenty-odd years after the introduction of a national curriculum which sets out a requirement for children to sing, relatively few take part in regular singing lessons. When it was optional, schools chose to be guided by the BBC in London. Once they were expected to be guided by decisions from Westminster, they stopped taking part. Is there a message here?

Has Michael Gove delivered on curriculum? On balance, no. Why not? Basically, he is driven by ideology in the way he decries his doubters. He pretends to consult and seek consensus but does not. He was over-influenced by the even more ideological Nick Gibb, his minister now departed. Gove is always right and never wrong, except for the occasional error of detail on lists of playing fields sold off or BSF cancellations, where he has been subtly portrayed as taking responsibility for a mistake made by officials. He has messed up school sport and physical education, the arts, culture, design and technology, indeed most things he touches. The proposal for the English Baccalaureate, even though now rescinded, is skewing learning for young people beyond the reasonable. On the one hand, he and his prime minister say school leaders know best and do not need regulatory control (for example, in the spending of the pupil premium or conforming to school food nutrition standards). On the other hand, they tell schools that there must be competitive sport and it will be delivered through the national curriculum. By the way, all the pontificating matters little to an academy or free school which has the flexibility to move away from the national curriculum.

Which brings us to a consideration of the national curriculum – but only in the context of the whole-school curriculum.

# … on the national curriculum

I have never been particularly moved by the national curriculum. People who ask me what I think of the latest proposals or revisions tend to look surprised when I tell them it all leaves me a bit cold. When I was at QCA, I was director of curriculum and part of my job was to help lead reviews of aspects of the national curriculum. I have always believed that the intense detail, which is debated for many hours and every feature pored over, is rarely read within a very short time and school teachers are guided by what they *think* is in the curriculum, what publishers produce and what is inspected or tested.

As the country engages in a debate about values, beliefs, identity and history, the national curriculum has become more than simply the framework for what is taught in schools. It is easy to focus upon the national curriculum as the starting point for addressing the ills of society. From obesity to climate change, from law and order to the performance of international sports teams, the national curriculum becomes the focus for advocates of this or that. Similarly, frustrated ambassadors for social change often blame the perceived outdated curriculum for the lack of progress they encounter.

The national curriculum has therefore become an easy target, open to question, criticism and manipulation. It can be used by government to state policy positions and it is attacked by opponents to score policy points. Argument is often less than measured, subject to cheap shots and invariably at the extremes of the generalised and specific.

Given the emphasis on knowledge content in the first national curriculum, the focus now is often in the subject detail. In the current review of the curriculum the media has feasted on content – what is in and what is out – with great excitement about various claimed important omissions and additions, often without a basis in fact. So while the principle of a national curriculum is not often contested, content is; Shakespeare, phonics, authors and artists have all become iconic battlegrounds. Many who comment most loudly and negatively about the curriculum have not looked closely at it and instead choose to enjoy their sport. The national curriculum, therefore, can be a public scapegoat, even though its intent and endeavours are appreciated by the vast majority. After all, in England at least, there is a tendency to criticise most of our national institutions.

A search for status leads lobby groups to demand that their agenda is recognised as a subject; although becoming a subject does not guarantee a good curriculum experience. There are many Cinderellas trying to go to the national curriculum ball and there are also some wallflowers that get little chance to dance. Music, drama, even dance itself are often neglected as schools focus on their best bets for success in the accountability stakes. Languages, engineering and mathematics need good teaching, resources and a strong qualification framework but they also need a new emphasis on curriculum design. The hierarchy of subjects is regularly brought into question, often by subject communities themselves. For the young, there must be confusion in being offered learning with which a significant proportion of the adult population seems at odds.

It is widely accepted that the original national curriculum was too backwards looking, born of attempts to ensure that those elements of knowledge and understanding necessary for success in a previous age were not lost. There emerged too much emphasis on summative assessment and not enough stress on skills, values and personal development. Because of the detailed specification, the weakest teachers gained a prescribed content and clear expectations but the strongest teachers lost influence over planned learning and professional intellectual curiosity.

Since then, there has been a gradual recognition of the need to keep the best and adjust the rest. Successive reviews have sought to reshape the national curriculum. The need for pupils to learn about the local, the national and the international aspects of their lives has become more accepted. The recognition that children learn through good explanation and exposition, strong instruction, effective questions, fieldwork, practical application, meeting influential people, going places and taking part is voiced by most representative groups, often with a wish to see their own agenda well represented. A minority see the national curriculum as sterile – to be endured while other experiences elsewhere offer enjoyment. A few seem to want it that way.

## The current national curriculum review

We are at an important time for the national curriculum. The coalition government is in a muddle over it, but on the scale of all its other educational messes, it is not too important. However, their work on the curriculum provides a wonderful example of the paradoxes permeating current policy and thinking. Encouraging schools to move away from their maintained status and enjoy the freedoms and autonomy of academy status is accompanied by inducements – one of which is deregulation of the curriculum. If your school becomes an academy you won't have to teach the restrictive national curriculum. Instead, you can have the independence to teach what your school and community decide is needed.

Meanwhile, in 2011, the secretary of state announced that a review had been set up in order to devise a highly specific national curriculum to ensure that pupils in England are well served by their education and that the nation improves its standing in the world. Either way it is bizarre. It is almost as if the national curriculum is being designed with the intention of driving every school over the cliff into academy status in order to avoid it. We are left to ponder whether the national curriculum is to be an entitlement for all pupils, a requirement for schools, a benchmark against which to gauge the individual school's curriculum offer or simply a talking point. Personally I am convinced that the national curriculum now serves primarily as a talking point for politicians and the press. When the government needs to deflect the media from a new crisis or period of poor news, a Sunday splash on a minor national curriculum issue will usually stir up a few headlines as the press scent another story with plenty of controversy.

However, the current review of the national curriculum seems particularly awkward and poorly managed. Early draft proposals for some subjects of the new national curriculum appeared in the 2011 report of the Expert Panel for National Curriculum Review. To some embarrassment, members of the Expert Panel have distanced themselves from the new proposals. They claim undue ministerial influence and a lack of adherence to the established principles agreed in their report. Instead of engagement with subject communities, employers, higher and further education, schools, parents, governors and pupils, we have poor Tim Oates, charged with seeing the review through to conclusion, trying to write programmes of study for the curriculum supported by Department for Education officials and dancing to the tune of a few on the inner circle of political favour.

Trying to justify the mess that is emerging as a means of ensuring that England does well as a nation on international tests would make most sane people ask why we want to do well if this is the price we have to pay. It might be more honest for Michael Gove to say, 'We are ideologically driven to return schooling to a bygone age. We have no time for the learning of skills, except the skill of memory. Educational aims are what other people have.'

Members of the original Expert Panel had been concerned to ensure a number of key attributes in the new national curriculum: the need for curricular breadth, constraints that would be imposed by any move towards year-on-year specification, the importance of oral language development, transitions from the Early Years into Key Stage 1, and the need to specify educational aims to preserve curricular breadth and frame light-touch accountability.

The likelihood is that, in due course, the new national curriculum will be brought in with accompanying sponsored textbooks on a year-by-year basis. This will lead to a short-sighted examination syllabus. Pupils and teachers will then have the 'complete guide to what to teach and learn' as they race through the schooling experience. The government is proposing content that is backward-rather than forward-looking, in syllabus and course programmes that only some schools will be required to teach. What is proposed isn't new, it isn't national and, worse, it isn't even a curriculum. What a mess! Word lists sum it up – there are 210 selected words that children should spell by the age of eleven. There are an estimated 170,000 words in the English language; we have a government that seems to think that just a few hundred of these are vital and impose them on the schools run by heads whom the government proclaim 'know best'. It could be argued that these words contain all the possible spelling combinations, but really it is an indication of the certainty and confidence in traditional approaches that has served so many so badly and which fly in the face of a literacy strategy developed some fifteen years ago. The word lists take up more space than the entire content of citizenship when pupils experience it for the first time in Key Stage 3.

Managing a national curriculum review is a challenge for many reasons. The main one is that what sounds straightforward is, in fact, very difficult. Those of us in middle age are often under the misapprehension that what we think about, know, understand and can do was learnt at school. Therefore, all that needs to happen is to put schools in order. The fact that much of what we now know has been acquired since leaving school, and that much of what we did learn at school has been forgotten, seems to escape most of us, as we point to young people and assert how poorly they perform compared with our day. There are two main problems with this viewpoint. First, we never know what we don't know and we dismiss what we failed to learn as unimportant because we have managed without it. Second, this fails to consider what children today might need by the time they leave school. What sounds so eminently sensible as a sound-bite appears daft when reality strikes.

Take Michael Gove's pronouncement that history is a narrative and should be learned as a series of facts in order. There should be fewer historical themes such as 'toys through the ages', he says, and less need for skills of historical enquiry. A new set of textbooks should sort that out then; until we start to look at the detail. Under the Gove system, given nine school years to cover just the thousand years of history since 1066, we would need pupils to learn at the rate of twenty-seven years per hour. Victorians would be allocated 2.37 hours, the Second World War would be addressed in 0.22 hours but extended to 0.24 hours to include victory in Japan. The Battles of Waterloo and Trafalgar would receive three seconds each, longer to say than study. The Magna Carta and the importance of the constitution would be taught at the start of Year 2 and the Irish Question, including the influence of Cromwell and Milton, would occur at age nine. Of course this is silly … but then so much of the debate in this area is silly.

Over the years, the approach to the curriculum, driven by the account-abilities of testing and inspection, has meant that the pupil experience is like sitting through the educational equivalent of the Reduced Shakespeare Theatre Company's production of the complete works. Political spite, malevolent score settling, personal crusades and vendet-tas direct so much of what the pupils meet, rather than the careful analysis of what they really need to learn in order to achieve our hopes for them. The history, comedy and often tragedy of the chase through volumes of content is condensed into just a few pages.

The framework document for consultation, including proposed con-tent of the new national curriculum, made public in February 2013, contains 'victories' for lobby groups. There are groups exclaiming they are delighted, pleased, concerned and even grateful to the secretary of state for his support. The Crimean War nurse Mary Seacole is to remain despite rumours that she was going to disappear from our his-tory. Cooking is in alongside personal finance, both of which were in the 2008 secondary national curriculum, though at the time were questioned by the Conservative Party in opposition. The PE commu-nity is pleased that their subject is at the heart of the new curriculum proposals and suggest this is evidence of a commitment to the legacy of the Olympics. The cultural and creative lobbies are reportedly reas-sured that their subjects have some protection. The traditionalists are delighted that there are expectations for children to know facts such as locations in geography and the names of famous characters and dates in history. There is nothing wrong with general knowledge or facts; it is what we do with them that matters. There is everything right with health and cooking and personal finance. However, the proposals have been greeted with announcements about 'winners' and 'losers': the learning of young people is still a battleground.

It was all such a lovely opportunity; the chance to start afresh after twenty-odd years and restate the national curriculum. Even allowing for the preconditions of political persuasion set out in the remit for the review, there was a chance to galvanise thinking around what we want for our children in the future. The old problem persists though; most people see the *national* curriculum as the *entire* curriculum and afford it too much emphasis.

Children in England today are growing up in a world where opportunity is greater than ever before. They are also facing challenges more complex than ever before. Their schooling is just one part of their upbringing and the curriculum they experience will, for some, be a supplement to what they learn from their home, family and community. However, too many young people still live in abject poverty – poverty of experience, ambition and spirit. Some of the children in our schools have seen things that most adults would rather not. There are children who are carers, children who are neglected or groomed. They all deserve a chance to do well and succeed. Is this the task of the individual school in which the children find themselves or is it possible to produce a national curriculum that helps schools to enable every youngster to flourish? Moreover, age and stage are different. Children grow at different rates and growth spurts occur at different times for different pupils. We will need to be careful about defining expectations in too limited a timeframe and will surely steer clear of year-by-year subject-by-subject textbooks, won't we?

It has always been the case that the curriculum of the school is bigger than the national curriculum, which constitutes the expectations that are an entitlement for all pupils. The best schools offer a vibrant, challenging and well-structured learning experience and, somewhere within it, the expectations of the national curriculum are met. Basically, the curriculum is all that happens in a school: lessons, events, routines and the range of activities around and beyond the school day that make up the entire learning experience. Good schools design learning for their pupils and cross-check against national expectations to verify they have done right by all the nation's children. Good schools get on and do things: dance, drama, music, art, using the outdoors, speaking in other languages, finding out about the past and other places, growing things, cooking, going places, using ICT and paint brushes, making things, experimenting, learning about their own bodies, working out how to get on with others in the real world. Above all, they use all these experiences as vehicles to do amazing English and mathematics to support the structured literacy and numeracy programmes and at the same time bring purpose to learning for pupils. Many children are natural performers in a physical sense – they dance, do gymnastics, sing, speak out. They strive to improve, to have more impact and to reach a peak of performance. We need them to build the same effort for quality into writing, mathematics and every subject discipline. They need to understand the concepts of hard work, endeavour, depth, polish, finish and to work with panache to show what they can achieve.

Subjects matter – for their knowledge base, for their discipline and for the appreciation of their impact on our world. Mathematics is about proof, art about observation and appreciation, science about hypothesis and testing, history about evidence, design and technology about fitness for purpose. A true historian shares the excitement of the discovery of the Staffordshire Hoard, the true scientist lives the Hadron Collider, the geographer is excited by clouds and ash dieback, the true mathematician brings alive the work of Alan Turing, the true artist kindles interest in the passing of Louise Bourgeois and her impact on sculpture. We enjoy with learners the unveiling of the Olympic mascots and explore their naming as a way into debates about fitness, lifestyle and big horizons in adversity. Teachers who are true subject enthusiasts know that their subject discipline is a living thing to be enjoyed and explored as it unfolds in the modern world. The best educated, however, are not limited by subjects but possess that critical skill of making those vital connections between disciplines.

In the end, the curriculum is what pupils in schools meet day in day out. As a profession we owe it to our pupils to offer them learning that will give them the knowledge and skills to manage their own lives, instil in them a desire to go on learning and allow them to look back, years later, and reflect that it was all worth it. For the nation's next generation the world really is their oyster. We have to help them learn how to open it.

## What could we do?

- An elected National Council for Schooling, at arm's length from government, could be important in building consensus, helping to balance different and competing influences, and communicating with schools. A national body could help to avoid coercive prescription and facilitate a drive towards a world-class education system. Engaging with the widest community, including children and young people, their parents and carers, could help a plurality of interests to be represented. A national body, which builds credibility with schools and the teaching profession and is looked on as an authoritative resource, could support the nation's endeavours in raising the performance of schools and the achievements and successes of young people.

- The national curriculum should be treasured. There should be real pride in 'our' curriculum: the learning that the nation has decided it should set before its young people. Teachers, parents, the wider education community, the media and the public at large should all see the curriculum as something that they embrace, support and celebrate. Most of all, young people should relish the opportunity for discovery and achievement that the curriculum offers to them.

- A clear framework for core knowledge and understanding, skills, attitudes and values would give schools the opportunity to shape the learning experience for their pupils in the context of local circumstances.

■ The national curriculum should aim to sustain motivation in young people and develop learning which is irresistible. Most people recognise that a well designed and implemented curriculum has a significant part to play in stretching the most able and talented, closing the gap in attainment, supporting the respect agenda, building healthy lifestyles, promoting civic participation and encouraging long-term involvement in education, employment and training. The achievements of the curriculum are not intended to be limited to any particular key stage but as setting young people on a path to lifelong learning and improving their life chances for a successful, responsible and enjoyable adult life. If we are to inspect our schools, we should inspect the whole curriculum. What gets tested or inspected tends to get taught. At present, most of the national curriculum goes untouched because of the game theory emphasis upon a narrow range of measurable outcomes. Even in English, speaking and listening struggles for prominence in spite of its influence on everything else a pupil learns. If the national curriculum is an entitlement, let's ensure it is well done. If it is an entitlement, that is ...

■ We should be approaching learning internationally and interactively.

It is amazing that, in the twenty-first century, we have not managed to teach the world to read. The might of the big computer companies ought surely to be able to come up with a 'world curriculum' which would sort out reading, writing and mathematics. So much in these areas is universal. There are also basic principles in science, geography, design and technology, art and so on which will be the same in the national curriculum for every country that has one. Geometry doesn't change and nor does displacement or density. Erosion is the same in Italy as Thailand. Refraction is the same the world over, as are forces and colour mixing. Map referencing seems pretty multinational in approach, time seems to be a universally agreed concept and profit and loss function in the same way worldwide. History might be viewed differently by different nations but, in the main, many subject disciplines have universal concepts.

Can the multinationals not get together and sort out some of the things that the whole of the world's population could learn through IT? Of course, some would worry about the danger of teaching the world according to Google or Apple, but there is a bigger reason why this has not happened. No company would be able to guarantee that every child using their approach would be successful. Big business relies on a significant proportion of users returning to their product, process or service, and they accept that not all will do so. They rarely claim that 100% success is achievable, except for manual tasks where the machine can take over. Learning requires the learner to commit, to persevere and overcome failure. That is why teaching is a very difficult task and one that nobody can yet guarantee will always be successful.

Shouldn't we try, though, for an international curriculum and an approach through ICT rather than continue to invest in competitive tests?

# … on a few aspects of the school leadership outlook

As educationalists, the question is do we want game theory to dominate our professional lives, to achieve the arbitrary measures set by others and to dance to the tune of national politicians intent on a market-driven high-stakes accountability model of schooling? Or do we want to exert professionalism, hold true to our basic values and fulfil our hopes for our young? Of course, these do not have to be polarities. It is perfectly possible to be accountable and hold true to basic values. It would simply look different. Many school leaders tell me that they feel their professionalism is compromised by the unending ratcheting up of pressure on results, the whims of the latest inspection framework or the latest measurable outcome they are expected to chase. They talk of what they want for the school they lead and of important aspects of their work that are not noticed or valued. They doubt themselves. Are they wrong to believe these aspects are important? Or are they simply out of step? Some school leaders can accommodate it all and some positively relish the quest for results and grades. Others see it as a way of keeping up the pressure on staff and pupils.

Most people in schools, although not all, have always been committed to transforming the life chances of their pupils. I don't think I realised when I was first a head teacher that I was doing that. I was trying to make our school the best it could be in terms of pupil experiences. I wanted our school to be a beacon for learning. I wanted to prove that schools could be better than they generally were. I wanted to innovate for learning's sake. We helped other schools and they helped us, we worked in partnership with teacher training to support people wanting to be teachers – because I always thought part of the role of the head teacher was to push others on a path towards leadership and influence.

It had been the same when I was a class teacher; teaching the best lessons ever, sometimes making learning real, the innovations and the dynamism that I felt was lacking in so many classrooms would be there in mine. The notion of 'going the extra mile' had not been developed. We just worked as long as it took and willingly gave time to take pupils to places like theatres, on residential fieldwork, or to sports events because that is what had been expected for years and that was what teachers did.

I sought out people to be with who were of like mind. With others, I was at the 'cutting edge' not by design but because others seemed to think my classroom and my schools were breaking new ground and exploring new territory in schooling. I was often asked to talk and work with others who wanted to see the world of education change and who wanted to see youngsters enjoying learning and achieving; I did this humbly as I thought the entire profession was excited by the prospect of a rising dawn in schooling and by professional challenge. At the time, we had no central touchstones for measuring the quality of our schools other than the professional recognition of others, including the rare inspection by HMI.

What I saw only later as the broader view, a bigger picture, was the link between the 'good' school and the future prosperity of society. Good schools were not just about the educational experience of the pupil and the joy of learning and achieving highly, they were also part of the quest to improve society.

The cynical critics of the approaches that I and others were advancing in our 'innovative' schools were always talking about pendulums swinging back and forth and what goes around comes around. I was so often frustrated that they did not seem to want to make improvements for the pupils; for childhood and youth to be better than it was previously. They seemed complacent, lazy and resigned on behalf of their pupils; they seemed to lack professionalism in its essence.

So, some of the jolts to the system from central government seemed much needed, and still are in some schools. At the time, the tremors from the centre were a novel phenomenon. Nowadays, we might be in a new era of complacency and resignation, even de-professionalisation, coupled for some with the excitement of a new dawn. Are those who are less enthusiastic about current developments the equivalent of the cynics of many years ago? Can those who are so positive about the unfolding agenda see things that their colleagues cannot or are they just better at game theory?

It was surely right that central government questioned and challenged the terrible outcomes of education for many pupils. In the mid-1990s, there were many schools where less than 10% of pupils achieved five GCSEs or Level 4, mostly in poor social circumstances. This was not due solely to a lack of innovation or lower effort, but in so many cases it was the result of lack of belief in pupils, resigned acceptance by parents, poor aspiration by staff and pupils with a tolerance for lowliness.

The regime of targets, inspection and league table comparators made a difference and transformed approaches to schooling in a way that structural change had never previously accomplished. However, many in the profession could never really seem to accept the impact. There was only grudging acknowledgement of the progress of schools from head teachers themselves. Sir Michael Barber, the government adviser on school standards, commented that he could not understand head teacher hostility to government policy when their school results had risen nationally by 6% on average in a year.

There were four main reasons. First, if results had risen so swiftly it gave a lie to the notion that schools had previously been achieving well – with the knowledge that questions would now be raised around that lie.

Second, many head teachers realised that there was now to be no excuse for accepting poor performance from some teachers and other staff, though it has taken fifteen years for the system to realise and state this through Ofsted.

Third, was the nagging impression that the focus on measurable results would distort the overall learning experience for pupils. If we viewed success through the narrow end of the telescope, then the lens would eventually limit the image of education and the quality of learning experienced, and nothing beyond the measurable would matter or, essentially, count.

Fourth, that sometime, sooner or later, the pace of the now recognised improvement must slow. Was 6% per year sustainable? The thresholds between the rational/logical and the cynical is so narrow that many educationalists believed the lemon would be squeezed dry before all pupils achieved the results demanded, meaning that those who questioned the strategy might be categorised as lacking professionalism. Some attacked the new agenda with the energy, belief and innovation that had always been prevalent, but it now focused upon the narrow end of the telescope. Many, for the first time, had a definition of school success. Here lay the opportunity for recognition that a generation ago had been almost entirely professional appreciation. The new recognition was professional and social: letters from the secretary of state – knighthoods and honours, Ofsted judgements, league table positions; all accolades not experienced a decade ago.

As accolades spread so did influence: access to national politicians, professional status (plus a deal of jealousy at times), recognition such as National Leader in Education status, increased responsibility in terms of chains of schools to lead and more money. All of these created a status that would, by some, be viewed with suspicion of motives and methods. Cynics, sometimes as an excuse for their own laziness or ineptitude, suggest that the integrity of schooling was being damaged by the recognition afforded to their colleagues.

The important questions should focus on whether overall schooling is improving and continuing to improve, and whether the focus of the telescope needs to shift to ensure that schooling represents what society needs and expects, or whether it distorts the purpose of schooling and our hopes for our young. I think the policy changes of the last twenty years have provided generally positive benefits for the system. The challenge is to keep them in check. I remain an optimist, an innovator and, fundamentally, a teacher. I want to see our young realise the hopes we have for them.

I now have what I did not have all those years ago: a wider view. A perspective about what might be happening to the heart of schooling – a heart that beats stronger because of its greater achievements and commitment and at the same time is saddened by the distortion of the school experience for our young and by the reduced professionalism of staff. The attitude of teachers is generally more professional than it was just a few years ago, inasmuch as there are fewer lazy, slovenly and uncommitted teachers in schools. There are many though who are unthinking – sleepwalking into the next target without questioning why, marching to a drum beaten by others when they don't like the sound of the drum beat or the tune. They cannot, however, explain why they are dissatisfied, except in terms of the pressure they feel. But why should we feel sympathy? They should want to embrace pressure, work hard and achieve for their pupils.

Some leaders have the certainty of a goal: a positive inspection judgement, a good place on a league table, a measure of progress. They embrace the language, the vocabulary and the associated actions. They march forward, clearing a new path. Others question the philosophy and risk being called the cynics that they witnessed all those years ago. When they laugh wryly about the column method returning in mathematical subtraction, and declare that they are now in vogue by teaching as they did at the start of a long career, they also feel that pang of uncomfortable guilt as they recognise the return of a pendulum. The problem, I feel, is the inner tension that many teachers feel in 'delivering' the sorts of results with which they cannot argue, in schools that they acknowledge should be good or better, while always wondering if the focus on results and the inspected quality of schooling are really what they came into the job to offer.

Many leaders believe that their own hopes for our young are not being realised in our schools. They want to achieve more but realise the telescope will not focus on the bigger image of successful schooling. They are professionally frustrated, bewildered and worn down by the pressure, while others are excited by the confidence of understanding first the new agenda and then being at its forefront.

This section of the book casts a light on leadership. There is plenty written on the subject – how to be a good leader, how to manage change, how to plan for the achievement of priorities, how to build learning communities. In terms of game theory, though, we might need to simply recognise what is happening and question our personal leadership outlook.

There is rarely a debate about whether we want young people to experience quality schooling. Of course we do. The current vogue is to talk about every child having the right to attend a 'good' school. How do we define 'good'? Surely the output measures used in inspection are not the only definitions that count, so there is much discussion about what quality schooling actually means and what it looks like in practice. School leaders, and everyone else in the community of the school for that matter, should have a stronger educational reference point than that which is determined by Ofsted or ministers.

I meet school leaders in a variety of settings, almost always by invitation. I get asked to speak at conferences at an average of two or three a week and I visit schools about three times a week. Most of the school leaders I meet are naturally concerned about covering their back, coming to terms with the latest set of indicators and ensuring compliance. Who wouldn't be? Over the last twenty years, the combined pressures of umpteen new Ofsted inspection frameworks, league tables, national strategies and directives on every aspect of schooling have made leaders very aware of what their role is. Policies abound. I was in a school recently that had received its academy chain's policy on shredding; it began by explaining that a tie should not be worn when shredding – (so much for reduced bureaucracy). Another chain has a policy for ladders – presumably it is about tights. Data is everywhere, so FFTD and RAISEonline are talked about with gravitas even though they are entirely built on the suspect data from testing and based on some questionable social assumptions. Policy is constantly changing, so there is a calculated switch in schools towards the proposed EBacc subjects or a move towards a new emphasis on the teaching of phonics. The whole movement is brought into harmony around the potential for forthcoming inspection, with Ofsted calling the tune.

Most school leaders work out how to win this game. They see the next attack coming – it was 'safeguarding', now it's 'performance manage-ment' – and they establish ways to head it off as though they were moving chess pieces to defend their king. Some struggle against the odds; just as the bishop moves to fend off the assault from the attend-ance diagonal, so the castle gets caught out with the pupil premium vertical shift.

Sir Michael Wilshaw, recently described 'outstanding' school leaders as 'sunny'. The question is whether the sun comes out because they are outstanding or whether being sunny causes the school to be outstand-ing. If the climate is so sunny, why are so many teachers who are deemed to be outstanding leaving the profession?

Despite such sunshine, the problem with endless compliance is that it causes clouds; clouds of self-doubt, of conformity, of threat and of stagnation. Those clouds can gather over the heads of those in the sun. Can I maintain my outstanding status? Can I cope with the shame of being downgraded as the goalposts shift? Is outstanding teaching sus-tainable? Is it worth it? Could I have an easier life leaving the profession and travelling around schools inspecting and telling other people to be outstanding while freeing myself from the very same pressure?

Most school leaders want to be in a school with a degree of self-deter-mination. They wish to set their own challenges with their own communities and work out how to meet them. They know there are some givens but, after that, they need to create, invent and sparkle. They want the talk of autonomy, innovation and collaboration to be reality rather than rhetoric. Yet we know that it is very hard to unleash exploration. Apparently, turkeys that are kept penned in a barn for a few weeks are reluctant to step outside when the door is opened. The first ones may risk being picked off. It is safer in the confines we know than to be alone on the outside. Exposure is lonely and dangerous but we do need the free-range experience and the possibly golden eggs that come with it.

Yet many school leaders do it. They innovate quietly. A primary school in Dudley uses tablet computers to encourage parents to help with homework and assist reception-aged children to begin forming letter shapes. A secondary school in Essex organises their learning to the extent that learners talk of their teachers as 'guides' and 'mentors', recognising that spoon-feeding is futile and knowing that their teachers will not give up on them, though the mindset is theirs to develop. A secondary school in Hull has work experience and civic contribution sitting alongside academic and vocational pursuits as an alternative to the proposed government imposition of narrow learning for teenagers. These are a few examples, among many, where the school leadership knows there has to be another way, where they remember what they said at the interview that so excited the panel and secured their appointment.

The big question, now, is how we encourage school leaders to *really* lead. The National College had taken on this challenge but a couple of years in a stranglehold of government pressure and the amalgamation with TDA has just about provoked submission. The professional instincts of school leaders burn as strongly as ever – we need to encourage each other and cease looking over our shoulders to cover our backs. People who continually look backwards eventually miss their footing. Instead we need a forward-looking, dynamic, engaging, active leadership approach that makes head teachers believe everything might be possible and that it is worth having a go. Rather than the sign outside the school telling us what the compliance checkers thought, our accolades should come from each other and from the pupils, families and communities we serve. We need to think of ourselves as professionals with the confidence, ability and desire to make the world a better place. You get the picture. Lead on.

# The need for frameworks in decision-making

It is essential that school leaders are able to articulate a framework around which their school operates and within which they make decisions about the day-to-day, long-term and strategic running of their school. Frameworks exist in all sorts of forms. Some people offer analogies or metaphors which describe the way in which they see their school's purpose. It could be a tree to show the way the roots underpin everything that happens above the surface. Maybe they use the symbol of a maypole to show how perfect patterns can only be created when everybody dances in step and somebody calls the tune. Whatever it is that becomes the framework for our school, it is essential that everyone understands it, which means that it is essential that the school leadership can articulate the idea succinctly.

Here is one example. If we want a *high quality* school then it seems obvious that the area we most need to work on is that of *qualities*. It seems to me that there are only three possible areas of quality to which leadership in school can make a difference: environment, experience and personnel. I will deal with each in turn but not in the sense of priority order.

First, there is the quality of the school *environment*. There is no denying that our surroundings speak to us clearly about the purpose and promise of the experience we are about to receive. In schools, children spend a significant amount of time in their classrooms and these make a statement to them about the intended purpose and impact of their learning. If we sit in a room where history is taught does the pupil get a feeling that history is about the way in which civilisation has developed, the achievements that have been secured and the conflicts that have occurred? In the mathematics classroom does the child get a feeling of excitement that mathematics and patterns are all around us in the everyday world, that problems can be solved by mathematics and proof is at the root of the subject discipline? If we were to move to a room where business studies was the focus of teaching, would youngsters understand that this is a discipline about economic viability, the way businesses are made or the extent to which people understand strategic planning? The room should speak to the pupils. I have often sat with children in a history lesson in a secondary school and then moved at the end of the lesson into a modern languages room, only a little while later to wonder why we changed classrooms in the break, for there was so little difference in the two environments except, of course, the teacher.

In primary schools, children typically remain in the same classroom for much of their time. Hence, you would expect the room, as you would in every secondary classroom, to convey to children the joy of learning itself. The room should pose questions about the big wide world. The way it is organised should help children to organise themselves. Is it tidy? Do things know their place? Are they put in their places? Is the room somewhere that can accommodate long-term work as well as short-term activity? Can everybody see when something is being explained? Is there a feeling that this is a learning community? What speaks of curiosity, achievement, wonder and challenge? Put simply, classrooms should ooze with learning.

But it does not stop at the classroom door. The good school knows that surroundings matter wherever we look. Whether it is the corridors, the stairways, the entrances, the exits, the outdoor environment, the library, the IT suite, the workshops or the gymnasium, the way in which the environment is presented matters. Imagine being a pupil who spends many hundreds of hours in the school hall during assembly. Sit where they sit and see what they experience. For most children assembly takes place in a carefully managed environment with attention paid to the ceremony of celebration, wonder, acknowledgement or discovery. The worship element is delivered in space that is peaceful, organised, gentle and reflective. However, many children attend assemblies which should be a celebration of good in the school, but as they look behind the adult leading the experience they see upturned stage blocks, stacks of chairs and tired curtains; little about their physical environment would tell them that this is a special moment in their day.

Many schools now have an entrance foyer to behold. I remember going to a school in the north-east of England where the entrance hall was splendid. It contained artefacts, sculptures, trophies and photographs of children from the school from times past and present. There were numerous examples of high quality student work and every message given out was that the visitor was stepping into a place of educational excellence. The problem was that, when I walked around the school with some of the senior leaders, the children's experience was anything but what was on display in the foyer. The stark breeze-block walls and concrete floors spoke volumes about the institutional life they were experiencing. At one point we came to an entrance towards the rear of the school where children made their way in and out, sometimes three or four times a day. Again, this was bare breeze-blocks leading to large metal doors which led out to a muddy, litter-strewn area. The contrast was dramatic. Upon re-entering the foyer from within the school, I noticed a sign on the face of the door which said 'No students past this point'. It became clear that the very people that the school was there for were unable to see the vision of what the school might become, or indeed the achievements of the school over the recent past. The only students who would pass this point on their way to see the head teacher would be those who were of the chosen few or those who had transgressed. It was a shame.

With the arrival of Building Schools for the Future, many schools gave much greater thought to the way in which the environment of the school might be presented. As a consequence there have been some dramatic developments in the architecture and decor of schooling. More schools have realised that it is possible to present and display the work of pupils in classrooms and hallways, even corridors which are used as a thoroughfare, through the use of Perspex coverings. However, the proposals for the modular school building currently proposed by the government – the limited space given to corridors and libraries, the ban on curves and glass, the requirement that all walls should be rendered – miss an opportunity to shape environments that really work for learning. Architects are up in arms. Would it not be better, for example, to give an indication of the cost per square metre and demand that the building come in on budget so that there is scope for each school to design its structure according to the needs and imagination of those who use it? Or is this yet another backdoor means by which the government is enforcing its view of pedagogy, while stating that teachers know best? Whatever environment we present will convey a message to the children; surely we would want surroundings that say learning is worth it.

The second quality about which the school can do something is the *experience* of learning. There has been much emphasis on the learning experience in recent years and this is gaining pace again as Ofsted inspections focus on what pupils are learning. Teaching and learning experiences go hand in hand and clearly we want young people and their teachers to enjoy positive ones. I have been asked so often if I believe in the basics of learning and my reply has always been the same: yes, I do believe in the basics. The basics are art, dance, drama and music; learning outside the classroom; making things, mending things, growing things, cooking; the opportunity to speak with people in different languages and enjoying scientific, historical and geographical discovery. If children do all of these basic things then the opportunities for English and mathematics are enormous and they should be woven into every experience that children have. There are plenty of examples where it happens: the primary school in Hertfordshire with the musical playground, the values-led curriculum in the primary school in Herefordshire, the school in east Sussex where the pupils make public information films about stranger danger and recycling to be shown in the foyer. Teachers from across Gateshead work together to explore ways to 'Construct the Curriculum' and produce advice booklets to help each other and schools beyond. There are secondary schools, such as the one in Nottingham, where Key Stage 3 is a joined up experience as pupils learn about themselves and their community while being helped to understand the skills they will need to cope with what lies ahead. Their experience of self-organised residential visits, structured observation in local industry and organising charity events is structured to fit in with the formally taught modules of subject discipline studies. A secondary school in Somerset runs a business around orchid production and through it pupils learn science, economics, business, trade and a range of employability and entrepreneurial skills. Good pupil experience is happening all over the place.

There is no doubt that the way in which we manage the experience of schooling will lead to the sort of quality schooling we want pupils to enjoy. So do we stick with the institutional traditions that have dominated schools since they began in the 1870s or should we instead be looking for experiences that enable learning? There is an important distinction to be made between enabling learning and pandering to children or the fad of the moment. Shouldn't we look again at the way in which time is used – the extent to which all children have to be in school at the same time – and the way in which aspects of the timetable could be part-compulsory, part-mandatory and part-optional? Two schools in North Tyneside have attempted to break the traditional format of pupil experience. One has changed the shape of the school day, with a later compulsory start and finish but options at either end, building upon what we know about adolescent alertness. The other has set out to actively teach pupils how to learn and apply techniques for success across their curriculum. Both are viewed with interest, or called brave or dismissed rather than being the focus for long-term research to consider system-wide implications. There are all sorts of approaches we could use to make the teaching experience more human, more sensible and yet more rigorous, in order to extract every piece of learning from the organisation that we do.

The third quality around which we can make a difference is that of *personnel*. It almost goes without saying that the people the children meet will have a massive impact on their futures. Naturally this applies to teachers but also to the rest of the staff and community. The point of being a teacher is to make a difference. In the primary school, children still spend much of their time with one designated teacher, though this is beginning to change. How their teacher presents learning will have a marked effect on performance for the youngster. In the secondary school, pupils meet a whole range of teachers over the course of a day and week. Do they each impart the same images of teaching – the same excitement, the same levels of enthusiasm – or do they offer a puzzling range of expectations?

The good teacher is someone who brings their subject discipline alive, who starts from the child's point of view and helps them to cross learning thresholds, climb learning hills and enjoy the learning valleys. The good teacher explains things carefully, instructs with precision, questions with subtlety, answers with honesty, wonders aloud, laughs, moans, puzzles and fails occasionally. The good teacher is highly prepared for teaching lessons and endlessly prepared to improvise. The good teacher shares their happiness and sadness with the children and appears as a real person. There is truth in the saying that children mirror their teachers. It is also accurate to say that pupils want to emulate the teachers they respect. Of course, the good teacher is not simply an accomplished educator in the 'purveyor of lessons' sense but is someone who makes a difference to the outlook of young people, cares about their well-being, spends time with them on the building blocks of learning and enables them to believe that they can achieve the things that matter in life.

Obviously the range of people that pupils meet extends well beyond their teacher. Whoever the children meet – be it the teaching assistant, technician, librarian, catering staff, cleaning staff, secretarial staff or the site manager – they need to be courteous, polite and good role models. Equally, each of them needs to take a full part in the life of the school in respect to learning and education.

These three qualities, *environment*, *experience* and *personnel*, are probably the only three things that leadership teams can work on within their own school. However, qualities alone are easy to state but much more difficult to actually address without the fundamentals of leadership – some *strategies*. So let's outline five key strategies which will interweave with the qualities in order to create the sort of school we want to see.

The first and most important strategy that will make a difference to the qualities relates to *attitudes*, *values* and *relationships*. If I were the head teacher of any school, the first thing I would work on with staff and children would be common understandings of these three issues. The school needs to have clear understandings about how it treats its surroundings, its attitude to work and its respect for people. This means how we treat each other, how we take responsibility for ourselves, how we treat our environment, how we celebrate our strengths, how we accommodate and overcome our weaknesses and how we support and take responsibility for each other.

For example, what function does assembly play in the daily life of the school? How do we use it to bring about the attitudes and outlooks which will foster the sorts of behaviours we want to see? What is the school attitude to rewards and sanctions (carefully thought through in terms of the qualities we need to see in our school)? We would hope to see a thoughtful approach to the way in which we acknowledge, reward and reprimand and thereby avoid some of the pitfalls of resorting to traditional conditioning approaches. We need careful thought about how we acknowledge children with gifts, talents and abilities without leading them into embarrassment. We must have sensible thinking about what we do to enable young people with special educational needs to be supported and helped to make progress, without falling into the trap of patronising or over-supporting them.

Next comes clarity of strategy about the *curriculum*. What do we want to offer the children in our school? How will we organise learning to make sure we realise what we want to achieve, and how will we know it is working?

As I've said above, the national curriculum is only part of the school curriculum, so how do we make it fit in such that it makes sense and is exploited as part of our learning offer? There is much more about the curriculum elsewhere in this book, so this will suffice for now.

Our third strategy applies to *learning approaches*. How do we think children can be best placed to learn? Do we want them to see learning as a transmission process, where, in the main, teachers transmit and pupils receive and they either get it, or they are bored, or they don't understand or they couldn't care less? Would we rather learning were an experience like a greasy pole, where eventually youngsters are expected to be unable to hold on any longer? Or do we want it to be a sticky experience where children are sucked into learning and unable to let go? What sort of teachers will be needed to make learning authentic and enable it to come alive? What sorts of spaces will we need and how will learning be organised? How much learning needs to take place in classrooms and how much could occur in situations which reflect real life?

Of course, every school needs *internal systems*, ways of looking at themselves and making sure they are an effective institution. The term 'internal systems' refers to everything from the way in which responsibility allowances are allocated through to the detail of what to do at playtime when it is raining. It is the macro and micro of management of schools and is applied to everything from environment to experience to personnel. It is budget, data management, performance management of staff and premises management. It is cloakrooms, buses and routines. It will determine whether the school is efficient or not. The most efficient schools are often the most effective schools. The weakest schools are ones with relatively few systems. How do we run an organisation so that the internal systems support what we do rather than dominate, such that the systems do the bidding of the school rather than the other way round?

Lastly, we need to think about the way in which the school manages *external relationships*. So, if it is a primary school, how does it relate to the secondary schools to which its pupils move? A secondary school might need relationships with all its feeder primary schools. Every school needs to link with its community, with its governors, local businesses and employers, the local university and teacher training partnerships, and with social services, health and police professionals who can bring that roundedness to children's experiences.

If we take the notion of qualities, linking them carefully with strategies, and fuse that with the idea of the warp and the weft in a piece of material, what emerges is something that might be seen as the *fabric of school leadership*. Our schools are successful when the qualities we seek are supported and enhanced by the strategies that help us to achieve them.

## THE FABRIC OF SCHOOL LEADERSHIP

Qualities

|  | Environment | Experience | Personnel |
|---|---|---|---|
| Attitudes, values, relationships |  |  |  |
| Curriculum |  |  |  |
| Learning approaches |  |  |  |
| Internal systems |  |  |  |
| External relationships |  |  |  |

Strategies

The notion of the fabric of leadership provides one framework for explaining the decision-making processes in a school. Every decision should slot in somewhere on the tapestry, and how it fits indicates our approach to achieving the quality of schooling that we seek. The purchase of a set of mathematics textbooks, for example, would fit on the coordinate of experience and learning approaches. Do we want a set of textbooks that offer a drill-and-practice experience or one that sets and applies practical challenges? If we cancel a games session because of wet weather, we might argue that there is a link between curriculum and environment. Often it is more likely to be a decision made to avoid conflict with potentially irritated parents, faced with muddy children and clothing. If that is the case, the decision fits on the environment and external relationships coordinate. Decisions about lost property might fit with environment and internal systems in most schools; however, it might correspond better with environment and attitudes, values and relationships. In schools where pupils are taught about taking responsibility for their belongings, lost property ceases to become an issue. Where schools use internal systems as a dominating force, they might consider what pupils might learn about personal attitudes from a different approach. What is the purpose of the school drama production? Is it about the quality of experience, linked to teaching approaches, or is it to satisfy external agencies, particularly parents who want to watch their own children and feel that well of pride without being overly concerned about the purpose or quality of the overall learning experience? If it is the latter, and we need it to be the former, we have some work to do.

Some schools are a beautiful tapestry and a joy to behold. The way in which qualities and strategies overlap creates a pattern which entices the whole community to believe in education in its truest sense and ultimately enables youngsters to achieve. Some schools are stretched along one strand, so that something like the school production becomes the dominant factor for a short while or perhaps the physical and aesthetic environment dominates everything that happens. The beautiful displays are still delightful but they don't seem to emerge from an embedded outlook for the school. They look good on the surface but when we peer underneath there are knots and tangles. In a way the knots and tangles are useful; they show the history of problems that have been overcome or challenges that have been met. And some schools, very few, are beset with holes in the middle and are unravelling because of a lack of purpose or direction.

Some expectations, often arising from outside the education system, got stuck in the institutional mindset of schools many generations ago. We often refer to this rigid institutional behaviour as 'traditional values' because it sounds so much better. The leadership point in all this is to be able to articulate a framework that helps the school to move forward and gives everyone concerned a sense of the importance of various aspects of our work without letting any particular aspect dominate.

# Institutional features

I have visited various prisons, purely in an effort to understand the educational opportunities available to those at Her Majesty's pleasure. They are frightening places. Just getting in is dehumanising: the endless locking and unlocking of doors, being kept in a holding pen while searches are done. The pervading smell of cabbage (really), all day, every day, whatever the menu offers.

I have also visited hospitals, both as a patient and as a visitor to friends and family members. I usually experience a feeling of uncertainty as the signs, with ever more complex ward names, guide me towards my destination. Not knowing the systems induces a lack of confidence. Those who spend their time in these, staff and inmates or patients, are much more at ease. Most prisons and hospitals are well-managed institutions run for efficiency. Some people also see schools as institutions. The difference between school leadership and school management comes through to me when considering the features of the organisation. How far does the efficient and effective management of the institution support or hinder the overall hopes for our young people and how much do the systems become an end in themselves?

So, what are the features of an institution and how well do they apply to schools?

- Once enrolled you have to be there. Not only that, but checks are regularly made to ensure that you are present. Hence, roll calls and registers and all sorts of alarms when someone goes missing.

- There are bells which ring to tell people it is time for the next phase of the day and to take away decision-making on the part of the individual.

- An inordinate level of importance is placed on routines – who should be where, who has access to space and when, movement around the building, keeping to the correct side of corridors or stairs.

- Some of the inmates are trusted more than others. They have earned their special treatments and have privileges denied to the majority.

- There are 'no-go areas' that are understood by staff and inmates almost as a conspiracy. These are places that staff are known not to frequent, and therefore don't do so for fear of finding things they might not want to see. Somewhere in most hospital complexes you will find a shivering group of people sucking on cigarettes while holding their various drips and physio equipment.

- There are also 'no-go inmates', the ones who know the wrinkles and ways around the system. These are the individuals whom it is best to avoid, unless you are within their inner circle, and even that can be a worrying place to be.

- There is a worry about the inmates 'running loose'. The institution therefore controls movements and keeps people busy or pinned down for extended periods of time.

- Contact with the outside world is minimal and restricted. Consultation about the inmate happens on the institution's terms.

- Wearing uniform matters and there are gradations of uniform to denote privilege or status.

- Badges and labels spell out minor rewards and privileges. There are rotas that explain duties.

- Specialist or valuable resources are kept under lock and key and inmates are not allowed access unless under special conditions.

- Feeding time is a perfunctory period of each day. It is often chaotically routine and the management of the routine becomes more important than the value of the occasion.

- Movement and transport of inmates is a complex and awkward arrangement and, as such, it is a relatively dehumanising experience; but then, so is a lot of the management of the institution.

■ When inmates leave the institution they are not expected to return. In prisons, they are hopefully reformed and in hospitals with any luck they are cured. Those who keep their heads down and play the game, keep in with the officials, take their medicine and do their exercises are seen as model inmates.

How far does this represent our idea of a school? The real question is whether the characteristics of an institution dictate or are a by-product of the way it works and is led. Try reading the features of an institution again, this time within the context of images of schools as institutions.

Schools, hospitals and prisons have become places of more sensitive, purposeful and human routines over recent years. There is generally more dignity afforded to the inmates, more recognition of the need for positive outlooks and more concern for the importance of relationships in the overall process. Has the progress of schools matched most hospitals and prisons, or are schools being persuaded by public pressure to continue to run as historical institutions rather than modelling the needs of the future?

## What does this have to do with leadership? SMSC

There is an increasing amount of leadership talk about schools being effective in a technical sense: getting the job done well, an unrelenting focus on evidence and indicators and making them travel in the right direction. There are, though, other sorts of effectiveness. We can be morally effective: responsible, accountable, flexible, adaptive and accommodating in our leadership approach to our community. We can also be ethically effective: managing power, authority and justice in sustainable ways. The way we lead our school as an institution is about all of these elements.

We can always tell when we are in an effective school. We do not necessarily need to ask for the latest inspection report or look for the sign or letterhead that announces its latest performance results in examinations and tests. Nor do we need the slogans that appear on published posters around the school imploring us to be the best we can by emulating Olympians or climbing impressive peaks.

The tests for effectiveness can be much more subtle, yet also more obvious. How 'comfortable' is the school to walk around? Do pupils look relaxed without appearing slovenly? Are adults at ease with youngsters while still showing authority? Do young people take responsibility? Are they looking after equipment, property, plants, creatures, each other, themselves? Is there an absence of litter and gum marks on the floor and scrawl on walls and windows? Are there queues and lines and crowds? (If there are, there will more likely be indiscipline.) Do adults keep talking about wearing the uniform properly, announcing unintentionally that few are doing so and thus encouraging the war of attrition of spirit that can be such for fun for those with little else to be concerned about? Is there pupil work exhibited around the school – sculptures, models, writing, art, photography, write-ups of experiments or proofs in mathematics – that shows the standards that have been achieved by some and to inspire the rest? Is the real world, particularly the world of work, evident to pupils as they spend their days in school? Are there examples of educational visits that extend subject disciplines or examples of visitors who have been to school to extend and enrich the learning of pupils?

The assembly speaks volumes about what matters in our school community, for good or ill. Does the assembly celebrate the collective achievement of the school, acknowledge the achievements and applaud the successes? Does it help students to reflect upon the way they might behave in a fair and just society? Are they being taught to ask questions about the ways in which people are exploited or controlled? Are the young people resolving to do something to help others locally or internationally? Is managed protest encouraged?

Dare adults address awkward matters of concern that affect teenage lives? Are matters of national interest – such as racist comments by famous sports personalities, the predatory behaviour of a celebrity, the grooming of young girls or teenage knife crime – avoided as a taboo too far or used as a vehicle for preparing innocent people for thresholds we would not want them to cross?

Are pupils encouraged to perform and show their talents in sport or arts? Do adults join them, sharing their skills, playing in the same band, appearing alongside one another in a drama production and enjoying each other's company?

Are youngsters praised or complimented by adults and each other? Or are they rewarded by adults in authority? Are they punished when something goes wrong or are they encouraged to atone for misdemeanours? Are there charts showing stars or stickers – the results for all to see of the relative behaviours of Pavlovian conditioned people? Do examples of inappropriate behaviour remain recorded for all to see for weeks after the event, encouraging some young people to actively seek to accrue punishment as a means of demonstrating their prowess at something?

Most of all, are young people proud of each other and themselves? Do they appreciate progress and success? Do they recognise that the school community is on their side and that they are all learning together about this complex thing called growing up?

An effective school does all these things, and more, and may decide to call them social, moral, spiritual and cultural (SMSC) education. The renewed emphasis in inspection on SMSC means that there will be a rush to systems and records to give evidence of standards and effectiveness. But the evidence is all there in the way the young people treat their school and the people within it.

## Leadership levers

When leaders in schools try to get things done they often apply four very subtle levers in order to encourage their staff to take the action that they believe is needed.

First, although not in any sense of greater importance, leaders offer the *promise of an enhanced professional lifestyle*. They suggest to their staff that the best way forward would be to try something new that brings greater efficiency, is more economical in the use of time, is more enjoyable and saves reinventing the wheel.

A second lever that many leaders use is *reference control*. Basically the leader puts the reference point for the intended action somewhere else. We see teachers do it in classrooms when they say to children, 'Would you do that at home?' The point of this question is to place the reference point with the parents rather than with the teacher in the classroom. (Of course, when the child replies 'yes' it leaves the teacher stumped for what to say next, usually something like, 'Well, don't do it here then.') In schools, leaders use reference control to encourage staff. They say things like, 'Well, you know that Ofsted inspectors are looking for ...' or 'This is important from the governors' perspective' or 'The parents are very keen on this course of action' or even 'The children in the school council have stated this very clearly'. Basically the school leader is saying, 'Please don't blame me, it's other people who are putting pressure on me.' The burden of accountability is clearly understood by the staff and there is respect for the individual who is 'carrying the can'.

The third lever that leaders often use is to appeal to *professional conscience*. 'You know why we came into the job – the children in this school come from some of the most difficult circumstances and it's our job to give them the best possible opportunity' or 'Come on, you know these children have got real gifts and talents and the challenge for us is to stretch them as far as we can.'

And lastly, a leader uses a *reasonably argued case for change*. The sort of conversation would be along the lines of, 'We know that the twenty-first century is more unpredictable than any period in the past. Therefore we've got to offer our children the capacity to be flexible and adaptable in the way we teach and the way they learn. We know that technology is influencing so many aspects of everyday life, therefore we must make sure the children we teach are capable in that respect.'

School leaders use these four levers with subtlety, depending on circumstances and the task in hand, to encourage their staff to behave in the way they require. Reflect for a little while on the recent decisions in your own school and you will see what I mean.

If we take this forward we can start to see the influences upon a school in the way they organise their development. These four levers are placed on a quadrant and it is worth reflecting on the way in which the shape of a school can be depicted, both in leverage terms and the pressures upon it. In this first diagram we can see that the professional lifestyle aspect is emphasized.

This is the sort of school where, on showing a visitor around, the leader would emphasise the efforts made to increase the facilities for staff and to create a more productive working environment. Similarly they might talk about the new approach to parent consultation evenings that are more economical or more valuable for the parents or the staff.

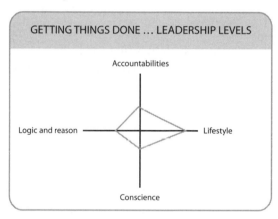

They might describe the way in which school reports are now produced to a common format, so that staff are working in a more efficient way and feel better about the finished product.

In this second example, the school is driven currently by pressure, accountability and conscience. Typically the head teacher will say

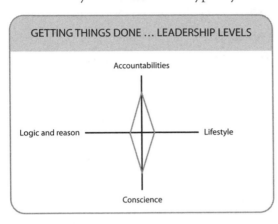

things like, 'We're near the bottom of the league, and it's essential that we get out of this position. Therefore some of the things we do may not have all the logic and reason that I would want to

encourage in an educational sense, but we have to get away from the bottom of the league because these children do not need tainting with that image. And, in any case, it's our job to give these children the best possible start we can, so I'm not having them seen as people who are not worthy; our conscience cannot allow it. Lifestyle? We don't really have one. We're so busy, we're here before it's light in the morning and we don't leave until it's dark. In fact, some of our staff think we work in Finland.' (Maybe it could be a new government strategy to raise performance – teach in the dark and pretend we are in Scandinavia.)

In this next example, we see the school driven by logic and reason and professional conscience, with less emphasis on accountability and

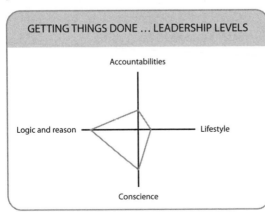

lifestyle. In this school you hear the sort of conversation that goes, 'Well, we don't bother with the league tables and what Ofsted inspectors say. What we believe is our children need to be prepared for life in the twenty-first century and we're driven by doing the best we can for the children that we teach. Therefore we work ourselves to the bone, hence the lack of emphasis on professional lifestyle, and we're going to give our children the best we can regardless of what the powers that be say about our efforts.' This is a high and noble outlook and most of us recognise it will last just as long as the next Ofsted inspection.

In the last example the leverage is pretty well in balance, a state that schools will sometimes recognise.

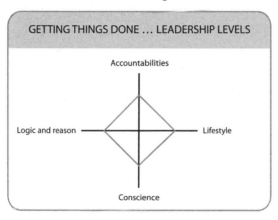

Maybe you would like to reflect for a moment on where your school is at the present time. Of course, schools shift in terms of the pressures upon them and the pattern of today may be very different in just a few weeks' time with altered demands. The promise of Ofsted coming over the hill will create a leverage shape that is likely to be unlike the one when they said 'Farewell' a couple of months ago. What does matter is that head teachers and school leadership teams are very clear about the pressures upon the school and the way in which it is being driven in certain directions by the circumstances in which it finds itself. Only with a clear awareness will the leadership team be able to address any necessary adjustment.

## Political leverage

The notion of leadership levers within schools can be taken one step further to consider the way in which national and local politics can affect and influence the system overall. To revisit those four levers (logic and reason, accountability, lifestyle and conscience) from a political perspective would see just a slight change in the wording. The promise of enhanced professional lifestyle is, at the current time, being represented in political terms by the word *freedom* – the promise of enhanced professional autonomy. The notion of *reference control* is being emphasised politically by a continual focus upon accountabilities and comparisons; on a school-by-school basis and with other nations and jurisdictions on an international scale. When we come to professional conscience, politicians at the moment are emphasising society's *conscience* and the wish for us all to do our best by the children of the current generation. Who could disagree with that? And lastly, everybody thinks they offer a reasoned case for change!

The National College for School Leadership's Future Leaders programme has been a very successful development over the last ten years. By selecting highly qualified entrants to the profession, a small and growing annual cohort has been 'fast-tracked' to leadership positions through high quality coaching, induction into leadership approaches across the globe and internships in schools with recognised leadership expertise in 'challenged school communities'. The success has been significant as these schools have seen dramatic progress and the Future Leaders have responded to the personal challenge. Typically the Future Leaders are dynamic, convinced and convincing. They also possess that leadership characteristic so important in school success: confidence. They are, after all, selected and fast-tracked, and with the recognition and pressure goes a certain sureness. The schools with which they are associated have almost always seen improvement in test scores and accountability measures, so there is a rightful acknowledgement of the success of the scheme. Interestingly, the Future Leaders organisation is now beginning to assert that there are other measures of school success and other professional concerns for school leaders. A school is more than the sum of its results in examinations and tests. The need to balance all of the pulls on the quadrant exists in all settings.

## Do we have a futures learning outlook?

With all the pressures on leadership, it isn't surprising that our image of where we are trying to go gets distorted. We might talk about heading to a new future but the reality is the future is not very far away if an Ofsted inspection is due. Consequently, the way in which we work might become a little distorted in respect of the children and their learning. Surely we need an outlook that focuses on the futures of the children. Take a look at the diagram below.

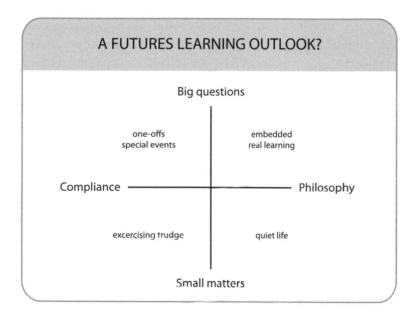

It seems to me that schools work in a pattern which is on a continuum between their wish to achieve compliance and their commitment to working towards their own philosophy. Equally, in terms of children's learning, schools deal with the really big questions as well as small matters. We handle the big concepts in science; we help young people to understand how technology can address some of the planet's major challenges; we study history to learn of human achievements and failings as civilisation has developed over time; our interpretation of the arts affects students deeply and is one of the ways that different cultures express themselves. These are all big picture issues, but this is a very different outlook from one that sees small gobbets of learning offered on a piecemeal basis as crumbs that will eventually make a loaf. The learning of isolated dates and names from history or the drill on number bonds and algorithms in mathematics are small matters unless integrated into the big issues of the subject discipline.

Each school could plot itself somewhere on this quadrant. If we work from a small matters starting point – achieving minor things in order to make progress towards test results – then the exercising slog will probably meet those needs. In order to sugar the pill many schools offer one-off special events for children so that they can see the purpose of some of the topics they are learning but also to experience those things that deep down inside we all know make learning more effective. If we want our philosophy to be achieved, but only deal with small matters, we are probably ducking the issue anyway and heading for the quiet life.

What makes the really big learning difference is when important questions are addressed within the context of the philosophical outlook of the school. This is when we get embedded real learning – when the learning makes sense not because it is a special event that we get excited about, but because it is just a natural organised part of the work we do in school. Children are doing authentic learning: working on actual problems, finding legitimate solutions, functioning with genuine audiences and dealing with a real world. In order to achieve what they care about they have to learn some structured, trudging things along the way. But they understand that their teachers need to teach *some* things in isolation and out of context – because that is what life and learning are about.

Taking forward the quadrant notion, the current situation across our schools is probably less equally balanced and more distorted, as in the diagram below.

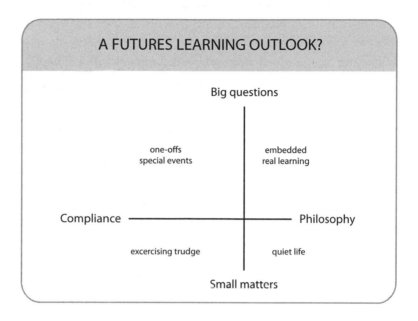

There are relatively few schools that seek a quiet life because they dare not challenge their own philosophy. But there are many schools which, under pressure, are engaging children in an exercising slog, whether it be through textbooks, the computer screen or interactive whiteboard. The daily life for these children consists of pencil-and-paper exercises, completing formatted sheets and making copious notes, all supported by the writing of lesson objectives at the start of it all, four times a day. The demands on teachers can be enormous and this transfers to the pupils, which means that the forthcoming one-off special event takes on significant importance for children and teachers alike. Hence the multitude of photographs that appear to demonstrate that school really is an exciting place, despite the generally awkward, and only sometimes exciting, tedium of many lessons. World Book Day provides the chance to emphasise the liveliness of literature as teachers and pupils alike arrive at school dressed as their favourite character.

The British Council's Connecting Classrooms programme offers the chance for a school to engage in an extended consideration of similar, shared and different lives of people in other parts of the planet. The Eco Week, Black History Month or LGBT fortnight help us to achieve our hopes for our young while bringing learning alive with a special focus for a short while. Each of these, exploited carefully, could move from being events into extended, embedded learning within school.

Of course, what most schools want, and some achieve, is embedded real learning, where big questions are addressed in the context of the philosophical outlook of the school. This is the sort of school where the young people are organising and managing the weekly routine as a natural part of school life and where events, when they do happen, emerge because the children see them as important. These happenings are driven by young people who, as the event unfolds, are using many of the skills that they are learning naturally in subject areas. In turn, the school will see that children's capacity in the exercising trudge grows dramatically as they are engaged in authentic learning and able to make sense of some of their learning in a structured way.

Until recently I was unsure about the impact of one-off events on top of the day-to-day exercising world of children. However, a visit to a primary school in Wednesbury in the West Midlands convinced me otherwise. As I walked around the school with the head teacher I couldn't help but notice the endless array of awards that the school had received – everything from Quality Mark to the Healthy Schools Award to the Art Schools Award to the Midlands Teaching Award and the Big Spring Clean. You name it, they seem to have been involved in it, and every aspect of school life, from sport and art to health and ecology, was incorporated. It suddenly felt as though they did very little other than special events and the school throbbed with excitement about what was coming up next. The children were always on visits, going somewhere new, taking their parents and enjoying the promise of a new experience. As we stopped at a noticeboard displaying photographs of a recent school musical, the head teacher showed me a picture of himself and his deputy. The head teacher and the deputy had been playing a part in the musical – they were the front and the back of the camel! There was no loss of dignity; there was an absolute commitment to being part of the excitement of learning in the school, and this transmitted to every aspect of what they did. True, the children did do exercises, and true, they were taught things formally from time to time, but in the main their learning had to make sense and the school made sure it was as fun and enjoyable as possible.

This effort to make the learning authentic and embedded is at the root of some of the most significant efforts in secondary schools. The school in Accrington that actively engaged pupils in the design of their new building – not in a token way but through a programme called 'A Class of Their Own' which brought engineering and the built environment together in a structured and accredited experience – offered an opportunity for youngsters to engage in the world of work for real purpose.

The primary school in Netherfield near Nottingham where pupils visit Silverstone race track and return to school to build their own powered buggies for their challenge, where there are reading sleep-overs to encourage the social aspects of books and where the school comes alive with the fantasy, but real to the children, purpose of unusual events that capture pupil and parent interests and set a context for literacy, numeracy and pretty well everything else.

Some schools seem able to communicate their purpose and encourage young people to see the point of the learning they do in terms of the hopes for our young people as expressed in the opening section of this book. A secondary school in Smethwick has worked to develop a Literacy for Life (L4L) curriculum that outlines competences that drive all teaching – it uses e-learning to the full and organises learning into themes that captivate the pupils to the extent that the pupils themselves opt for 'drive workshops' to target some of their needs – and has created a structure that embeds learning. The school even has pupils planning and leading sessions for staff.

Numerous secondary schools produce termly magazines that sum up the life of the school for the parents, community and pupils. However, a technology college in Solihull that captures every event in school in their publication – and makes a point about its value in terms of the bigger learning (including a 'Where are they now?' section with the reflections of ex-pupils) – somehow manages to produce a learning experience and expectation stapled into one. A federation of primaries and a secondary school in the south of Manchester shows through its magazine a continuum of learning, engagement with the community and an endless flow of experiences beyond the outside lanes of the track into which many children have been born. From working with older people to adventure, visits, performances, gardening, sport, debating, work experience, parenting events, working at the airport, cleaning up the area and special awards and recognition, these schools breathe life into their community and their pupils. These publications speak volumes about the embedded learning experience.

## What might be the leadership promise?

In times of challenge and difficulty leaders often wonder how they can hold true to what they believe. What they need is a promise that they make to themselves.

First, their response to changing and challenging circumstances should always be professional. There should be an outlook which is thoroughly committed to established and articulated principles, that holds fast to the vision of the school and its community and never sways from a commitment to the young people whose futures we serve.

Then, it is a case of making sure that we remember why we are in the profession. Are we simply purveyors of rations, people who are there to distribute a curriculum, fill young people with snippets of learning and ensure that targets are achieved? Most would argue that they are 'crafters of abundance', seeing themselves as educators who believe that young people have all sorts of talents and skills in immeasurable quantities and the challenge for the teaching profession is to help these youngsters make as much progress as they can, so that in the future they will be able to enjoy their lives in an enriched way.

This sort of thinking means that we have to see ourselves as a guide on the learning adventure rather than someone organising a marathon. In a running race, tiredness increases as we travel further, but fatigue sets in for some, while others have endless stamina. Those at the front make better progress and those at the back get more tired, until eventually the backmarkers drop out and fall by the wayside, leaving only the frontrunners to succeed. Is that really the ambition we have for our teaching profession and our children? Should we not be more like the organisers of the orienteering course who set out challenging markers to be visited, so that sometimes we go uphill through the brambles and against the wind, and at other times sail down the hillside with the wind on our backs, enjoying the elation of knowing where the next success might be found – and enjoying reaching it.

And then, of course, there is the leadership challenge of remembering why we are doing this and what our real targets are. Are we really working just for the next inspection, the next examinations or the next election? If we simply work for the next inspection, we may satisfy the scrutinisers and will certainly be good purveyors of rations, but will we actually be achieving what we hope for the young people we teach? If we satisfy next year's examinations or SATs targets, will we be secure in the knowledge that we have helped our young people to achieve a certain level of success? The next election obviously matters to politicians, local and national, but their policies usually have had little time to take effect. It shouldn't be the next inspection, examination or election but the next *generation* by which we should be seeking to measure our success. It is salutary to think that in twenty or thirty years time, the young people we teach in our schools today will recall moments from their own learning adventure. Surely we would want those images to be positive and for them to have happy memories of their time in our care.

A good piece of leadership advice is to always remember the interview. At most interviews, candidates talk about bringing richness to children's learning and creating links that make sense for young people at their point in life. They describe involving parents, making learning dynamic and giving children enthusiasm and motivation so that they will eventually succeed. Most interviews for headship do not dwell on the importance of today's online data and most head teachers do not promise to simply change the colours. It would be a good idea if interviews were recorded and played back to governors and head teachers alike on an annual basis. The governors might then remember what it was they asked, why they selected the candidate they did and, in some cases, not now be asking for different outcomes from the ones they required in the heady days of the appointment.

Whatever else happens, good leaders remember to keep the sunny side up, to laugh and smile to enjoy life and appreciate what they do. Schools have changed over the last twenty years. There is a lot less laughter and a lot less fun. But schools are strange places and funny places. The concept of having all our young people together with just a few adults, while the rest of the world gets on, is itself an odd concept. The institutional behaviours that have developed over a hundred and more years are also peculiar, sometimes absurd. We should change them or enjoy them for their silliness. We should also enjoy the children we teach. They are young, they are prone to mistakes in learning that will take them further, they will do funny things that make us and them giggle and we should laugh along with them, as opposed to at them, as they make their way through life. Schools that find laughter typically succeed. Childhood should be a joyous time and we should celebrate the fact that we, as people in the teaching profession, have the opportunity to be with such innocent and delightful individuals.

# … finally

In the story for very young children, Chicken Licken is chased by a whole group of creatures including Henny Penny, Goosey Loosey and Foxy Loxy. They all pursue each other, running around in circles. The story ends abruptly with 'and then the sky fell in'. There are so many parallels with our schooling system at the moment.

When I set out to write this book, my aim was simply to comment on the state of schooling, offer a perspective on our journey to the present day and then proffer a few thoughts on how we might move forward. It was to be a 'What is, what was and what might be' sort of book. The process of writing has led me through a series of explorations of some of our schooling dilemmas and has been, at times, more than a little frustrating. The absurdity, the seriousness, the common sense all around us that is so often ignored; the achievements, the obstacles and the futility of so much political action, however well intentioned.

Schools are confronted by accountability through examinations and tests. The inspection system chases the examination and test results and concludes that the best results are achieved in the best schools. The ways in which the best schools work are recorded as evidence of good practice and schools with less good results are expected to copy them. Success in the examinations and tests brings reward and non-compliance carries penalties. The reward can be the offer of academy status, with freedom from the very practices that brought success. Alternatively, academy status, can be forced upon failing schools so they can have freedom from the practices that brought success to others and which obviously haven't worked for them.

The examinations and tests therefore prove that the school is good or bad depending upon where they are in the accountability measures; and, good or bad, schools can release themselves from their chains in order to try to secure better results. Heads, teachers and governors are drawn into a world where they measure their success on the basis of their success in the examinations and tests. They push on every allowable tolerance in the system. As their results improve, they naturally quote the data that prove they merit the praise heaped upon them.

Inspection confirms the status indicated by the examination and test results and schools celebrate the shorthand terms that describe their efforts: outstanding, good with outstanding features. Heads are recognised as successful based on their capacity to improve results in examinations and tests and some accrue greater responsibility as they take on more schools, in turn requiring staff to secure yet better examination and test results.

We are told that leadership is stronger than ever, teaching has never been better and that teacher training is more effective than it has ever been. When told such things, why shouldn't the profession broadcast its successes? Except, of course, that the evidence of this improvement comes from the inspection system that has to demonstrate the source of the success they have registered.

The examinations and tests matter more than anything else. Sport provision is reduced, culture and the arts are marginalised, and practical activities such as design are neglected. Citizenship and PHSE are all seen as peripheral. Everyone is looking over their shoulder, force-feeding the one behind, while at the same time second-guessing the one in front. All that matters is the measurable data of the examinations and tests.

And then the sky falls in! We are caused to question whether the examination and test results are valid, whether as measures they are fit for purpose. If they are not, then the whole edifice of successful schooling has been built on sand for the last twenty years. Add to the chaos of examinations and tests, the mess of school admissions and the confusion of inspection, and we are looking at a very big sky that has fallen in.

In writing this book, I have come to realise that the schooling system is in greater disarray than I had feared, even though I was aware of the upheavals being faced through insights afforded by spending so much of my working time in schools. The single, overriding reason it is in such a muddle is without doubt the partisan involvement and influence of national politicians of all persuasions.

We are in a particularly difficult phase at present. As secretary of state, Michael Gove has wrought much upheaval and damage on the schooling system. This is not necessarily by design; indeed he poses some very relevant challenges. The problem is that, like so many national politicians, he is driven by short-term action, ideology and the need to show impact by the time of the next election. He is also making sure that many of his reforms are irreversible; this is dynamite politics. In order to sound plausible, his comments offer half-truths and inaccuracy rather than spin. Presentation relies on the polarisation of views and demonising the opposition rather than consensus.

The loss of school autonomy began as the influence of policy-makers grew under Keith Joseph, Margaret Thatcher's first secretary of state, and has continued under Tory, Labour and coalition governments ever since. The manipulation of what goes on inside schools through the targeting of funding and the building of accountability is a curse on all the national politicians who, over this same course of time, have lost general respect from much of the general public.

So, having written this book and come to terms with what is happening, am I now despondent?

Quite the opposite. Day after day I go into schools of all types all over the country. I am met by cheerful but confused professionals trying to make the best of it. Some are in the most challenging of circumstances, others the most secure, the most successful, the most pressured, the most privileged or the most frustrating, yet all seem to be somehow getting on with it amidst the political maelstrom all around them. Nearly all play the system in some way. Some exploit it, some work around it, some are cowed by it but have a good go anyway. All seem to have within them a sense of doing what they can and running a parallel race alongside the game theory of results to achieve the best educational outcome they can for the pupils they serve.

Some realise more than others that the very roots of democracy are being challenged by tensions in the schooling system. Some grasp that the sense of public service they value so dearly is being masked by the business outlook-led production of data that can be used to prove whatever onlookers need to see. Many can chant the mantras about standards and some recognise that they are talking with forked tongues, when what they really aim for is a rounded experience and secure future for young people which is based on something very different. Many have hung on for a long while and believed it couldn't get any further away from their core beliefs; yet most of those think that carrying the banner for their deep educational beliefs is worth it.

These educationalists mostly run exciting schools. Some run less exciting schools as a routine but can spice it up sufficiently on occasions to carry the pupils with them successfully. They too have become proficient at game theory.

Somehow, though, the profession must get back its professionalism and there has to be greater consensus about what goes on in schools and why. We need a version of a 'schooling spring'. Politicians have to back off. It is almost as though the face of schooling can be decided nationally, as Michael Gove is doing now with his free-for-all over the organisation of school types. The face might be decided nationally but the heart must surely beat locally.

We need to shift perceptions in the media towards campaigning for the improvement of teacher status and confidence. We must bring parent and school communities together so that they better understand each other. We should be challenging the idea that ministers are the best people to shape the futures of our young people. We need to be firm, focused, equipped with evidence and information and most of all proud – proud of our professionalism, proud of our purpose and proud of our youngsters.

An elected National Council for Schooling could present an opportunity to structure a system with which there is accord and pride. Our children need the adults of this country to get behind them and to help lift their expectation and performance. They need to feel the promise of good schooling and understand the investment being made in them and the opportunity being offered to them by the nation. Surely we want them to have enjoyed school enormously and be pleased to leave because they are ready to take on whatever the world can put before them.

# Bibliography

Allen, G. (2011). *Early Intervention: The Next Steps. An Independent Report to Her Majesty's Government*. London: Cabinet Office.

Alexander, R. (1991). *Primary Education in Leeds: Final Report from the Primary Needs Independent Evaluation Project*. Leeds: University of Leeds and Leeds City Council.

Alexander, R. (ed.) (2009). *Children, their World, their Education: Final Report and Recommendations of the Cambridge Primary Review*. London: Routledge.

Alexander, R., Rose, J. and Woodhead, C. (1992). *Curriculum Organisation and Classroom Practice in Primary Schools: A Discussion Paper* [Three Wise Men Report]. London: Department of Education and Science. Available at: http://www.educationengland.org.uk/documents/threewisemen/threewisemen.html (accessed 14 January 2013).

Bangs, J., MacBeath, J. and Galton, M. (2011). *Reinventing Schools, Reforming Teaching: From Political Visions to Classroom Reality*. Abingdon, Oxon: Routledge.

BBC (2012). 'Louise Casey Calls for New Approach on "Troubled Families"'. Available at http://www.bbc.co.uk/news/uk-politics-18881046 (accessed 14 January 2013).

Bell, D. (2005). Annual Report of Her Majesty's Chief Inspector of Schools 2004/05 [speech delivered on 19 October at report launch]. Available at: http://www.ofsted.gov.uk/resources/speech-david-bell-hmci-annual-report-of-her-majestys-chief-inspector-of-schools-200405 (accessed 14 January 2013).

Bennett, N. (1976). *Teaching Styles and Pupil Progress*. Cambridge: Open Books.

Bew, Lord (2011). *Independent Review of Key Stage 2 Testing, Assessment and Accountability. Final Report* [Bew Review]. London: TSO. Available at: https://media.education.gov.uk/MediaFiles/C/C/0/%7BCC021195-3870-40B7-AC0B-66004C329F1F%7DIndependent%20review%20of%20KS2%20testing,%20final%20report.pdf (accessed 14 January 2013).

Bullock, A. (1975). *A Language for Life* [Bullock Report]. London: HMSO. Available at: http://www.educationengland.org.uk/documents/bullock/ (accessed 14 January 2013).

Cameron, D. (2010). We Will Make Government Accountable to the People [speech delivered on 8 July]. Available at: http://www.conservatives.com/News/Speeches/2010/07/David_Cameron_We_will_make_government_accountable_to_the_people.aspx (accessed 14 January 2013).

Cockcroft, W. H. (1982). *Mathematics Counts* [Cockcroft Report]. London: HMSO. Available at: http://www.educationengland.org.uk/documents/cockcroft/ (accessed 14 January 2013).

Cohen, D., Voss, C., Taylor, M., Delextrat, A. and Sandercock, G. R. H. (2011). Ten Year Secular Declines in Muscular Fitness in English Schoolchildren. *Acta Pediatrica* 100(10): e175–e177.

Comber, C., Galton, M., Hargreaves, L., Wall, D. and Pell, A. (1999). *Inside the Primary Classroom: Twenty Years On*. London: Routledge.

Confederation for British Industry (2012). *First Steps*. London: CBI. Available at: http://www.cbi.org.uk/campaigns/education-campaign-ambition-for-all/first-steps-read-the-report-online/ (accessed 12 February 2013).

Crowther, Sir G. (1959). *15 to 18* [Crowther Report]. London: HMSO. Available at: http://www.educationengland.org.uk/documents/crowther/ (accessed 14 January 2013).

Delamont, S. and Galton, M. (1986). *Inside the Secondary Classroom (ORACLE)*. London: Routledge & Kegan Paul.

Department of Education (2012). *Darren Henley's Review of Cultural Education*. London: Department of Education. Available at http://www.education.gov.uk/schools/teachingandlearning/curriculum/a00204067/henleyreview (accessed 11 March 2013).

Department for Education (2013). *Draft National Curriculum programmes of study*. London:

Department of Education. Available at http://www.education.gov.uk/schools/teachingandlearning/curriculum/nationalcurriculum2014/b00220600/draft-national-curriculum-programmes-of-study (accessed 11 March 2013).

Dweck, C. (2007). *Mindset: The New Psychology of Success*. London: Ballantine Books.

Dweck, C. (2008). *Mindset: How You Can Fulfil Your Potential*. New York: Ballantine Books.

Eastoe, J. (2012). *50 Things to do Before You're 11¾*. Rotherham: National Trust Books.

Elton, Lord (1989). *Discipline in Schools* [Elton Report]. London: HMSO. Available at: http://www.educationengland.org.uk/documents/elton/ (accessed 14 January 2013).

Gladwell, M. (2009). *Outliers: The Story of Success*. New York: Penguin.

Gove, M. (2009). What is Education For [speech delivered on 30 June to the Royal Society of Arts (RSA)]. Available at: http://www.thersa.org/__data/assets/pdf_file/0009/213021/Gove-speech-to-RSA.pdf (accessed 14 January 2013).

Gove, M. (2012). Michael Gove Bores Students [video online]. Available at: http://www.youtube.com/watch?v=1qQL5L31-1E (accessed 14 January 2013).

Gove, M. (2013). The Progressive Betrayal [speech delivered on 5 February 2013 to the Social Market Foundation]. Available at: http://www.smf.co.uk/media/news/michael-gove-speaks-smf (accessed 12 February 2013).

Greevy, H., Knox, A., Nunney, F. and Pye, J. (2012). *The Effects of the English Baccalaureate*. London: Department for Education/Ipsos MORI. Available at: https://www.education.gov.uk/publications/eOrderingDownload/DFE-RR249.pdf (accessed 14 January 2013).

Gross, J. (2011). *Two Years On: Final Report of the Communication Champion for Children*. London: Office of the Communication Champion. Available at: http://www.rcslt.org/speech_and_language_therapy/commissioning/communication_champion_final_report (accessed 14 January 2013).

Hadow, Sir W. H. (1931). *The Primary School* [Hadow Report]. London: HMSO. Available at: http://www.educationengland.org.uk/documents/hadow1931/ (accessed 14 January 2013).

Higgins, S., Kokotsaki, D. and Coe, R. (2012). *Toolkit of Strategies to Improve Learning: Summary for Schools Spending the Pupil Premium*. London: Sutton Trust. Available at: http://www.suttontrust.com/research/toolkit-of-strategies-to-improve-learning/ (accessed 14 January 2013).

House of Commons (2010). Education Committee: Minutes of Evidence. The Responsibilities of the Secretary of State (28 July). Available at: http://www.publications.parliament.uk/pa/cm201011/cmselect/cmeduc/395-i/395-i02.htm (accessed 14 January 2013).

House of Commons, Committee of Public Accounts (2012). *Department for Education: Accountability and Oversight of Education and Children's Services. Eighty-second Report of Session, 2010–12. Report, together with formal minutes, oral and written evidence* (18 April). London: HMSO. Available at: http://www.publications.parliament.uk/pa/cm201012/cmselect/cmpubacc/1957/1957.pdf (accessed 14 January 2013).

James, M., Oates, T., Pollard, A. and Wiliam, D. (2011). *The Framework for the National Curriculum: A Report by the Expert Panel for the National Curriculum Review*. London: Department for Education. Available at: https://www.education.gov.uk/publications/eOrderingDownload/NCR-Expert%20Panel%20Report.pdf (accessed 14 January 2013).

Johnson, R. and Watson, J. (2005). *A Seven Year Study of the Effects of Synthetic Phonics Teaching on Reading and Spelling Achievement* (Insight 17). Edinburgh: Scottish Executive Education Department. Available at: http://www.scotland.gov.uk/Resource/Doc/933/0044071.pdf (accessed 14 January 2013).

Macdonald, A. (2009). *Independent Review of the Proposal to Make Personal, Social, Health and Economic (PSHE) Education Statutory*. Nottingham: DCSF. Available at: https://www.education.gov.uk/publications/eOrderingDownload/FINAL%20Macdonald%20PSHE%20Review.pdf (accessed 14 January 2013).

Mourshed, M., Chinezi, C. and Barber, M. (2010). *How the World's Most Improved School Systems Keep Getting Better*. London: McKinsey and Co.

Mortimore, P., Sammons, P., Stoll, L., Lewis, D. and Ecob, R. E. (1995). *School Matters: The Junior Years*. London: Paul Chapman.

National Numeracy (2012). *Facts and Figures: The Headlines for Numeracy in the UK.* Available at: http://www.nationalnumeracy.org.uk/news/16/index.html/ (accessed 14 January 2013).

OECD (2009). PISA 2009 Key Findings. Available at http://www.oecd.org/pisa/pisaproducts/pisa2009keyfindings.htm (accessed 7 February 2013).

Ofsted (2010). *The National Strategies: A Review of Impact.* Ref: 080270. Available at: http://www.ofsted.gov.uk/resources/national-strategies-review-of-impact (accessed 14 January 2013).

Ofsted (2012). *The Annual Report of Her Majesty's Chief Inspector of Education, Children's Services and Skills 2011/12.* London: TSO. Available at: http://www.ofsted.gov.uk/resources/annualreport1112 (accessed 14 January 2013).

Ofsted (2012). *Generic Grade Descriptors and Supplementary Subject-Specific Guidance for Inspectors on Making Judgements during Subject Survey Visits to Schools: Personal, Social, Health and Economic (PSHE) Education Survey Visits.* Ref: 20100015. Available at: http://www.ofsted.gov.uk/resources/generic-grade-descriptors-and-supplementary-subject-specific-guidance-for-inspectors-making-judgemen (accessed 14 January 2013).

Plowden, Lady (1967). *Children and their Primary Schools: A Report of the Central Advisory Council for Education (England)* [Plowden Report]. London: HMSO. Available at: http://www.educationengland.org.uk/documents/plowden/ (accessed 14 January 2013).

Riots Communities and Victims Panel (2012). *After the Riots: The Final Report.* London: Riots Communities and Victims Panel. Available at: http://riotspanel.independent.gov.uk/wp-content/uploads/2012/03/Riots-Panel-Final-Report1.pdf (accessed 14 January 2013).

Rose, J. (2009). *Independent Review of the Primary Curriculum: Final Report* [Rose Review]. Nottingham: DCSF. Available at: https://www.education.gov.uk/publications/eOrderingDownload/Primary_curriculum_Report.pdf (accessed 14 January 2013).

Royal Commission (1868). *Schools Inquiry* [Taunton Report]. London: HMSO.

Rutter, M. with Maughan, B., Mortimore, P. and Ouston, J. (1979). *Fifteen Thousand Hours: Secondary Schools and Their Effects on Children.* Cambridge, MA: Harvard University Press.

Smith, E. (2012). *Luck: What It Means and Why It Matters.* London: Bloomsbury.

Swann, Lord (1985). *Education for All* [Swann Report]. London: HMSO. Available at: http://www.educationengland.org.uk/documents/swann/ (accessed 14 January 2013).

Syed, M. (2011). *Bounce: The Myth of Talent and the Power of Practice.* London: Fourth Estate.

Taylor, T. (1977). *A New Partnership for Our Schools* [Taylor Report]. London: HMSO. Available at: http://www.educationengland.org.uk/documents/taylor/ (accessed 14 January 2013).

Tickell, C. (2011). *The Early Years: Foundations for Life, Health and Learning. An Independent Report on the Early Years Foundation Stage to Her Majesty's Government* [Tickell Review]. London: TSO. Available at: http://media.education.gov.uk/MediaFiles/B/1/5/%7BB15EFF0D-A4DF-4294-93A1-1E1B88C13F68%7DTickell%20review.pdf (accessed 14 January 2013).

Tomlinson, M. (2004). *Final Report of the Working Group on 14–19 Reform* [Tomlinson Report]. Nottingham: DfES. Available at: https://www.education.gov.uk/publications/eOrderingDownload/DfE-0976-2004MIG839.pdf (accessed 14 January 2013).

Walker, P. (2012). 'Business Leaders Criticise Slipping Standards of "Exam Factory" Schools'. Available at http://www.guardian.co.uk/politics/2012/nov/19/business-standards-exam-factory-schools/ (accessed 12 February 2013).

Warnock, H. M. (1978). *Special Educational Needs* [Warnock Report]. London HMSO. Available at: http://www.educationengland.org.uk/documents/warnock/ (accessed 14 January 2013).

Wolf, A. (2011). *Review of Vocational Education – The Wolf Report.* London: Department for Education. Available at: https://www.education.gov.uk/publications/eOrderingDownload/The%20Wolf%20Report.pdf (accessed 14 January 2013).

# Index